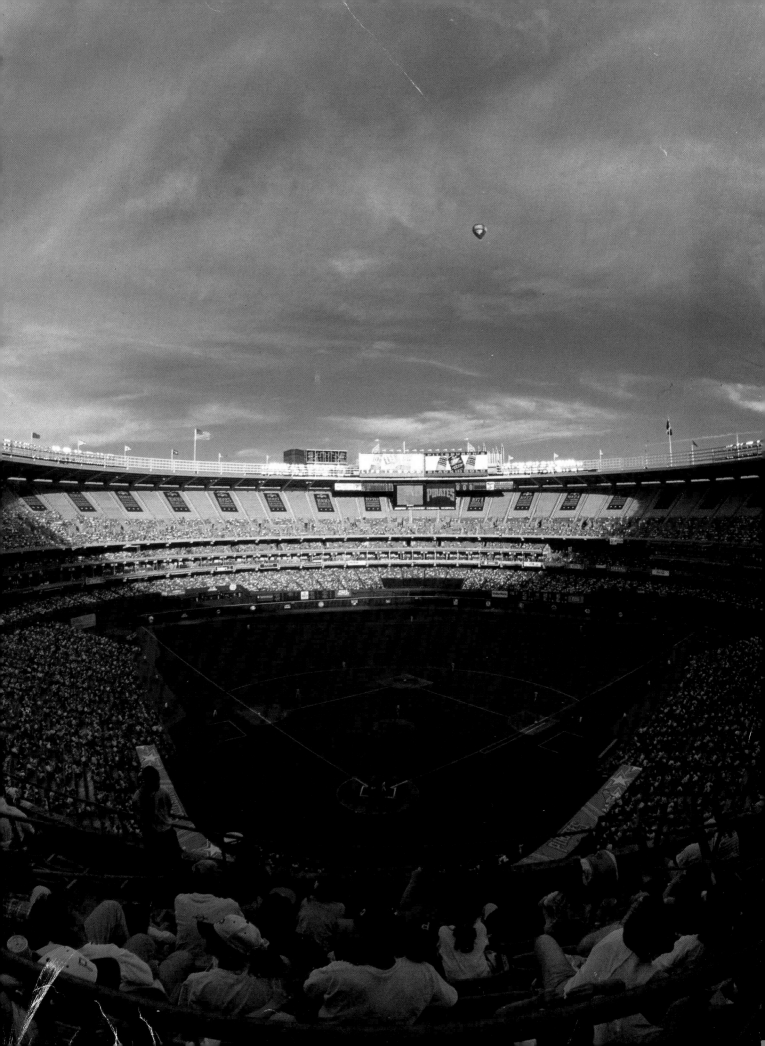

THE BUCS
THE STORY OF THE PITTSBURGH PIRATES

BY JOHN MCCOLLISTER

FOREWORD BY RALPH KINER

WELCOME BY KEVIN MCCLATCHY

ADDAX
PUBLISHING
GROUP

Bob Snodgrass
Publisher

John Lofflin
Editor

Brad Breon
Managing Editor

Darcie Kidson
Publicity

Anita Stumbo
Art Direction/Design

Dust jacket design by Deborah Ramirez

Cover photos courtesy Pittsburgh Pirates

Select photos courtesy Pittsburgh Pirates and A.P./Wide World Photos

Production Assistance
Michelle Washington, Gary Carson, Sharon Snodgrass, Jeremy Styno

Published by
Addax Publishing Group
8643 Hauser Drive · Suite 235
Lenexa, Kansas 66215

Distributed to the trade by
Andrews McMeel Publishing
4520 Main Street
Kansas City, Missouri 64111

Printed and bound in United States of America

1 3 5 7 9 10 8 6 4 2

Library of Congress Cataloging-in-Publication Data

McCollister, John
    The Bucs : the story of the Pittsburgh Pirates / by John C. McCollister.
        p. cm.
    ISBN 1-886110-40-9
    1. Pittsburgh Pirates (Baseball team) — History. I. Title.
    GV875.P5M39 1998   97-53243
    796.357'64'0974886—dc21   CIP

Dedicated to . . .

My grandfather, William Lyman Hall,
who taught me to love, live and breathe baseball

DR. JOHN McCOLLISTER

Contents

Acknowledgments

THE FRENCH-BORN AMERICAN AUTHOR JACQUES BARZUN once wrote: "Whoever wants to know the heart and mind of America had better learn baseball." Plenty of people agree. Perhaps that is why President Calvin Collidge was the first Chief Executive to proclaim: "Baseball is our national game."

Among those who endorse these observations are those loyal to the tradition of baseball, especially the fans of the Pittsburgh Pirates. To all of you who have supported this venture, I give my sincere thanks.

Deserving special note are those who went the extra mile in furnishing material for these pages. Jim Trdinich, Director of Media Relations for the Pirates, was there from the beginning of this project. His encouragement and assistance were of enormous help. Mike Kennedy, Media Relations Assistant, was extremely helpful in gathering photos. Also, I thank Pittsburghers Frank Morgan, Rich Corson and Dr. Robert Ruck for their assistance in research.

Thank you, too, to Mr. Frederick "Fritz" Huysman, Assistant Managing Editor/Sports, and the rest of his staff at the *Pittsburgh Post-Gazette* for their assistance in research, publicity and photos.

Sportswriter Kenneth Shouler has been instrumental in supplying background material as has Sam Sirkis, premier agent of baseball.

The eagle eye of editor John Lofflin demonstrated why he is such a valued professor of journalism at Park College in Kansas City.

Special thanks to Kevin McClatchy, President and CEO of the Pirates, who supported this project and who proved that you can field a quality team with dedicated players using motivation other than large salaries.

—J.M.

Foreword
by Ralph Kiner

*T*HE STORY OF THE **PITTSBURGH PIRATES** is also a big story in my baseball life. While I was with Pittsburgh, I received my baptism of fire in major league baseball.

I was blessed with a God-given talent to hit a long ball. I was fortunate, too, to work with managers who never tried to mold me into a different kind of player. And, of course, there was Hank Greenberg who was more than a teammate; during our brief association together with the Pirates, Hank was not only my teacher, he became more like an older brother that I never had.

Then there were you Pirate fans who rank with the greatest in the world. Although our team had years of struggle, you showered me and your Bucs with praise and support. I shall never forget you. You made my stay in Pittsburgh the pinnacle of my career. Everyone should have that experience.

May the Pittsburgh Pirates continue to bring joy and glory to you.

"THE GREAT ONE"

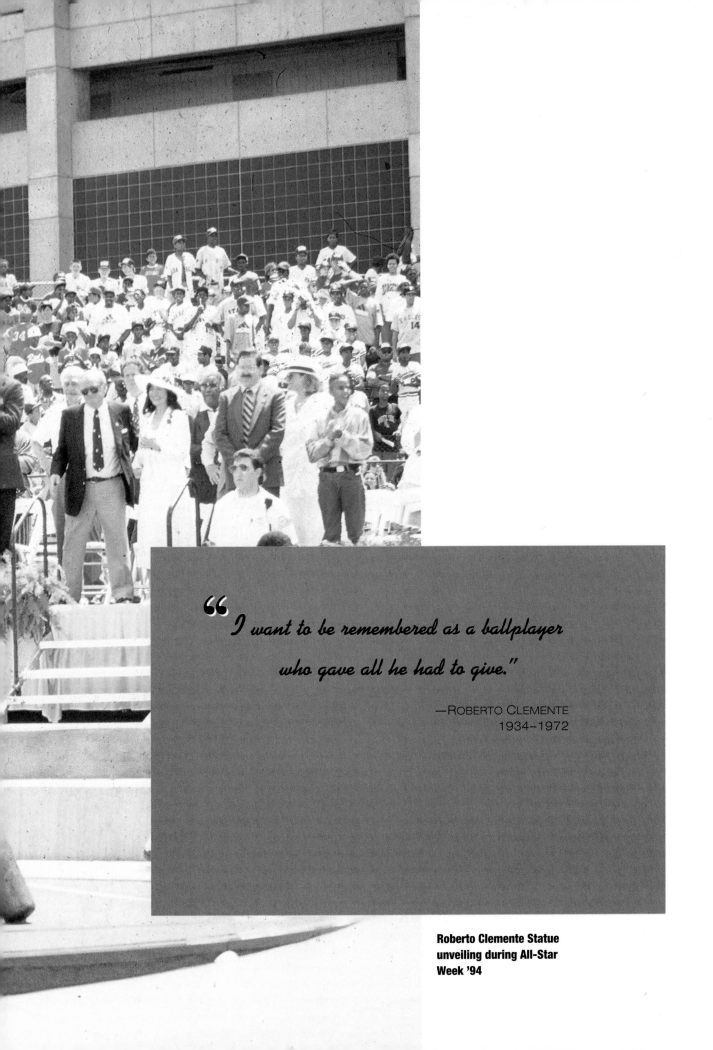

" *I want to be remembered as a ballplayer who gave all he had to give.*"

—ROBERTO CLEMENTE
1934–1972

**Roberto Clemente Statue
unveiling during All-Star
Week '94**

Introduction

THIS IS THE STORY OF A BASEBALL CLUB.

The word "story" is purposely used in lieu of the common designation "history." A baseball club rarely has a history in the strictest sense of the word. Instead, the record of its formation and growth more closely resembles a biography. A baseball club, perhaps more than any other entity, assumes a human personality—usually because each club mirrors the character of the individuals who nurtured its development and wore its uniforms.

The Pittsburgh Baseball Club is no exception.

Each generation of Pirate fans has been blessed with its own pantheon of godlike heroes of the game: Honus Wagner, "Deacon" Phillippe, Pie Traynor, Paul and Lloyd Waner, Ralph Kiner, Bill Mazeroski, Roberto Clemente and Willie Stargell—their names are spoken with near reverence. They have given us unforgettable thrills, and they have become as much a part of our lives as have any other historical figures.

Pirate fans also have been blessed with the characters of the game: "Rabbit" Maranville, whose pesky antics tormented both opposing players and his own manager; Fred Clarke, a scrappy manager who never ran away from a fight; Albert K. "Rosey" Rowswell, who described a home run unlike any other radio announcer. We remember them, as well.

Supporting those who have donned Pirate uniforms are the Pittsburgh fans: knowledgeable, faithful, opinionated, vocal, but always appreciative of players who give a 100 percent effort.

The following pages describe those heroes and characters who have written the record of the Pittsburgh Baseball Club during each of its 100-plus years of history.

Not all years receive equal treatment. Some stories, frankly, are more exciting than others; to comment extensively on years which failed to produce memorable events would be a waste of time for the reader. Other seasons, however, were filled to overflowing with magical moments and dynamic personalities.

Sometimes, the Bucs limped through seasons of frustration; at others, they celebrated world championships. But through it all, nobody can deny one obvious truth: The story of the Pittsburgh Pirates is unlike that of any other team in baseball. While other organizations have enjoyed the benefits of seemingly unlimited funds and heavily populated areas from which to draw fan support, the Bucs have had to work overtime for whatever success they have enjoyed. Owners had to count pennies. Ball players often were required to play for the love of the game instead of astronomical paychecks. Yet they were able to pull it off. *USA TODAY* labeled them the surprise contender of the year in 1997.

Relive with me the story of this wonderful baseball club. May these accounts trigger fond memories of a bygone era and, at the same time, stir you to eager anticipation of witnessing even greater thrills as the Pittsburgh Pirates, with each game, continue to write their incredible story.

—JOHN MCCOLLISTER

From the Owner's Box

THE STORY OF THE **PITTSBURGH PIRATES** mirrors the story of the great city it represents. There are no pretentions. Both the city and the team appreciate dedication to hard work with a no-nonsense approach to life. Both have had to struggle for recognition against the giant cities that dominate the news.

Most of Pittsburgh's citizens have been products of a working-class environment. At the same time, the Steel City has produced some of our nation's more affluent people: Andrew Carnegie, H.J. Heinz and Andrew Mellon, just to name a few. Each of them chose to give back much of their hard-earned money to the city they loved.

The Pittsburgh Baseball Club has had much of the same attitude. Former owners such as Barney Dreyfuss, John Galbreath and others were not just businessmen; they were also fans. They did whatever they could to give Pittsburgh the best baseball possible.

When I became a part of the Pittsburgh Pirate organization in February 1996, I pledged to carry on the tradition.

It wasn't easy at first. Baseball still smarted from the devastating strike less than two years earlier. In addition, both Pirate management and fans feared that Pittsburgh would not be able to compete in a market dominated by escalating salaries. Gossip around town predicted that the club would have to move elsewhere if it had any hopes of surviving.

I entered this arena totally aware of the risks involved, yet I was firmly convinced that Pittsburgh would rally around a ball club that filled its roster with dedicated, young, scrappy players who played for the love of the game.

Your support of your Pirates says that you agree with me. The enthusiastic play and second-place finish of the '97 Bucs proves that they could compete with teams who filled their rosters with mega-buck superstars.

Anyone who knows me can testify that I am honored to be a part of Pittsburgh and of baseball's most exciting team.

I speak for General manager Cam Bonifay and the rest of the Pirate organization that we are proud to represent a franchise steeped in the rich tradition of the Pirates.

This book reflects that pride. It was written from the only perspective that really matters—from that of a fan. It

KEVIN McCLATCHY

blends the magnificent history of our club with its dynamic goals for the future.

Sit back, relax and relive the excitement of the past as we do whatever we can to match, or even exceed, that excitement in future games.

In the meantime, if you're at the ball park, stop by to say "Hello." You'll be sure to find me there.

— KEVIN S. McCLATCHY
CEO and Managing General Partner

CHAPTER 1

IN THE BEGINNING

> " *The action of the Pittsburgh Club is piratical.*"
>
> —ATTORNEY FOR
> AMERICAN ASSOCIATION, 1890

DATELINE: FEBRUARY 2, 1876.

The place: New York City.

The event: The formation of The National Baseball League. America was not yet 100 years old. Grover Cleveland was president. Alexander Bell had just invented a new contraption called the "telephone." The experiment called a "democracy" was still licking its wounds from a Civil War that concluded just a bit more than a decade earlier.

In an attempt to put aside bitter memories, the young nation turned its attention from battle fields to ball fields. Bats and balls replaced rifles and cannons.

Residents of the callow city of Pittsburgh, Pennsylvania, also shared in the passion for baseball. The city that had grown during the Civil War by becoming a supplier of ammunition to the North, fielded three rather noteworthy amateur teams — the Enterprise Club, the Olympics and the Xanthas.

This three-cornered rivalry played most of its games at Union Park (with its 2,500 capacity stands) within the city limits of

James Galvin not only pitched the 1877 Alleghenys to a surprise 1-0 shutout of the National League's Boston club, but also homered for Pittsburgh's only run.

Allegheny, now known as the North Side. Eyewitness reports indicate many of the players on these teams looked quite good, although all the players were amateurs.

Spurred by the praise of local fans, one of Pittsburgh's teams, the Olympics, sailed down the Ohio River to challenge baseball's premier all-professional team, the Cincinnati Red Stockings, during the summer of 1869. It was a slaughter. Cincinnati won its 43rd consecutive victory by a devastating 54-2 score. For the next six years, Pittsburgh teams stuck to playing amateur ball.

On February 2, 1876, National League franchises were awarded to Chicago, St. Louis, Cincinnati, Hartford, Boston, New York, Philadelphia and Louisville. Quite possibly because of its humble showing against the Reds six years earlier and because the city was not yet considered a major market, Pittsburgh was left only with a promise by league officials: "If one of these teams decides to drop out of the league, we'll be happy to reconsider your application."

Unwilling to wait for one of the teams to exit the league, 20 days later — on George Washington's birthday — Pittsburgh formed its own professional team known as the "Alleghenys" (sometimes spelled "Alleghenies") and joined the International Association, which might be considered baseball's first minor league. The Alleghenys played their first game against the Xanthas at Union Park and won by a score of 7-3.

The next year, Pittsburgh got serious. On May 2, 1877, led by the masterful pitching of James Galvin,

the upstart Alleghenys challenged the National League's Boston Red Caps and won 1-0. Galvin knocked in the game's only run with an eighth-inning homer.

Sparkling moments such as this, unfortunately, were far too few. Following the 1877 season, many of the athletes abandoned the team out of frustration, leaving the Pittsburgh club with inferior players. Lacking fan support and enthusiasm for the game, the Pittsburgh Alleghenys disbanded on June 8, 1878, after posting only three wins in its first 26 games.

Over the next four years, Pittsburgh fans had to be content with games played by local, independent, amateur teams such as the "Keystones," one of the nation's first all-black teams.

A second major league — the American Association — was organized in 1882. The National League, formed just six years earlier, had suffered significant set backs. Philadelphia, St. Louis and Cincinnati all withdrew from the league, yet the league made no attempt at that moment to add new teams. Owner H.D. "Denny" McKnight and his Pittsburgh club were invited to field a team and join the new American Association. It was an invitation they could not refuse.

The Pittsburgh Alleghenys were alive once again.

Joining Pittsburgh were five other charter members of the league: the Philadelphia Athletics, the Louisville Eclipse, the St. Louis Brown Stockings (changed the next year to the "Browns"), Cincinnati Red Stockings (the former National League team) and the Baltimore Orioles.

Al Pratt, former star pitcher with the Pittsburgh Enterprise club, was the team's first manager. Games were now played in Exposition Park located near the site of the current Three Rivers Stadium.

Players on the 1882 squad included Cyrus "Ed" Swartwood, a left-hand-hitting outfielder who hit .329 and led the club with five home runs. Pittsburgh's first 20-game winner was right-hander Harry Salisbury (20-18). Denny Driscoll (13-9) led the league with an impressive 1.21 ERA. To the surprise of everyone, including the Alleghenys themselves, Pratt and his ballclub did amazingly well in their

first year with the league, compiling 39 wins and 39 losses.

Just prior to the 1883 season, two more teams — the New York Metropolitans (the name served as the basis for today's "Mets") and Columbus (Ohio) Buckeyes — joined the American Association. Pittsburg (the name of the city was listed without the final "h" in the league standings) had a season that was one notch lower than ugly, finishing seventh with a 31-67 mark.

The horrible record was certainly not the fault of Ed Swartwood who lead the league with a .356 average. The weakest link in the Pittsburgh

Although the 1883 Alleghenys posed no threat to the more powerful clubs in the American Association, it did produce some good players such as Ed Swartwood who led the league with a .356 average. Pictured players are:

Front Row: (L–R) Denny Discoll (P), Johnny Peters (SS), and Frank McLaughlin (SS)

Middle Row: Jackie Hayes (C), Buttercup Dickerson (OF), Al Pratt (Manager), Mike Mansell (OF), and Ed Nolan (P)

Back Row: Henry Overbeck (1B), Ed Swartwood (1B, OF), Billy Taylor (OF, P), Joe Battin (3B), and George Creamer (2B)

chain was pitching. Although Denny Driscoll won 18 games, he lost 21.

The 1883 Alleghenys had set into motion some changes with the hope that they would improve the current state of affairs. After playing two years at Exposition Park, the club moved back to the former Union Park, now called "Recreation Park." But the change in venue did nothing to alter the team's record or fan attitude.

"We saw better ball playing when they were amateurs," moaned some of the more vocal supporters. "If this is major league baseball, we don't want it." This was the start of a trademark attitude with Pittsburgh fans; they were forbearing, but would tolerate a second-division club only so long.

Pressure from the fans and media during this campaign became too much for management to endure. Manager Pratt resigned midway through the season with a 12-20 record and was replaced by Ormond Butler who didn't fair any better. After leading the club to 17 victories and 36 defeats, he, too, stepped down in favor of Joe Battin who closed out the miserable season with only two victories and 11 defeats. Even President Denny McKnight resigned from the club; his position was filled by E.C. Converse.

Four more teams — the Brooklyn Trolley-Dodgers, Indianapolis Hoosiers, Richmond Virginians and Toledo Blue Stockings — were added to the league in 1884.

Logic dictates that expansion would provide easier competition for the more experienced Alleghenys. Not so. The 1884 Pittsburgh club plunged even deeper in the standings, finishing, this time, in 11th

place with a .277 winning percentage (30-78). This was a team only a mother could love.

The season was the most frustrating for the team's two best pitchers. Joseph Neagle compiled an 11-26 record, while his fellow moundsman, Florence "Floury" Sullivan, chimed in with a 16-35 mark. This was the only year both Neagle and Sullivan were with the Pittsburgh ball club.

Pittsburgh fans and the press endured the club's share of losses during the initial seasons in the American Association. But, after seven years, with no perceived improvement, they voiced their displeasure by shouting cat calls as the Alleghenys took the field during their home games. Normally loyal-to-the-end Pittsburgh fans had enough. They were fed up especially with the dismal records of the past two years.

The 1884 campaign resulted in a clubhouse revolving door of managers — five in all — none of whom could generate a winning record.

Following the 1884 season, four teams dropped out of the American Association, including the powerful Columbus franchise. Through quick action by Pittsburgh management, some of the Buckeye's top players — pitchers Ed Morris and Frank Mountain, outfielders Tom Brown and Fred Mann, infielders James "Jocko" Fields, Charles "Pop" Smith, Billy Kuehne and John Richmond, and catchers Fred Carroll and Rudolph Kemmler — joined the Pittsburgh squad. In addition, the club added Hank O'Day from the Toledo Blue Stockings. O'Day, a noted fastball pitcher, later became a respected National League umpire.

The infusion of new blood helped.

Pittsburgh climbed to third place in 1885 finishing with a 56-55 record under the watchful eye of Horace Phillips — the last of the five managers who piloted the club the previous season.

Workhorse of the mound staff was Southpaw Ed "Cannonball" Morris who pitched a league-leading 581 innings in 63 games. His 39-24 record coupled with a fine 2.35 ERA showed both skill and stamina.

Offensively, the team lacked potency. Only one player batted over .300 — a left-hand-hitting right fielder from Liverpool, England, Tom Brown. Brown hit .307 and also topped the Alleghenys in the home run department with four.

The next year, 1886, Manager Phillips led Pittsburgh to a better finish — one rung higher, second only to the St. Louis Browns. Cannonball Morris won 41 of the team's 80 victories, good enough to lead the league despite the fact that nobody hit over .300 and the entire club hit a grand total of only 15 homers all year.

Although the American Association called itself a major league organization, baseball insiders knew that the National League was the "show." The American Association, with teams representing Louisville and St. Louis, was sometimes written off by baseball reporters as little more than a "beer and whiskey league" because most of its backers were brewery and distillery people. Even ticket prices endorsed the claim of National League superiority. Cost of admission to a National League game was 50 cents; you could see an American Association game for only a quarter.

One of the National League teams in 1886 was the Kansas City Cowboys. Travel to western Missouri became too costly in terms of time and money for teams such as Boston, New York and Washington. Rumor reached new Pittsburgh owner William A. Nimick that the National League was looking for a club to replace the Cowboys. Just before the league's annual meeting in New York City, Pittsburgh took a gamble. It resigned from the American Association and applied for admission into the National League. The gamble worked. Pittsburgh's application was quickly accepted.

In 1887, the Alleghenys were finally part of big-league baseball. The team, representing the thriving metropolis of 200,000 citizens, joined the Detroit Wolverines, Philadelphia Quakers, Chicago White Stockings, New York Giants, Boston Beaneaters, Washington Statesmen and Indianapolis Hoosiers.

Team owner Nimick worked in concert with Manager Phillips to prepare for battle. The club bought three established players — pitcher Jim McCormick and outfielder Abner Dalrymple of the Chicago White Stockings plus first-baseman Alexander McKinnon of the now defunct St. Louis franchise. Manager Phillips predicted the club would do as well in the National League as it did in the American Association.

On April 30, 1887, more than 4,000 fans squeezed inside the tiny Recreation Park to see the Alleghenys play their first National League game against Chicago. They were rewarded with a 6-2 victory. Two days later, Pittsburgh played Detroit — another established National League team.

Again the Alleghenys were winners, 8-3. Manager Phillips appeared to be a prophet. With powerful hitters such as McKinnon and Dalrymple, Pittsburgh looked like it would be a suitable match for any team.

Phillips' earlier prediction turned out to be a wee bit optimistic. Experience took its toll as the season wore on. The Alleghenys finished the season in sixth place in the eight-team league with a 55-69 record.

Utility outfielder-infielder-catcher Fred Carroll hit .328 and slammed six home runs. Leading the team in average was Alexander McKinnon at .340. And the first Pittsburgh player to lead the National League in any department was third baseman Art Whitney who notched a .924 fielding average.

In the pitching rotation, Pittsburgh's standout was James Francis Galvin who, at 5'8" and 200 lbs., earned the nickname "The Little Steam Engine." Galvin huffed and puffed his way to a 28-21 record.

Some of the reasons for the rather disappointing season lay not so much in what happened on the field as what happened off the field. Abner Dalrymple, hard-hitting left fielder, fell sick in June, thus limiting his play. He only batted .220 times all year. Pittsburgh management concluded this was why Chicago let him go.

An even more devastating twist of fate happened just prior to the July 4th doubleheader in Philadelphia. It involved Pittsburgh's star first baseman, Alex McKinnon, who had never missed a game all season. McKinnon was a baseball manager's dream. He was the first on the field during batting practice and the last to leave the stadium after a game. He was not only the team's leader in hitting and fielding, but also in passing along to his teammates a positive attitude. This July 4th, he was anything but positive. He called in sick and could not leave his hotel room. The next day he was no better, and left for his home in Boston to visit his doctor who was unable to diagnose his illness. Less than three weeks later, Alexander McKinnon was dead.

Without McKinnon and Dalrymple, most fans considered the Pittsburgh club "good field, no hit."

Jim McCormick was the backbone of the pitching staff in 1887, working 36 games. Shortly after the last game of the year, he announced he was retiring from baseball and going back to his home in Paterson, New Jersey. He was at the height of his career and he offered no reason for retiring. No amount of persuasion could change his mind.

You can tell a club has a poor year when its most memorable event was a ballpark burial. Fred Carroll, who hit a career-high .328 that season, owned a pet monkey that accompanied him everywhere. The primate, quite possibly big league baseball's first mascot, was a fixture around the clubhouse. When the pet died, it was buried with honors directly beneath home plate of Recreation Park during a pregame ceremony.

Prior to the 1888 season, with a depleted pitching staff (most clubs carried only three starters) and no power hitter, the Alleghenys combed the open market for any kind of seasoned player. They purchased center fielder Billy Sunday from

The Pittsburgh "Burghers" were the city's representatives of the ill-fated Players League in 1890. Players on this rival to the Alleghenys were: 1. Harry Staley (P), 2. Jake Beckley (1B), 3. Jocko Fields (LF), 4. Jerry Hurley (C), 5. Billy Kuehne (3B), 6. Ed Morris (P), 7. Hank Robinson (2B), 8. Al Maul (P), 9. Jerry Visner (RF), 10. Tommy Corcoran (SS), 11. Tommy Quinn (P), 12. Ned Hanlon (CF), 13. Jon Tener (P), 14. Fred Carroll (C), and 15. Pud Galvin (P).

Note that neckties were part of the uniform.

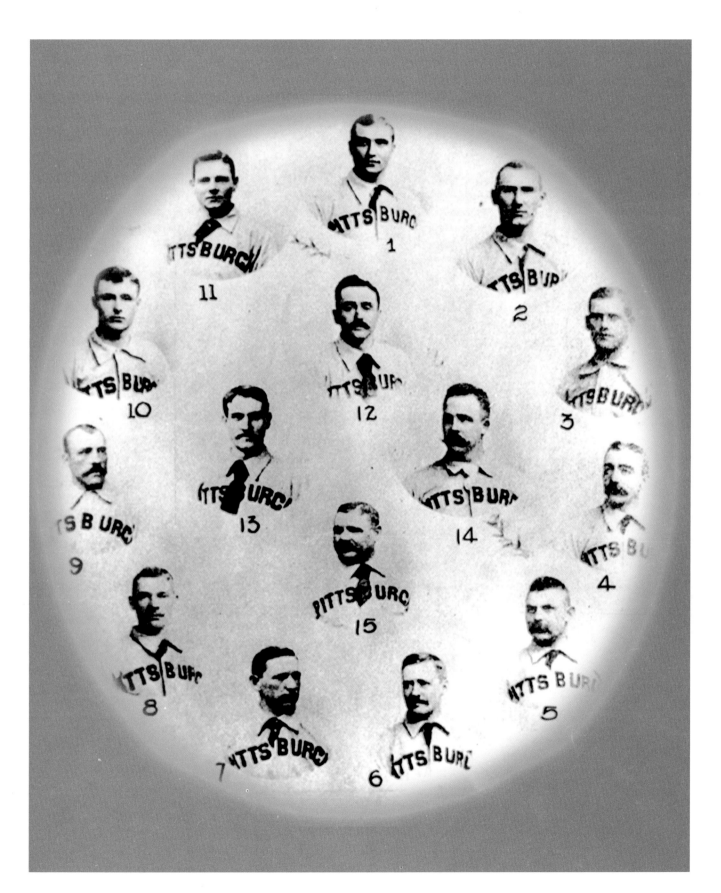

THE PITTSBURGH "BURGHERS"

Chicago. Sunday was swift in the outfield and on the bases; nobody who ever saw him play could doubt that. Unfortunately baseball rules would not allow a batter to steal first. Sunday's weak bat and average throwing arm were not enough to earn him Hall-of-Fame credentials.

Billy Sunday was not your usual ball player. In a game dominated at that time by loud-cussing, two-fisted drinkers who spent more time in bars than at batting practice, Sunday was a man who "found religion." And, he did not care who knew about it. Following his eight-year career in baseball, Sunday became one of America's legendary evangelists, filling revival tents everywhere. Often he peppered his fiery sermons with a visual demonstration of "sliding into God's home plate and being called 'Safe.'"

In spite of that perceived pipeline to higher powers, the Alleghenys could do no better than finish sixth in 1888, with a record of 62-68.

Part of the reason for the mediocre record in '88 was that only one batter — rookie first baseman Jake "Eagle Eye" Beckley (.343) — hit over .300. But Beckley, with not one home run to his credit, lacked the power normally needed in a first-sacker. Beckley was not alone. The entire Pittsburgh team was gossamer-thin in power; they could muster only 12 homers all year.

By now, all of America was caught up in the excitement of baseball. The Alleghenys tried to add to that excitement by shopping for players with power. Just prior to the start of the 1889 season, Pittsburgh's top brass assumed they had purchased third baseman "Deacon

Jim" White and shortstop Jack Rowe from the struggling Detroit franchise (replaced that year by the Cleveland Blues). However, both White and Rowe held out for a portion of the purchase money and did not join the Pittsburgh club until July 8 — more than halfway through the season.

The pressure-cooker atmosphere proved to be too much during the 1889 campaign, even for the crafty veteran Horace Phillips. He was challenged on one side by fans who demanded: "When are you going to give us a winner?" and on the other by upper management who wanted to know why he wasn't getting more out of his talented ballplayers.

Suddenly, and without warning, Phillips snapped. He became incoherent in his talk. He could not remember who had won the game the day before. He even imagined conversations with players that never took place.

Club owner Nimick gave his good friend a two-week leave of absence beginning July 31 to pull himself together. On August 9, Fred Dunlap was named interim manager. Horace Phillips returned after two weeks, but lasted only a few days at the helm. On August 24, Phillips mercifully was sent home and replaced by Ned Hanlon.

Horace Phillips would never again don a major league uniform. He suffered a nervous breakdown and spent his remaining years in a sanitarium for the mentally ill.

Fred Carroll hit a respectable .330. First baseman Jake Beckley batted .301 and finally found his home run swing as he blasted nine out of the park. In fact, Pittsburgh's home run production picked up

Al Buckenbeger served as both manager and club president during a turbulent relationship with the Pittsburgh club during the early 1890s.

AL BUCKENBEGER

noticeably with a year-end total of 41 round-trippers.

Pitching was a gnawing problem. Harry Staley won 21 games, but also led the league with 26 defeats.

With all the soap-opera-like scenarios and inconsistent play during the 1889 campaign, the Pittsburgh club did well to finish in fifth place with a .462 winning percentage.

Major quandaries for the Pittsburgh club as well as other baseball franchises in 1890 came not from opposing teams, but from within the ranks. Problems began three years earlier when the players of the National League voted to form a union they called the "Brotherhood." By 1890, that organization became strong enough to put pressure on the owners for a share of the clubs' profits in addition to their annual salaries. When negotiations broke down, the players rebelled and formed another major league which they simply called the "Players League." New clubs were established in Buffalo, New York, Brooklyn, Boston, Philadelphia, Cleveland, Chicago and Pittsburgh (a team that was known by two nicknames: the "Brotherhood" and, the more popular designation, the "Burghers").

Most of the marquee players of both the National League and the American Association jumped ship to join the new Players League. Nearly all of the Pittsburgh Alleghenys left as well, except for Billy Sunday (who had a religious conviction to stay with his old ballclub) and a run-of-the-mill pitcher by the name of Bill Sowers. Most of the other players, including

slugger Jake Beckley and player-manager Ned Hanlon, preferred to stay in Pittsburgh and signed on with the Burghers.

Guy Hecker was named manager of the Pittsburgh Alleghenys (sometimes called the "Nationals" or the "Innocents" to distinguish them even more sharply from the renegade Burghers). The Alleghenys recruited sandlot players and anyone else who showed some degree of talent for playing the game. No less than 50 players wore a Pittsburgh Alleghenys uniform that year.

The Alleghenys played their home games at Recreation Park; the Burghers played at Exposition Park. Because Hanlon and his crew had the much better team, the city of Pittsburgh supported the sixth place Burghers more than it did the Alleghenys. In one game, the Alleghenys drew only 17 paid admissions. In an effort to increase attendance, the Alleghenys played some "home" games in smaller towns in Ohio, West Virginia and Western Pennsylvania.

Where they played meant little difference in the outcome of the games, however; the Alleghenys ended the season mired in the league basement with an embarrassing record of 23-113.

The Players League lasted only one season because it lacked solid financial backing. Ballplayers who jumped teams were given an "all is forgiven" amnesty if they returned to the clubs they left. One of the leaping players — infielder Louis Bierbauer — had forsaken the Philadelphia Athletics of the American Association for the Brotherhood team in the same city. The Athletics, however, had failed to field a team in 1890, so the American Association laid claim to all the players who had elected to leave the Athletics following the '89 season. Through a clerical error, Bierbauer's name did not appear on the list of players now owned by the American Association. J. Palmer O'Neil, who had succeeded William Nimick as Pittsburgh's club president, was quick to discover this omission and persuaded Bierbauer to sign a contract to play for the Alleghenys the next year.

The American Association cried "Foul!" O'Neil stood his ground insisting that Pittsburgh acted within the letter of the law.

The two leagues submitted the matter to arbitration. Pittsburgh presented a case based upon logic and reasoning. For the Alleghenys, the American Association had no cause for protest: "The American Association did not reserve Bierbauer; he was a free agent, thus Pittsburgh was free to sign him." The spokesman for the American Association was much more emotional in his accusations. "The action of the Pittsburgh Club is piratical," he shouted.

The arbitration board sided with Pittsburgh. The ruling became even more significant because the name used by the American Association to brand the Pittsburgh club was now adopted by the management and fans as a badge of distinction. Henceforth, the club was no longer called the Alleghenys. Instead, its team name would be forever the "Pirates."

Only seven of the former players returned to the Pittsburgh club for the 1891 season. One was player-manager Ned Hanlon. An olive branch was offered him and the rest of the returning players by President O'Neil who simply said, "We'll just forget that the Players League ever happened."

One of the new players coming to the Pittsburgh Pirates that year was a tall, skinny catcher from Brookline, Massachusetts, named Cornelius McGillicuddy. Fans and teammates knew him better as "Connie Mack."

The club moved back to Exposition Park, even though the location was not ideal. The park got its name because circuses camped there when they came to town. Located next to the lower end of the Allegheny River near the point, the field was a superb venue except for one minor problem. During the spring, when the snow melted and the rivers overflowed, sometimes the water would creep into Exposition Park, making the territory more appropriate for swimming meets than baseball games. As a result, an early practice of the Pirate club was to schedule the opening games of a season out of town.

Even with a new name, a new ballpark and some personnel changes, the Pittsburgh squad again concluded the year in last place, although the team did manage to win 32 more games than the year before.

As one might expect, the manager's head was the first to roll. On August 1, one month before the end of the season, Ned Hanlon was replaced by Bill McGunnigle, who had won successive championships for Brooklyn in 1889 and 1890.

The National League and the American Association grew weary of fighting each other and agreed to merge into one league called the

The ruling became even more significant because the name used by the American Association to brand the Pittsburgh club was now adopted by the management and fans as a badge of distinction. Henceforth, the club was no longer called the Alleghenys. Instead, its team name would be forever the "Pirates."

Charter members of

the National League

and Association were

12 teams composed

of the nation's best

ballplayers.

National League and Association. Charter members of the league were 12 teams composed of the nation's best ballplayers. The Louisville Colonels, Baltimore Orioles, St. Louis Browns and Washington Senators from the old American Association joined the existing eight clubs of the National League. Players from the five disbanded clubs — Boston, Milwaukee, Philadelphia, Columbus, and Cincinnati — went on the open market and were considered free agents.

With the birth of the new league, the Pittsburgh club reorganized. Captain William W. Kerr, a top executive with Arbuckle Coffee, became the chief financial investor. Popular Pittsburgh sports enthusiast William C. Temple was elected president. Bill McGunnigle was not rehired; in his stead was Al Buckenberger. New faces also showed up on the playing field. Tommy Burns, the former Chicago third baseman, was the most famous addition. Also added were pitchers William "Adonis" Terry, Phil "Red" Ehret and Charley Esper. New outfielders included Joe Kelley, Elmer Smith, Pat Donovan, Jake Stenzel and George Van Haltren.

The 1892 Pirates finished with quite a respectable 80-73 mark, but that was good enough for only sixth-place in the new 12-team league. First baseman Jake Beckley — who had returned to the Pirates following his one-year hiatus with the Players League — led the club with 10 homers, while Irish-born right fielder Patsy Donovan, a mid-season acquisition from Washington, batted .294 in 90 games.

The sixth-place finish of the club in 1892 is quite remarkable, considering that the team's two top pitchers — local boy Mark Baldwin (26-27) and rookie Philip "Red" Ehret (16-20) had losing records.

In addition, the Pittsburgh club suffered from internal struggles generated by the front office. From all reports, the principal owner, William "Captain" Kerr, was a likable chap, but prone to second-guessing his manager. Both he and Al Buckenberger got into frequent heated arguments. During the year, in fact, Buckenberger was kicked upstairs and made acting president. Tommy Burns was named player-manager. A few weeks later, when the club did no better, Burns was relieved of the managerial duties and Buckenberger was brought back to serve as both manager and acting president. ∎

In his early year with the Pirates, Tommy Burns served as player/manager for part of the 1892 season. Burns was one of the players who elected to play without a fielder's glove.

TOMMY BURNS

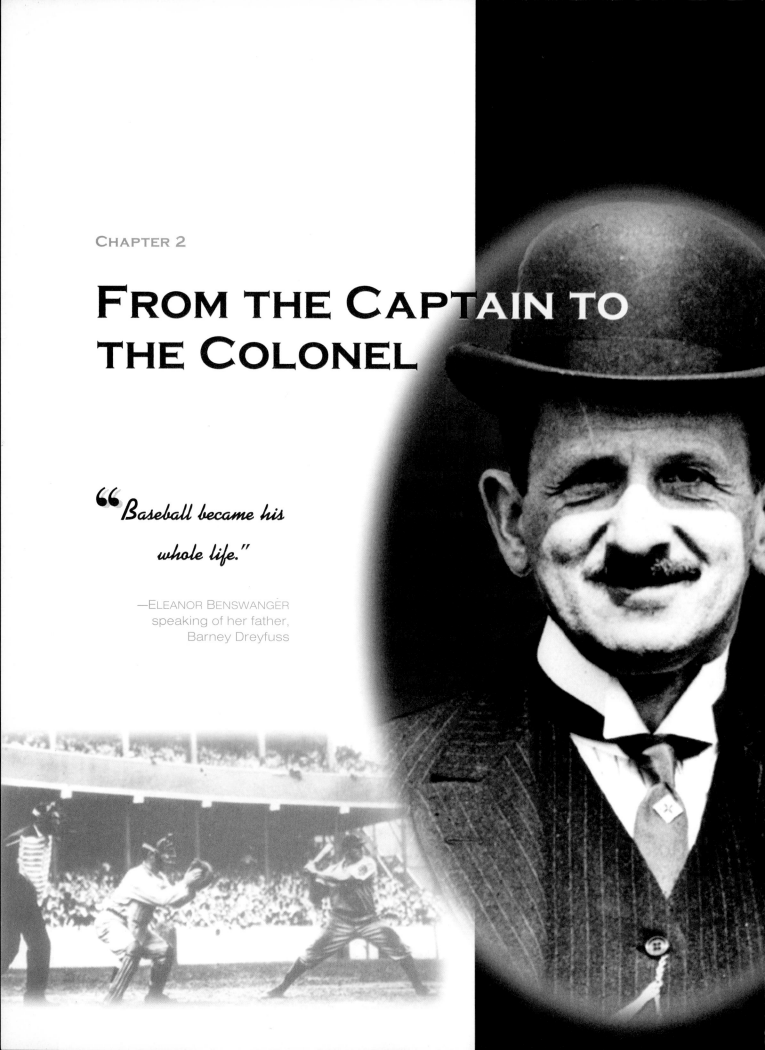

CHAPTER 2

FROM THE CAPTAIN TO THE COLONEL

❝*Baseball became his whole life.*❞

—ELEANOR BENSWANGER
speaking of her father,
Barney Dreyfuss

𝑃RINCIPAL OWNER, CAPTAIN KERR, had earned a reputation as a tough-minded executive with Arbuckle Coffee. From the day he invested in his baseball team in 1891, Kerr made changing managers seem as routine as changing shirts. Pittsburgh had finished in sixth place the previous season and Kerr was uncertain the club could earn a profit. To avoid fiscal chaos, he called a meeting in his office with the team's most popular player, Connie Mack, and 10 of his teammates.

"You fellows did your part to wreck us during the Brotherhood fight," he scolded them, "and most of the clubs are still in debt. Well, from now on, the league has decided that the top salary for any player will be $2,400. All of you fellows can sign now at that figure. But, if you hold off until next spring, it will be only $2,100."

Each of the players signed the agreement. "I felt the game that I had made my life's work was moving backward instead of going forward," said Mack.

Pirate fans thought they were heading for another dismal year at the start of the 1893 season. The Pirates did not win one game during the entire month of April. When fans walked downtown through the infamous smoke and haze created by the steel mills, some stuck their noses into the air and asked, "Is that the Pirate ballclub we're smelling?"

Almost overnight, something happened. Beginning in May, the Pirates became as hot as a Bessemer Converter. They won games

Owner Barney Dreyfuss was a determined owner who would not accept anything less than a 100-percent effort from his players.

with increasing regularity. Not only did they climb out of the league basement, they actually challenged the league's front-runners for first spot. The Bucs did not finish the season leading the league, but they did place a very respectable second to the powerful Boston club. Pittsburgh posted a phenomenal team batting average of .319.

Topping the Pirates in the hit parade were Elmer Smith (.366), Van Halen (.350), Patsy Donovan (.331), and Jake Beckley (.324). Left-hander Frank Killen led the pitching staff with a league-leading 34 wins. The only real casualty that year came when catcher Connie Mack was spiked by a runner (catchers did not use shin guards at the time) sliding into home plate. This accident stifled Mack's career as a starting catcher. The most positive conclusion was that the Pirates' 81-48 record that year told the fans and themselves that they could hold their own with anyone.

Momentum was on the side of the Bucs. Captain Kerr expected his club to succeed Boston as league champions. When he announced himself as a replacement for Acting President Buckenberger gossip around town was that Kerr wanted the glory that would come to the president of a pennant-winning team.

From the first pitch of opening day in 1894, however, signs pointed to another poor

season. Much of the reason was due probably to Connie Mack's limited playing time; he appeared in only 63 games that year. Whatever the cause, Mr. Kerr was not keen on representing a losing team. Something had to be changed. In line with baseball tradition, the first to feel the slings and arrows of criticism was Manager Buckenberger.

Midway through the season, Kerr summoned Connie Mack to his

His real name was Cornelius McGillicuddy, but he's best know as "Connie Mack." By whatever name he was called, he proved to be a superb catcher and manager for the Pirates.

office and asked him to take over as manager.

Mack was, at first, reluctant. "It's not Al's fault that we're doing so poorly," said Mack.

"But something is wrong," argued Kerr. "Our hitters aren't hitting; our pitchers aren't pitching. I think Buckenberger has lost control of his players."

Connie Mack who had gained a reputation for being a blunt, honest man, added, "Captain Kerr, I frankly would be afraid to manage a club for you. You're always second-guessing the manager. That doesn't help."

Kerr did not like the answer, but respected Mack for expressing himself honestly. He agreed to give Buckenberger a few more weeks.

The stay of execution didn't help. By September 1, 1894, Pittsburgh had slipped yet lower in the standings. Kerr again called Mack to his office and offered him the job. This time he spoke with much more urgency: "I have decided to make a change in the manager's position, so it's either you or someone else," he snapped.

Connie Mack reluctantly agreed to take the job and pledged to do the best he could.

Mack's first year as manager in 1895 resembled a roller-coaster ride. Fans cheered as the Pirates sat on top of the league during most of the spring. By June 2, they shouted obscenities as the Bucs slipped back to third place. Even *The Sporting News* observed: "The mighty have fallen. That class of fickle fans known as 'knockers' are making life miserable for Connie Mack and loyal supporters."

Injuries affected key players.

Southpaw ace Frank Killen was seriously spiked during a game with Baltimore on June 11. When he was finally able to return late that year, he was not in shape to give his usually sound performance. He won only seven games that year.

The 1895 Pirates ended the season in seventh place with a 71-61 record, although Manager Mack did whatever he could to win games. One report that Mack never denied was that the night prior to a home game, the genial manager placed some baseballs in a freezer in order to "freeze the life out of the balls." In those days, umpires reused foul balls. When the opposing team was at bat and a ball was hit onto the roof of the stadium, a young boy stationed there to retrieve foul balls would toss back one of the frozen balls. That made it more difficult for any batter to get substantial distance out of a solid hit.

Connie Mack's last season as manager in 1896 proved the adage that any manager is hired only to be fired. Although his ace pitcher, Frank Killen, regained his form and posted 31 victories, the remaining staff was unable to come close to imitating Killen's performance. One of the reasons for their sorry play was that many other Buc players preferred to spend time in bars and houses of ill-repute than at the ballpark. Mack's easygoing attitude did not impress his boss, especially in the middle of a ho-hum season.

Following a one-run loss on the road, Kerr sent a telegram to Mack asking why he did not lift a pitcher who was in trouble. Mack wired back that Kerr was not to second-guess him.

"The mighty have fallen. That class of fickle fans known as 'knockers' are making life miserable for Connie Mack and loyal supporters."

—THE SPORTING NEWS

That response irritated Kerr who called Mack into his office as soon as the club returned home. Captain Kerr advised him that his days as manager were over. Patsy Donovan, the Pirates' long-ball-hitting right fielder, became player-manager. The Bucs finished with a 66-63 record and a lock on sixth place.

Managing a major league baseball team is difficult. Managing it from right field is more challenging. But managing it under the watchful eye of Captain Kerr was virtually impossible. Patsy Donovan later would discover that the hard way.

When the 1897 club staggered home in eighth place, Kerr decided not only to fire the scrappy Irishman Donovan as manager, but also himself as president. He hired William "Wattie" Watkins, former manager of the World Champion Detroit Wolverines, as president-manager. Kerr also promised Watkins that he would have complete reign of the club, to make any trades he wants and to never fear being second-guessed.

The arrangement, appealing as it seemed, didn't work. The Bucs ended the 1898 season in eighth place with a 72-76 record. Patsy Donovan (.302) was the only regular hitting over .300, and the entire club hit only 13 home runs all year.

Leading the pitching staff was Jessie Tannehill (25-13). None of the other hurlers posted a winning season.

The Pirates got off to a miserable start in 1899 with only eight wins in 27 games. Watkins, who had been given full authority by Captain Kerr, made one minor change. He replaced shortstop Fred Ely as captain of the team with Patsy Donovan, the club's former manager.

Watkins made a horrible mistake. He didn't consult with Captain Kerr before initiating the change. In spite of Kerr's promise not to interfere with Watkins' work, Kerr was livid at being slighted. He let his manager know, in no uncertain terms, his displeasure. Four days later, Watkins resigned as manager of the Pirates.

Patsy Donovan took up where Watkins left off and led the club to a season-ending 76-73 record, good enough for only seventh place.

During the 1899 campaign, Pittsburgh made some moves to build for the future. Fresh faces included rookies Jack Chesbro, a renowned spitball pitcher (a legal pitch in those days), and Clarence "Ginger" Beaumont, a speedy outfielder with an educated bat. In one game on July 22 of that year, Beaumont got six hits, all singles, yet none of them left the infield.

In 1900, when the National League chose to reduce the number of teams from 12 to eight, club owners voted to eliminate Louisville, Cleveland, Washington and Baltimore. That left Pittsburgh, Brooklyn, Philadelphia, Boston, Chicago, St. Louis, Cincinnati and New York.

Owner of the Louisville Colonels was Barney Dreyfuss — a 34-year-old German Jewish immigrant who could never rid himself of a heavy accent. Dreyfuss, a Damon Runyon prototype of the American Dream, was born and educated in Germany. He emigrated to the United States when he was 17 years old. His friends say he was a pacifist and wanted to avoid the Kaiser's compulsory military training, although

> Managing a major league baseball team is difficult. Managing it from right field is more challenging. But managing it under the watchful eye of Captain Kerr was virtually impossible.

the young Dreyfuss never confirmed that claim. Whatever the reason, Dreyfuss landed his first job for six dollars a week cleaning whiskey barrels for the Bernheim Distillery in Paducah, Kentucky.

Working nine hours a day, studying English and taking classes at school, Dreyfuss improved himself and his worth to the company. Bernheim Distillery executives recognized this and promoted the ambitious young man up the company ladder. But his fast-pace life soon took its toll. The 5'7" Dreyfuss experienced headaches and nausea. A doctor ordered him to get outdoors and play baseball.

"I don't know how to play this baseball," confessed Dreyfuss.

"It's time you learned," said the doctor.

Dreyfuss not only learned to play the game, he used his organizational skills to form a semipro team. He even developed into a pretty fair second baseman.

The Bernheim Distillery moved to Louisville in 1888 and Dreyfuss, who was now its credit manager, went with the firm. While in Louisville, Dreyfuss predicted that baseball would not only become a popular sport, but would be a wise business investment as well. He bought a small block of stock in the local Louisville Colonels — a team in the American Association along with Pittsburgh, St. Louis Browns and Philadelphia Athletics. Two years later, when his club was admitted to the 12-team National League, Dreyfuss had become its treasurer.

Soon, young Barney obtained a majority of the stock and assumed

Wattie Watkins was promised full reign of the club as manager in 1898. One year later, he discovered this was not true.

the responsibilities of president.

"Baseball became his whole life," recalled Eleanor Benswanger, his daughter.

The conservative Dreyfuss, who neither drank alcohol nor touched tobacco, refused to tolerate a team that wasn't a winner. He didn't insist on first-place finishes each year, but he did demand that each team be competitive.

Dreyfuss was not out to win a popularity contest. He fought with players, fellow owners and sports writers. He was labeled dominating, stubborn, unreasonable and obstinate. But he always seemed to get the job done.

Honus Wagner at bat.

When Dreyfuss learned in 1900 that his Louisville team would no longer be part of the league, he mapped out his own plan. Friends in Pittsburgh revealed to Dreyfuss that former Pirate manager W.H. Watkins had put up $5,000 on an option to buy the Pirates. Watkins, however, was unable to obtain the remaining capital. Dreyfuss leaped at the chance and received enough backing from friends in Louisville to pick up the option.

But Kerr, no business lightweight

. . . the club had its first league batting champion — the mighty Honus Wagner.

himself, saw a golden opportunity to get much more. Since Louisville was not yet officially out of the National League, the Captain insisted that Dreyfuss bring the best of his players with him. The arrangement was made to resemble a trade.

Pittsburgh gave up five players and $25,000. In turn, the Pirates received 14 top-notch players — including future Hall-of-Famers. The impressive list included Fred "Cap" Clarke, Honus Wagner, Claude Ritchey, Tommy Leach, Charley Zimmer,

Cliff Latimer, Charles "Deacon" Phillippe, Pat Flaherty, George Edward "Rube" Waddell, Walter Woods and Elton "Cunny" Cunningham.

At its reorganization meeting, Barney Dreyfuss was named president, and 27-year-old Fred Clarke became player-manager. Tough decisions had to be made right away. The merger of the Colonels and the Pirates left the new team with more players than management could afford. Some, including Cunningham, were given unconditional releases. Cunningham would never forgive Barney Dreyfuss for what he thought was a slap in the face.

When 27-year-old player-manager Fred Clarke filled out his lineup card for the start of the 1900 season, he wrote: Beaumont, middle field (the popular designation for that position until 1945); Clarke, left field; Williams, third base, Wagner, right field; Cooley, first base; Ritchey, second base; O'Connor, catcher; Ely, shortstop; and the pitcher's slot.

On the bench also were some pretty fair country hitters, including young Tommy Leach — a diminutive infielder who would later compile amazing statistics — and some pretty fair pitchers, Jesse Tannehill (20-6), Charles "Deacon" Phillippe (20-13), Sam Leever (15-13), Jack Chesbro (15-13) and George "Rube" Waddell (only 8-13, but with a league-leading 2.37 ERA and 130 strikeouts). Tannehill's record was good enough to lead the league in winning percentage (.769).

Playing managers such as Clarke were not uncommon, especially during baseball's early years. Some of Clarke's contemporaries who managed and played for major league clubs at the same time were Bob Allen of the Reds, "Patsy" Donovan of the Cardinals (who had managed the Pittsburgh club in 1897), Clark Griffith of the White Sox, Jimmy McAleer of the St. Louis Browns and Jimmy Collins of the Boston team which, at that time, had several different names, including the "Somersets," the "Puritans" and the "Beaneaters."

The Pirates gave Exhibition Park fans plenty of thrills in 1900 as the Bucs finished in second place (79 wins, 60 defeats), six games behind the Brooklyn Dodgers. On top of that, the club had its first league batting champion — the mighty Honus Wagner.

Wagner hit .381 that year, beating out the Phillies' Elmer Flick by only a few percentage points. "Winning that first batting title was my greatest thrill in baseball," said Wagner. "The league race had been decided, but there was a lot of interest in the batting championship. Everything apparently hinged on what Elmer and I did on the last day. The press figured we were tied and they kept us abreast of what was happening in Philadelphia that afternoon.

"I got one more hit than Flick that afternoon, and the Pittsburgh reporters were happy to announce that I had won the championship by two percentage points. After reviewing the official hits and times at bat, however, I learned that I had actually earned a seven-point margin over Flick."

Not only did Wagner lead the National League in batting average, he also topped the list in slugging

The Pirates gave

Exhibition Park fans

plenty of thrills in 1900

as the Bucs finished

in second place . . .

six games behind the

Brooklyn Dodgers.

average (.573), doubles (45) and triples (22).

The Dutchman was the club's only .300 hitter, but other teammates were not far behind. Claude Ritchey hit .295, Ginger Beaumont posted a .283 average, and Clarke had a respectable .281.

Pirate President Barney Dreyfuss and his feisty player-manager Fred Clarke did not always see eye-to-eye. Dreyfuss, the consummate gentleman, advocated good sportsmanship and clean play. The unpredictable Clarke, however, exercised a more aggressive approach to the game.

During one Sunday afternoon contest in Chicago that year, Clarke twice slid hard into second baseman Clarence "Cupid" Childs in attempts to break up double plays. "Do that one more time," warned Childs, "and I'll punch you right in the nose."

Clarke viewed that as a challenge. Three innings later, Clarke was again on first base and, at the crack of the bat, ran toward second and slid with his spikes high. "Immediately, Childs punched me," said Clarke. "Naturally, I hit back. Soon we were in a bench-clearing brawl.

"Both the Chicago and Pittsburgh newspapers made the most of the incident. It just so happened we were to play the Cubs the very next day at Exposition Park. The papers suggested that on our return to Pittsburgh, Childs and I would finish the fight." As soon as he got off the train back to Pittsburgh, Clarke received word from Mr. Dreyfuss that he was to come to the owner's office the first thing Monday morning.

"Fred," demanded the usually mild-mannered Dreyfuss, "I'm tired of your rowdy tactics. If you don't cut them out, I'll have to get rid of you."

"Mr. Dreyfuss," responded Clarke in a subdued tone that belied his image, "how many Monday games have we played at home this year?"

"Seven," answered Dreyfuss. "Why do you ask?"

"What's the average attendance for a Monday game?" asked Clarke.

Dreyfuss opened his finance books. "About 2,200," said Dreyfuss.

Fred Clarke did not say anything else and left to get dressed for the game. Contrary to the predictions of the sports writers, nothing unusual happened during the nine innings, and Pittsburgh soundly defeated its Chicago rivals.

The next day, Dreyfuss greeted Clarke: "Fine game yesterday."

"Yeah, and a nice crowd," said Clarke. "What was your official count?"

"Ah . . . a bit more than 7,200," admitted Dreyfuss.

Clarke playfully grabbed Dreyfuss by the arm. "Barney, those rowdy tactics are just going to ruin you," he said. Dreyfuss never again criticized Clarke's aggressiveness.

Finishing second place in 1900 gave the Pirates their first profitable season in decades. Nonetheless, the Pirate front office was about to sail into rough waters.

Barney Dreyfuss acted as though he was the one chiefly responsible for the Pirates' success. Few could argue the point. But, Captain Kerr felt it was his ability to get championship-quality players that made the difference. The rivalry between the two became obvious even to the casual observer.

Finishing second place in 1900 gave the Pirates their first profitable season in decades. Nonetheless, the Pirate front office was about to sail into rough waters.

Dreyfuss did not help matters when he remarked jokingly that he outranked Captain Kerr because he was made an honorary Kentucky Colonel during his days in Louisville. "A colonel is always considered a superior to a captain, no matter whose army you're in," said Dreyfuss. Kerr saw nothing funny about that remark.

In a stockholders meeting in January 1901, Kerr made a calculated move to gain control of the club. Kerr had allegedly lined up enough support from investors to elect his handpicked board of directors. Yet through a shrewd move and the help of his attorney, Pennsylvania State Senator William Edwards, Dreyfuss revealed at the meeting that Kerr had disqualified himself as a director because he acted as a teller at a previous meeting. The argument convinced the investors to elect Dreyfuss president. Kerr screamed in protest; he even tried to stop Dreyfuss with a legal injunction. The attempt failed.

In a last-ditch effort to gain control, Kerr sent a representative to Barney Dreyfuss and asked him to sell his stock to the Captain for a substantial profit. "Sell nothing," shouted Dreyfuss. "I'm buying." He, in turn, made a generous offer to the Captain. Kerr, totally exhausted from fighting, agreed to sell.

New owner of the Pittsburgh ballclub was now young "Colonel" Barney Dreyfuss, a man who had spent barely half his life in America.

Manager Clarke and owner Barney Dreyfuss had a healthy respect for one another. Dreyfuss was the owner and signed the paychecks. Clarke knew that he served his role at the pleasure of the owner. At the same time, they followed a sharp division of responsibility. Once, after a loss by Pittsburgh brought on, at least in part, by ragged play, owner Dreyfuss burst into the team locker room and demanded to know why the players did not give their all.

Clarke, although as angry with the players as was his boss, abruptly ordered Dreyfuss out of the players' quarters. "Get out and stay out!" he shouted.

Barney Dreyfuss was aghast. "You mean I can't come into my own clubhouse?" he asked.

"Exactly!" Clarke said. "Anytime you want to find fault with the team, you talk to me in private. I'll take the blame. As far as these players, if there is criticism, they'll hear plenty from me, and me, alone."

Dreyfuss knew Clarke was right and seldom stepped foot again in the locker room immediately before or after a game. ■

The chiseled features of the face of Honus Wagner showed the rugged determination of a coal miner who turned out to be the greatest shortstop in the history of baseball.

HONUS WAGNER

CHAPTER 3

PENNANT FEVER

"He was the best shortstop in the league, the best third baseman, the best outfielder, the best second baseman, and the best first baseman."

—TOMMY LEACH
on Honus Wagner

Pitcher Sam Leever's sore arm may have cost the Bucs a chance for their first World Series crown in 1903. Note: Although some pitchers began wearing fielding gloves as early as 1893, others elected to play without them.

*B*UDGET RESTRAINTS VS. ESCALATING SALARIES. That sounds similar to headlines that dominate today's sports reports on the evening news. That same conflict nearly paralyzed baseball as early as the turn of the century.

Realizing the potential success of the National League's remaining eight clubs, some farsighted baseball enthusiasts conspired to form a competitive major league. Leading the charge for that venture was the energetic Ban Johnson, youthful president of the old Western League. He convinced others — Charles Comiskey, Connie Mack, Charles Somers, Clark Griffith and Jim McAleer — to wage an all-out, no-holds-barred fight to recruit the best players in the nation for their new league.

In 1901, Cleveland, Detroit, Baltimore and Washington — the four teams unceremoniously dismissed by the Nationals — were the first venues of what was dubbed the American League. Chicago, Philadelphia, and Boston fielded crosstown teams that rivaled clubs already in the National League. The eighth entry to the American League was a team from Milwaukee.

Not only did the new league open new doors for more baseball players, it also refused to impose the National League's $2,400-per-player limit on salary. That was a potential nightmare for Barney Dreyfuss who had exhausted nearly all of his funds in the purchase of the Pirates.

Some of the game's top stars reached out for higher paychecks. Pittsburgh, fortunately, lost only two players — infielder Jimmy

PITTSBURGH BASEBALL CLUB

National League Champions 1902 and 1903

Top Row: Zimmer, Sebring, Phillippe, Merritt, Leever, and Phelps
Middle Row: Chesbro, Bransfield, Clarke, Dreyfuss, Wagner, Beaumont, and Smith
Botton Row: Burke, Conroy, Leach, Ritchey, and McLaughlin

Henry "Father" Chadwick, editor of the 1901 *Spalding's Guide*, wrote about the Pirates' accomplishments:

It [the Pittsburgh Club] was more harmonious as a team than its adversaries and did less kicking, the latter being a weakness that characterized every team in the league in 1901 to a more or less extent, the rule of the season in this respect being "the more the kicking the nearer to the last ditch" and the less of that nearer the goal.

Mr. Chadwick's complimentary editorial about the Bucs painted a far different picture than did a report in the June 8, 1901, edition of *The Sporting News* that described a near disaster in which the quick thinking of Fred Clarke and Honus Wagner prevented Umpire Elton Cunningham from being attacked by irate Pittsburgh fans. Cunningham, a former pitcher with Barney Dreyfuss' Louisville squad, was one of the players released from the Pirate roster prior to the merger of Louisville and Pittsburgh in 1900. According to *The Sporting News*:

There is a difference of opinion as to the cause of the hot time in the old town last Saturday, when 2,000 men and boys chased Umpire Cunningham off the grounds and would have injured him if Manager Fred Clarke and big Honus Wagner had not acted as his bodyguard. Some people say that Cunningham's umpiring angered the crowd, while others claim that the players of both teams worked up the indignation by nagging the umpire all through the game.

The Pittsburgh players were around him twice and made so many noisy objections at various times that when in the ninth Cunningham called [Kitty] Bransfield out when he was safe by two feet on a bunt . . . the loyal rooters needed only someone to lead them to become a howling mob.

Williams who went with John McGraw to Baltimore and catcher Harry Smith. That ability to keep its key personnel may have been the major reason why Pittsburgh would go on to win its first pennant in 1901 with a record of 90-49, seven-and-a-half games ahead of their cross-state rival Philadelphia Phillies.

The Pirates also picked up their share of rather colorful players to fill out the '01 team, including Ed Doheny, a "live life with gusto" type of left-hander from the Giants. Doheny would later give Barney Dreyfuss more than his share of grey hairs.

Honus Wagner had another one of

his "typical" years, hitting .353. He showed all-around athletic ability when he topped the league in RBI (126), doubles (39) and stolen bases (48). Although he was brought to the Pirates as an outfielder, Wagner was pressed into service during the 1901 season as a shortstop for 62 games. Wagner, however, did not look like a typical infielder. This 5'11", 200-pounder resembled a college fullback. He was unusually broad-shouldered and his bowed legs resembled parentheses. His immense hands were once de-scribed as looking like bunches of bananas hanging on his long arms. Appearances notwithstanding, Wagner would develop into the game's greatest shortstop ever.

Pirate pitching also gained attention around the circuit. Heading the league in earned run average were Buc hurlers Jesse Tannehill (2.18) and Deacon Phillippe (2.22). Jack Chesbro (21-10) led the league in winning percentage (.677).

Arguably the greatest Pirate team in history was the 1902 Bucs. With a remarkable 103-36 season, Pittsburgh finished in first place, 27½ games ahead of second-place Brooklyn — the widest spread in games in major-league history between any pennant winner and a second-place team.

Obviously, this was a year when the Pirates completely dominated the league. Not only did the team over-power the second division clubs, but it easily handled both the Brooklyn Dodgers and third-place Boston Beaneaters by identical 14-6 mar-gins.

Part of the reason for the Pirates'

JACK CHESBRO

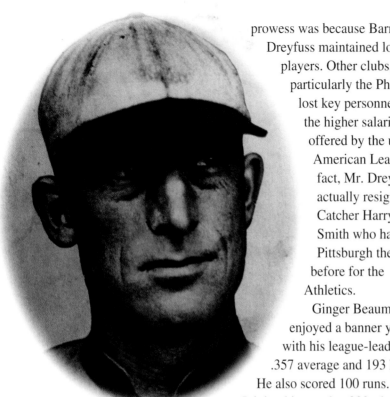

FRED CLARKE

prowess was because Barney Dreyfuss maintained loyal players. Other clubs, most particularly the Phillies, lost key personnel to the higher salaries offered by the upstart American League. In fact, Mr. Dreyfuss actually resigned Catcher Harry Smith who had left Pittsburgh the year before for the Athletics.

Ginger Beaumont enjoyed a banner year with his league-leading .357 average and 193 hits. He also scored 100 runs. Joining him on the .300-plus batting average honor roll were Honus Wagner (.329), Fred Clarke (.321) and Kitty Bransfield (.308). Honus Wagner led the league in slugging average (.467), RBI (91) and stolen bases (42).

Pitcher Jack Chesbro showed everyone that he had learned how to control his spitball by posting a 28-6 season to lead the league. Other Pirate pitchers who dominated the opposition were: erratic Ed Doheny (16-4), Deacon Phillippe (20-9), Jesse Tannehill (20-6) and School-master Leever (15-7).

One of the more shocking statistics that year was that little Tommy Leach ranked third in the league in slugging average. He had 15 doubles, 20 triples and six home runs. Amazingly, those six round-trippers were enough to lead the National League. It was the lowest home run output ever to lead a major league.

The 1902 season might well have featured a headline about some outfielder being drowned at Exposition Park. Following heavy rains, when the Allegheny River over-flowed its banks and existing sewers were not able to handle the onrush-ing water, the Pirates' home field felt the effects. On more than one occasion parts of right and center fields were under water.

The July 4th doubleheader that year left no doubt that Exposition Park was possibly the most challeng-ing field in major league baseball.

A heavy downpour for several days sent water cascading over the banks of the Allegheny, so at the beginning of the morning game on Independence Day, the entire center field was covered by an inch or so of water. A special ground rule ac-cepted by both teams allowed a runner one extra base if the ball landed in the water.

During the morning game, the water became deeper. A young boy was hired to dry off wet baseballs with a towel in order to keep them in the game. According to eyewitness reports, by the seventh inning of the afternoon game, both center field and right field were nearly knee-deep in water. In fact, neither of the two right fielders — Wee Willie "Hit 'em where they ain't" Keeler of the Dodgers and Alfonzo "Lefty" Davis of the Pirates — recorded a single putout in the afternoon contest. Instead, they both found a little island in the outfield water from which they did not move. Center fielder, Ginger Beaumont of the Pirates, high-stepped through the water to catch a fly ball for the final out and celebrated by diving head-first into the mini-lake that had engulfed a major portion of the outfield grass.

The most lasting impact upon baseball that year, however, happened off the field. After the turn of the century, America's pastime was influenced by a group of men who were not fond of always following a gentleman's code of ethics. John McGraw, manager of the New York Giants, was a tough competitor. And the Pirates' Fred Clarke, by his own admission, was no angel. Owners, including Barney Dreyfuss, realized that if these managers and players were not kept in check, baseball could deteriorate into a game for rowdies.

When it came time to elect a league president that year at the annual meeting of club owners, Dreyfuss nominated the Pirates' secretary, a 32-year-old native of Kentucky, Harry C. Pulliam. "Harry and I have worked close in Louisville and Pittsburgh," Dreyfuss told the other club owners. "I can promise you that Harry Pulliam is the soul of honor. If he is elected, I expect no favor and I shall ask no favors."

Dreyfuss' words were persuasive. Pulliam was elected and began a campaign to clean up the league. He was especially aware of the importance of players and managers respecting umpires. He promised heavy fines, even suspensions, for those who failed to heed his warning.

Also, at the same baseball meeting, the National League recognized the American League as an equal rival in baseball. Contracts previously signed by certain key players were now accepted as legitimate. Leaving the Pirates for the so-called "junior circuit" were ace pitchers Jesse Tannehill and Jack Chesbro who had won 48 games between them that year.

Out to spoil the Pirates' domination of the league were John McGraw and his Giants, led by one of the all-time-great pitchers, Christy Mathewson. Through solid hitting and masterful pitching, the Giants leaped from eighth place to second in 1903. The Pirates were able to play only .500 ball against the upstart Giants, yet maintained their hold on first place by overwhelming second-division clubs such as Philadelphia and St. Louis.

The Pirates fielded a superb team in 1903. Winning six of their first seven games, the Bucs gave strong indication that they were the ones to beat that year. During the next month, over a 15-game winning streak, the Pirate pitching staff set an all-time record by tossing six consecutive shutout games.

Pitching for the Bucs that year were Sam Leever (25-7 and a league-leading 2.06 ERA), Deacon Phillippe (24-7), Ed Doheny (16-8), William "Brickyard" Kennedy (9-6) and Kaiser Wilhelm (5-3). Honus Wagner (who was often dubbed "Old Bowlegs") once again won the league batting crown in 1903 with a .355 average; Fred Clarke was a close second at .351, but led the league with a .532 slugging average. Wagner led the senior circuit with 19 triples and his 101 RBI fell three short of the league lead by Sam Merles of New York. Ginger Beaumont's 209 hits led both leagues.

In spite of the wealth of talent, the

After the turn of the century, America's pastime was influenced by a group of men who were not fond of always following a gentleman's code of ethics.

1903 Pirates endured their share of internal problems. Manager Fred Clarke occasionally embarrassed Barney Dreyfuss with his on-the-field outbursts and obscenities yelled at umpires. One arbiter, James "Bug" Holliday, spent only this one year in the big leagues. It was long enough, however, to gain for him an unexpected education. Following a blistering attack on his umpiring skills one afternoon, Holliday was called names by Fred Clarke he had never before heard. Holliday gave Clarke the thumb. Afterward, Holliday confessed, "I knew what he called me must have been some bad names, but only after I went to my hotel room and looked up those words in a dictionary did I know just how bad they really were."

The most devastating problem involved pitcher Ed Doheny. The likable Irishman was a solid pitcher with a wicked curve and an over-powering fastball. However, in July, for some unexplained reason, Doheny developed a lame arm. Frustrations mounted for him and everybody could tell it. In place of his normal, happy-go-lucky approach to life, he suddenly turned angry at himself, his teammates and the world. He was not able to pitch for the remainder of the season. Just prior to the last game, Doheny was escorted out of the dressing room and sent to a mental hospital in Danvers, Massachusetts — bringing back memories of the fate of Horace Phillips in 1889.

Doheny did not respond to treatment. Instead, he attacked a physician and a nurse. He remained a patient at the hospital until his death 13 years later.

In 1903, the Pirates agreed to participate in an experiment that made baseball history. Prior to the season's end, Mr. Dreyfuss called Henry Killilea, president of the American League Champion Boston Pilgrims, and asked if he would like to stage a series of games between the two teams. That was the beginning of what came to be known as the World Series.

A one-page contract between the two teams spelled out the terms of the only nine-game Series.

Immediately following the signing of the agreement, the Boston Pilgrims and the American League dropped all hints of diplomacy. Pressure was put on Killilea. "You must beat them," ordered American League President Ban Johnson. To show the seriousness of the rivalry, Killilea made Barney Dreyfuss pay his own way into the ballpark.

The Pirates won the first game in Boston; Deacon Phillippe bested Denton True "Cy" (short for "cyclone") Young 7-3. Pirate outfielder Jim Sebring had the distinction of hitting the first World Series home run in the contest.

In Game Two, Sam Leever was yanked after the first inning because of a sore arm. Boston won by a score of 3-0.

Game Three invited the largest crowd to that date in Boston history (18,801). Another 10,000 had to be turned away. Phillippe and the rest of the Pirates, however, made them drown their sorrows at the neighborhood pubs when they overpowered the Pilgrims 10-3.

Back in Pittsburgh for Game Four, Phillippe again pitched, notching his third consecutive Series victory, as the Pirates won 5-4.

Boston surged back behind the pitching of the immortal Cy Young, and won Game Five 11-2.

Game Six was no better for the Bucs. Sore-armed Sam Leever was unable to keep Boston in check. The final score: Boston 6, Pittsburgh 3.

Still in Pittsburgh for Game Seven, ace hurler Deacon Phillippe got a welcomed extra day's rest due to a rain delay. But that was not enough as the Pilgrims won 7-3 on a sloppy, wet field.

Weather conditions were no better in Boston for the final game of the Series. Following another one-day rain delay, the Deacon again took the mound, establishing an all-time record of five starts in a World Series. During the game, Clarke bunted down the first base line. Boston's first baseman, "Candy" LaChance, fielded the ball and hit Clarke with the throw. Players and fans ran onto the field. It took umpires Tommy Connolly and Hank O'Day a half hour to restore order.

Phillippe pitched well, yielding only three runs, but his mound opponent, Bill Dinneen (who later became an American League umpire) did better. He shutout the Pirates 3-0.

The Boston Pilgrims, representatives of the upstart American League, became baseball's first World Champions.

Although they lost the Series, the Pittsburgh players lit a spark of excitement in Pittsburgh. Solid fan support resulted in the club showing a profit of more than $60,000 for the year. When the World Series money was sent to Pittsburgh, owner Dreyfuss, as a gesture of appreciation for the loyalty of the players during the recent American League raids, added his entire club owner's share to the players' pool, giving each Pirate $1,316.25. For the only time in history, each player of the losing team took home more Series money than did a player for the winning team.

That gesture of benevolence notwithstanding, Barney Dreyfuss and the rest of the National League owners were devastated because of what they deemed to be a humiliating loss in the World Series to the new American League representatives.

In 1904, the New York Giants continued their hot streak; two of their pitchers — Christy Mathewson and Joe McGinnity — together won a remarkable 68 games. The Pirates, on the other hand, started cold and remained that way throughout the season. And it all began in spring training.

For the previous few years, owner Dreyfuss preferred to hold spring training in Hot Springs, Arkansas, rather than somewhere farther south or in California. He was fond of its mineral baths and thought they would provide benefits for the team. This year, however, because of an unseasonable cold snap, most of the players were unable to work themselves into shape.

Several key players, consequently, saw limited duty. Honus Wagner was out of the lineup for 24 games, Kitty Bransfield missed 27 and player-manager Fred Clarke was bedridden much of the year and could appear in only 70 games. A poor start to the season in April was impossible to overcome and the Bucs had to be content with a fourth-place finish.

Although they lost the Series, the Pittsburgh players lit a spark of excitement in Pittsburgh.

Honus Wagner assumed his rightful perch as the league's best hitter for average (.349) and for slugging (.520). He also led the circuit in doubles (44) and stolen bases (53). Ginger Beaumont banged out 185 hits to lead in that category.

Even the purchase of a package of new pitchers that year failed to help. Added to the staff were William "Doc" Scanlon, Jack Pfiester (his real name was Pfiestenberger), Mike Lynch, Lew Moren, Roscoe Miller, Charles Case, Howard Camnitz and Anthony "Chick" Robertaille.

Because of the humiliation suffered by the Pirates following the 1903 World Series loss to Boston, the Giants refused to play a World Series against the Pilgrims, who repeated as American League Champions. Giants President John Brush vowed he would not be dragged into a contest with "minor leaguers." Manager McGraw agreed. The Pilgrims were disappointed and felt insulted by Brush's slur, none-theless they proclaimed themselves World Champions by default.

Barney Dreyfuss truly appreciated the loyalty shown to him and his organization by players. Dreyfuss did not demonstrate the same loyalty, however, to those whose performances indicated that their skills were failing. Kitty Bransfield, a fixture at first base for four years, had slipped to a .223 average in 1904. At the winter meetings in December, Dreyfuss traded the steady Bransfield to the Phillies for a minor league prospect named George "Del" Howard. Dreyfuss was so eager to make the trade that he also threw in outfielder Harry McCormick and utility man Otto "Oom Paul" Krueger.

The Pirates did show substantial improvement in 1905 over the year before and became the Giants' biggest threat. John McGraw, the aggressive New York manager, let it be known that "Pittsburgh is the team we have to beat and there are no holds barred." In short, McGraw declared war on Pittsburgh.

The bad blood between the two clubs came to a head in April during a game at New York's Polo Grounds. Fred Clarke was coming in from his left field position to remove a pitcher. McGraw, who coached third base for the Giants, screamed insults at both the pitcher and Clarke. "You're nothing but quitters," he shouted.

Clarke became furious. He ran towards McGraw and, within seconds, both managers were swinging wildly. Neither would be a candidate as a champion prize fighter; umpires were able to separate them before one blow was struck.

The next day, before the game, McGraw spotted Barney Dreyfuss at the park. "Hey, Kraut!" he yelled at the Pirate owner. "Are you going to lose more money and bet on today's game?"

When Dreyfuss refused to acknowledge his insult, McGraw accused him of welshing on past gambling debts. Dreyfuss became so angry he fired off a letter to League President Pulliam who, in turn, slapped McGraw with a $150 fine and suspended him for 15 days.

This was the sort of instance that made John McGraw perhaps the most universally despised representative of major-league baseball in his era.

On the playing field, Honus Wagner, for one of the rare times in his career, failed to lead the league in hitting in 1905. His .363 average was good enough only for second place behind Cy Seymour of Cincinnati who hit a career high .377.

The Pirates finished in second place that year, nine games behind McGraw's Giants. That certainly did nothing to ease the tension still seething inside Barney Dreyfuss and the rest of the Pirate faithful.

Neither did the cold winter months. By the start of the 1906 season, Dreyfuss pledged to do whatever it took to finish ahead of John McGraw and his Giants. John McGraw was just as determined not to let the Bucs take away his title. Perhaps this was one of the reasons why Dreyfuss was willing to gamble on a pitcher named Vic Willis of the Boston franchise. Willis had raw talent, nobody could argue that fact, but he had lost an astounding 29 games the previous season. Nevertheless, Dreyfuss thought Willis could win when backed by the consistent hitting of the Pittsburgh club.

Barney Dreyfuss was so confident in his opinion, he was willing to part with three players, including Del Howard, the man he received in the infamous Bransfield deal one year earlier.

Both Dreyfuss and McGraw were so focused on destroying each other that neither of them seemed to notice the whirlwind series of victories by the Chicago Cubs. Led by their new manager, Frank Chance, the Cubs posted an amazing record of 116 victories and only 36 defeats. Pittsburgh and New York had to be satisfied with battling for second place, which the Giants eventually captured.

The Pirates — who became the first club that year to use a tarpaulin to cover the infield when it rained — finished third in 1906, yet the season provided some bright spots. The pitching staff, for example, tossed a club record 26 shutouts. Vic Willis, that same 29-game loser when he was with Boston, led the Bucs with 23 wins; Sam Leever had 22; Albert Peter "Lefty" Leifield, who came from the Cardinals, won 18; and old reliable Deacon Phillippe posted 15 victories. Two no-hitters were thrown that year. Howie Camnitz pitched a 1-0 shutout of the Giants. The game, the second of a double-header, was called after five innings because of darkness. Nick Maddox also threw a no-hitter on September 21 against Brooklyn, and won 2-1.

The Buc offense was dominated by Honus Wagner who led the league once again in hitting (.339) and in doubles (38).

The focus of attention for the Pirates switched in 1907 from getting McGraw at all costs to dethroning the Cubs. Dreyfuss thought that second sacker Claude Richey — a player left over from his Louisville days — had lost a step or two. He had his eye set on Boston's second baseman, Ed Abby (real name: Abbaticchio) who hailed from nearby Latrobe. Boston was agreeable to a trade for Richey as long as Pittsburgh sweetened the pot by including Ginger Beaumont and Pat Flaherty. Dreyfuss reluctantly agreed.

The trade was not enough to unseat the Cubs who, again, won the

Vic Willis was a gamble that paid off for the Pirates in 1906. He had lost 29 games the year before while with Boston, but bounced back to lead the Bucs with 23 victories.

The focus of attention for the Pirates switched in 1907 from getting McGraw at all costs to dethroning the Cubs.

Three teams — the

Giants, Cubs and

Pirates — were

neck and neck in

the standings until

the last game of

the season.

league championship with 107 victories, 17 games ahead of the Bucs. With the Phillies in third place that year and the Giants back in fourth, Barney Dreyfuss still retained some bragging rights. "I didn't win the pennant," he said, "but I am happy that two Pennsylvania clubs finished ahead of New York's Muggsy McGraw."

Other rewards of the season included the fact the Pirates led the league in team batting average (.254) and in stolen bases (264). Thirty-three-year-old Honus Wagner once again earned the batting crown, hitting the ball at a .350 clip, as well as leading in slugging average (.513), doubles (38) and stolen bases (61). The Pirates also had two 20-game winners: Vic Willis (21-11) and Lefty Leifield (20-16).

Ginger Beaumont, one of the players swapped for Ed Abby, had some Pirate fans second-guessing Barney Dreyfuss; he finished the year with a .322 average and led the league with 187 hits. Abby batted .262.

The fate of the Pirates that year might well have been better had Mr. Dreyfuss listened to one of his salesman friends who sent back glowing reports of a young pitcher from Weiser, Idaho. The salesman lost himself in arm-waving and superlatives when describing this big fastballer who averaged 20 strike-outs a game. But Barney Dreyfuss was unwilling to put up the money to bring the youngster to Pittsburgh for a tryout; the salesman, he thought, was trying too hard to make a sale. So, Mr. Dreyfuss declined to look at this young pitcher. His name was Walter Johnson. Johnson was

eventually signed by Washington of the American League and the "Big Train," as he was called, pitched 21 years for the Washington Senators racking up 413 major league victories before retiring in 1927.

Prior to 1908, the unbelievable happened. Honus Wagner, one of the most loyal Pirates of them all, refused to sign a contract. Wagner had asked for a $10,000 salary; Dreyfuss felt that was too much money, even for a league batting champion. Throughout spring training, the "Flying Dutchman" didn't pull on a Pirate uniform. In fact, it wasn't until April 19, four days into the season, that Dreyfuss finally offered him an acceptable contract.

"I really wasn't a holdout," insisted Wagner. "I was going to retire and go into the garage business in Carnegie. But Barney had to convince me that $10,000 a year in baseball was better than the garage business."

The Pirates that year needed every ounce of talent. Three teams — the Giants, Cubs and Pirates — were neck and neck in the standings until the last game of the season. Unfortunately, Pittsburgh ended the year in a second-place tie with New York, one game behind league-leading Chicago.

Pitching was again a strong factor for the Pirates. Vic Willis showed his usual finesse (23-11) as did second-year man Nick Maddox (23-8). Howie Camnitz (16-9) and Sam Leever (15-7) were also on the winning side. Lefty Leifield (15-14) had, for him, a mediocre year.

Some critics thought that Pittsburgh fell short because of the trade of Kitty Bransfield who, with a .304 average, was only one of four players in the league to hit better than .300. One of the others to hit more than .300, as usual, was Honus Wagner (.354) who led the league in that department.

This year, as much as any other in Wagner's illustrious career, demonstrated his domination in every dimension of offense. Not only did he repeat as National League batting champion, he also led in hits (201), doubles (39), triples (19), RBI (109), slugging average (.542) and stolen bases (53). He was second in home runs (10) and runs scored (100).

One of his teammates, Tommy Leach, was one of those who saw Wagner up close. He, too, was overwhelmed by Wagner's talent. Following his retirement from baseball, Leach described Honus Wagner this way: "He was the best shortstop in the league, the best third baseman, the best outfielder, the best second baseman and the best first baseman. That was in fielding. Since he led the league in hitting eight times between 1900 and 1911, you know he was the best hitter, too."

Wagner literally mesmerized the fans of his era. He was not only quick, but tough. Opposing ballplayers gawked in silent reverence when this barrel-chested native of Carnegie stopped ground balls with his bare hand. Even the caustic John "Little Napoleon" McGraw, per-

Third baseman Tommy Leach led the 1902 Pirates with six homers. He was also instrumental in the Pirates winning the National League Championship in 1903 and playing in the first World Series ever.

petual arch enemy of Barney Dreyfuss and the Pirates, once confessed to Wagner: "You're a great ball player. I surely wish I had one like you."

Once, the gruff McGraw was asked by one of his pitchers: "How should I pitch to Wagner?"

"Just throw the ball," answered McGraw, "and duck."

"Coming from McGraw, that wasa real compliment, and I was proud of it," the Dutchman admitted later.

Honus Wagner became the most famous person in Pittsburgh. He was idolized by everyone from President Howard Taft (who named Wagner his favorite ballplayer) to his friends at the Elks Club and St. John's Lutheran Church in Carnegie. Yet Wagner approached his status as a baseball star much differently than do most modern-era players. He felt it was below a player's dignity to endorse products or to be paraded on stage in vaudeville shows. One theatrical manager offered him $1,000 a week (a bundle of money at that time) to appear in a show with Ty Cobb and Nap Lajoie — two batting rivals. Wagner refused. Likewise, he rejected an offer for major dollars to appear at a Pittsburgh department store during the off-season just to greet customers.

Wagner's biggest, most violent "No!" was to any offer to endorse cigarettes or other tobacco products. During the 1908 season, Honus Wagner's picture appeared on a card placed inside a Sweet Caporal Cigarettes pack in an attempt by the company to increase sales. Placing photos of baseball players inside packs was a rather common promotional gimmick begun in 1886 by Old Judge Cigarettes. Nonetheless, the Sweet Caporal cards were printed without Wagner's knowledge or permission. The powerful shortstop, who was an evangelist for physical fitness, neither smoked cigarettes (although he enjoyed an occasional cigar) nor endorsed smoking. Of particular concern to Wagner was that some children might be tempted to buy the cigarettes just to get his picture.

Seven cards were printed and given away as a premium before the company received official word of Wagner's protest. Today, only one card is left and was recently purchased for more than $400,000. It's the highest amount paid for any baseball trading card in history.

The cigarette company had promised John Gruber, the Bucs' official scorer, a $10 bonus were he to get Wagner to sign an agreement to have his picture on a trading card that would be included in a pack of cigarettes. When Wagner heard about this, he sent a check and a note to Gruber that read: "I don't want my picture in cigarettes, but I don't want you to lose the ten dollars, so I am sending you a check for that sum." ■

> Honus felt it was below a player's dignity to endorse products or to be paraded on stage in vaudeville shows.

DEACON PHILLIPPE

CHAPTER 4

A FIELD NAMED FORBES

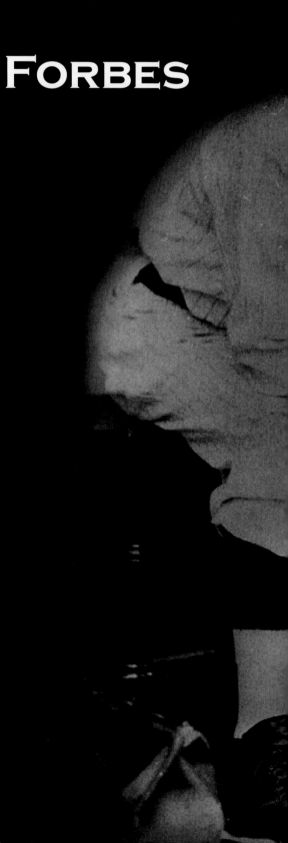

“ *A friend of mine bet me a $150 suit of clothes that the park would never be filled. We filled it five times the first two weeks."*

—BARNEY DREYFUSS
on his new stadium, 1909

WHEN HE WAS A BOOKKEEPER for the Louisville Colonels, Barney Dreyfuss defied the skeptics by predicting that a winning baseball team would be a solid investment. He backed his theory with his own dollars in obtaining quality players and a first-rate club. His Pittsburgh Pirates proved him right. But even his most loyal supporters raised an eyebrow or two in 1908 when he announced his plan to build a massive, three-tiered stadium for fans in the Steel City.

Most ballparks, even those in the larger cities such as Chicago and New York, were made of wood. Dreyfuss envisioned one made of steel and concrete — an engineering phenomenon designed to last decades longer than any existing stadium. The concept was a far cry from the modest facility of Exposition Park where fans often had to stand on tiptoe behind a roped-off outfield to see the field of play. And, who could forget those flooded outfields each time the Allegheny River overflowed its banks?

"When I first told people about the new ballpark and its location, they laughed," admitted Dreyfuss. "It was on property belonging to Schenley Farms, complete with livery stable while a few cows roamed over the countryside."

The new ballpark, dubbed by some members of the press as "Old Ironsides," was named Forbes Field after John Forbes, a British

Fred Clarke spent 16 years with Pittsburgh as a player and a manager.

general in the French and Indian War who captured Ft. Duquesne from the French in 1758 and re-named it Ft. Pitt. The new facility cost Mr. Dreyfuss and the Pirate organization a total of $1 million ($250,000 for the land, $750,000 for construction). It had a seating capacity of 25,000, making it a bigger park than the Polo Grounds of the New York Giants. "A friend of mine bet me a $150 suit of clothes that the park would never be filled," said Dreyfuss. "We filled it five times the first two weeks."

Forbes Field opened its gates on June 30, 1909. A standing-room-only crowd of 30,388 cheered as the Pirates took the field against the Tinker-to-Evers-to-Chance Chicago Cubs. Chicago won the game 3-2, yet that loss failed to dampen the spirit of the fans who saw what was considered then the most beautiful park in the majors.

It was spacious, indeed. Home plate was 110 feet in front of the stands, giving a catcher plenty of room to chase pop fouls. Left field was deep — 360 feet from home plate; right field was even farther away — 365 feet down the foul line. But center field was a pitcher's dream. Left-center field (the "power alley") was a whopping 457 feet, and the deepest part was 462 feet from the batter's box. Hitters referred to this area as "Death Valley." It was so deep, in fact, that the batting cage used in pregame practice was wheeled up against the center field wall and left there during the game; no player, so the experts believed, could ever hit a ball that far.

Barney Dreyfuss was proud of his new park just as he was of his 1909

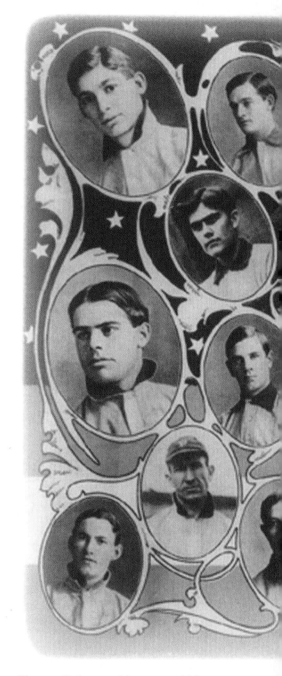

Pirates. Only one thing marred his exultation. His friend and longtime associate, Harry Pulliam, committed suicide in mid-season.

"No finer man was born into this world," grieved Dreyfuss. "I am heartsick."

In spite of his personal loss, Dreyfuss maintained his focus and that of his ballclub. With a revamped

infield of Bill Abstein at first, Jack "Dots" Miller at second, reliable Honus Wagner at short and William "Jap" Barbeau at third, the Pirates finished the season with 110 wins, six-and-a-half games ahead of the Cubs. It was the most wins in one year for any Pirate team.

Like the voice on a cracked phonograph record, the official statistician of the National League announced, to nobody's surprise, that Honus Wagner was, once again, the league's batting champion with a .339 average. Wagner also led in doubles (39), RBI (100) and slugging (.489). Although not enough to lead the league, his 35 stolen bases testified to the fact that he could still run with the best of them.

**WORLD CHAMPION PIRATES
1909**

Charles Benjamin Adams was called "Babe" because of his baby-face appearance. He was more than a kid on the mound, however, as he compiled a 194-139 record with Pittsburgh from 1907–1926.

Pitching remained a vital cog in the success of the Bucs. Although they saw limited duty, Phillippe and Leever combined for 16 wins and only 4 losses. Howard Camnitz tied the great Christy Mathewson with 25 wins, and Lefty Leifield won 22 contests.

Most surprising was a new kid on the block named Charles Adams. Most people knew him as "Babe" because he was so young among the sea of veterans on the club. Manager Clarke called him his "baby on the spot" when he posted a fine 12-3 record that year.

With the pennant won, it was time to think about the World Series with the American League champion Detroit Tigers.

It was an ideal match-up, a press agent's fantasy, featuring the two greatest hitters of the era — Honus Wagner and the feisty Tyrus Raymond Cobb. It was really no contest. Wagner batted .333 during the Series; Cobb hit a mediocre .231. In addition, Wagner loved to recall a personal confrontation with the "Georgia Peach" during the first game.

Wagner was stationed at his normal spot at shortstop. Cobb was on first. Cobb tried to tantalize Wagner by shouting: "I'm coming down on the next pitch, Krauthead."

As soon as the pitcher released the ball, Cobb took off for second. Wagner covered the bag. Catcher George Gibson threw a perfect strike into Wagner's glove. Cobb slid with spikes high. Wagner sidestepped the onrushing Tiger, then swung his gloved hand sharply across Cobb's jaw with vengeance. The blow was powerful enough to cut Cobb's lip and knock out two of his teeth. To add insult to injury, the umpire bellowed: "Yer out!"

It was payback time.

Until his dying day, the Dutchman insisted that this was one of his most satisfying moments in baseball.

Game One of the 1909 Series went to Pittsburgh 4-1, giving the hometown fans a chance to cheer the stellar pitching of Babe Adams. In Game Two, Ty Cobb stole home with ease. It was just one of the humbling statistics in a 7-2 loss for the Bucs.

Not to be outdone, in Game Three in Detroit, Honus Wagner got three singles, knocked in three runs and stole three bases as the Pirates won 8-6.

Detroit's "Wabash George" Mullin struck out 10 Pirates as Detroit blanked the Bucs in Game Four, 5-0. Back home in Pittsburgh, the Bucs and Babe Adams again came out on top, 8-4, in Game Five, but the quick trip back to Detroit may have exhausted the Pirate players as they lost Game Six to Mullin 5-4.

In the final game, held in Detroit, Pittsburgh, once again, called on its overworked ace, Babe Adams. He rose to the challenge and shutout the Tigers 8-0.

Only two home runs were hit during that entire World Series, both by player-manager Fred Clarke. But the real star of the seven games was the rookie pitcher, Babe Adams, who won three of the four games, including the seventh contest. No other pitcher before had ever won three games in a seven-game World Series.

More importantly, for the first time in its history, the Pittsburgh Pirates were the World Champions of baseball.

The 1909 Pirates so dominated the league that some reporters suggested the club start selling World Series tickets before the next season's opening day. Yet, a popular adage says: "If you wish to make God laugh, tell him your plans." The 1910 Bucs were living proof of how true that is. The euphoric memory of a World Championship of 1909 seemed light-years away. Shouts of celebration among Pittsburgh fans faded into distant echoes as the Bucs showed little resemblance to the players who wore the same uniforms only one year earlier. Their third-place finish behind Chicago and New York gave no reason for the Pirate faithful to pop more champagne corks.

"Our 1910 team was my biggest disappointment in baseball," admitted Barney Dreyfuss. "Never did I see a great team fold so quickly."

Of chief concern to Dreyfuss and Manager Clarke was the absence of a steady-fielding, hard-hitting first baseman. Several players, including Honus Wagner, tried to fill the slot, but Wagner was just too valuable at shortstop; the rest simply were not able to do the job.

The sharpest decline for the Pirates that year was in the pitching department. Indeed, some of the staff earned favorable stats. Deacon Phillippe had a 14-2 season; it was a year in which he issued only 9 bases on balls, making him one of the few pitchers in history ever to yield fewer walks than wins posted. Babe Adams notched an impressive 18-9 record. However, the three reliable aces of the mound — Camnitz, Leifield and Willis, who had combined for 66 victories in 1909 — slumped to a total of 36 wins.

Finally, the creeping consequences of age caught up with some of the other Pirate regulars. Honus Wagner failed to win the batting crown for only the second time since 1903; his .320 average placed him fourth in the standings. Fred Clarke, now 38 years old, was frequently hobbled by injury. "Dots" Miller was sidelined for over a month, thus opening the door for a native of Wilkinsburg, Bill McKechnie, to fill the second base slot.

Two rookie outfielders showed plenty of speed and baseball savvy. Not only were they talented, but each had a college education — a rare credential for a ballplayer in those days. One was Vince Campbell, fresh from the campus at Vanderbilt University. In 74 games that year, he hit an impressive .326.

The other rookie with promise was born Maximilian Canarius. He shortened his name to "Max Carey." Although he played in only two games that year, the switch-hitting, swift outfielder demonstrated that he could cover as much ground as anyone.

But it wasn't Carey's speed that surprised anyone. After all, he stole 86 bases in just 96 games for South Bend in the Central League the year before. Instead it was his academic background. Max Carey was

The 1909 Pirates so dominated the league that some reporters suggested the club start selling World Series tickets before the next season's opening day.

studying to become a Lutheran pastor.

Carey, already a college graduate, was in his second year at Concordia Seminary in St. Louis when he was discovered by Aggie Grant, then manager of the South Bend team. Although he was given an opportunity to play professional ball that year, Carey decided to return to the seminary. However, just prior to graduation and ordination, Carey announced he actually felt a call to play baseball and signed a contract to play for South Bend. "I decided not to complete my studies at the seminary," said Carey, "having come to the realization that baseball, rather than the ministry, was to be my life's work."

The 1911 campaign was a mirror image of the previous year. Once again, Pittsburgh, Chicago and New York battled for the National League lead. This year it was the Giants' turn to hang a championship flag in their ballpark. Pittsburgh finished third, 14½ games behind McGraw's front-runners.

Barney Dreyfuss became convinced that money could buy a pennant-winning club. Although unable to purchase the dependable first baseman he desperately needed, he did pay an astronomical $22,500 for Marty O'Toole, a pitching sensation from the American Association St. Paul club (a Boston franchise). In addition, so that O'Toole would feel comfortable in his new surroundings, Dreyfuss dug into the till for an additional $5,000 for O'Toole's catcher, Billy Kelly.

Barney Dreyfuss would have been wiser to invest his money in wildcat oil wells. Although Kelly batted .290 over three years with the Bucs, he was able to hit only one ball out of the park. O'Toole's pitching record was under .500 in his four years with Pittsburgh. He cited undue pressure from the hype prior to his arrival in the big leagues as the reason for his less-than-spectacular showing.

Honus Wagner won his eighth and last batting title that year with a .334 average. Babe Adams compiled an impressive 2.33 ERA, good enough for third in the league. Fred Clarke played in only 101 games but, aging legs and all, hit .324.

Vince Campbell, the brilliant rookie during the previous season, held out for more money and did not appear in a Pirate uniform until July 10. He played in only 42 games, hitting .312. But Barney Dreyfuss was no supporter of players who lacked loyalty. To him, holding out for more pay showed disrespect for both him and the team. At season's end he traded the rapid-running Campbell to the cellar-dwelling Boston "Rustlers" (as the team was called for that one year only).

The 1912 Pirates won 93 games, 10 short of McGraw's Giants who tore up the league.

Barney Dreyfuss chose logic in lieu of emotion in an attempt to bolster the team in mid-season. He traded Tommy Leach (who had been with him since Louisville) and pitcher Lefty Leifield to Chicago for Artie "Solly" Hofman and Leonard "King" Cole — neither of whom proved to be of genuine help to the Bucs.

He did not win the batting title, but Honus Wagner still clubbed a fine .324 and led the league with 102 RBI. Owen "Chief" Wilson was tops

The 1912 Pirates won 93 games, 10 short of McGraw's Giants who tore up the league.

Max Carey choked up on the bat in order to punch out many singles. Once he was on first, this former seminary student electrified the fans with his base running.

in the National League in triples (36). But it was Max Carey who brought genuine excitement to the game by hitting .302 and was league runner-up in the stolen base department (45).

Carey, like Ty Cobb of the American League, made base-stealing an art. The key to his success was his ability to study pitchers with the eye of a statistician. He memorized their mannerisms. At precisely the correct moment, he headed for second base. Those who saw this scientific base-stealer in action, testify that they had never seen a runner on a hit-and-run play fly from first to third so quickly.

No solid first baseman was added to the roster, yet the 1913 Pirate squad had a definite new look. Fred Clarke, a fixture as player-manager, knew that his tired legs would no longer allow him to play as he once did. With the permission of Mr. Dreyfuss, Clarke managed the 1913 season from the bench. And, as Clarke admitted later, it wasn't much fun. Clarke's lineup consisted mainly of young, unproved youngsters trying vainly to compete in the big leagues. Even the veteran Honus Wagner felt the impact of Father Time. An injured knee

limited him to 114 games and an even .300 batting average. This was the Flying Dutchman's 17th consecutive year hitting .300 or more . . . and his last.

Young Jimmy Viox, showing promise at second base, hit .317. Pitcher Babe Adams won 21 games and checked opposing teams with his 2.15 ERA, good enough for second place in the league behind the masterful Christy Mathewson.

Another bright spot that year was Arley Wilbur Cooper, a left-hand pitcher acquired late in the previous season from the Columbus, Ohio, farm team. Although his 1913 record was a modest 5-3, he showed Manager Clarke that he had the stuff to make it in the majors.

The 1913 Pirates could only earn a fourth-place finish in the National League standings. Of more importance, for the first time in years, the front office showed that it was willing to initiate a massive rebuilding effort.

"The Pirates have fallen into a rut, and I'm going to have to do something drastic to get us out of it," said Barney Dreyfuss prior to the league's annual December meeting in New York City.

That something drastic turned out to be one of the bigger — and worst — trades in Pirate history. It would later be known as the "Five for Three Deal."

Miller Huggins, diminutive player-manager of the St. Louis Cardinals, who would later gain even greater prominence as manager of the legendary New York Yankees, attended the December meeting along with Helene Hathaway, owner of the Cardinals. Huggins and

Hathaway were willing to offer for trade something the Pirate club desperately needed — a proven first baseman. His name was Ed Konetchy. Konetchy, the Cardinals' cleanup hitter, had led his club with seven home runs and had a respectable .287 average. In addition, St. Louis was willing to part with third-sacker Mike Mowrey and Bob Harmon, a right-hand pitcher.

Barney Dreyfuss sensed an opportunity to fill in some much-needed gaps. He desperately wanted these three players. He agreed to trade five of his established players — Owen Wilson, Jack Miller, Art Butler, Cozy Dolan and left-hand pitcher Hank Robinson.

Although the Pittsburgh fans and media felt uneasy about the departure of favorites such as "Chief" Wilson and Jack Miller, Dreyfuss attempted to convince them that this trade would solve the club's problems. "At long last we again have a high-class first baseman," he told them.

When Pittsburgh won 15 of its first 17 games in 1914, Dreyfuss looked like a genius. Suddenly, however, the Bucs took a nose-dive. Throughout the 1914 season, they had to fight just to keep out of the cellar and settled for a miserable seventh-place finish. Meanwhile, the Cardinals, led by the five former Pirates, clawed their way to third place.

Barney Dreyfuss focused much of the blame for the Pirates' demise on his new first baseman, Ed Konetchy, who hit only four home runs and a mere .249 — hardly the stats of the hard-hitting first-sacker he had in mind. Konetchy's performance so

frustrated Dreyfuss that the Pirate owner broke the promise he made years ago to Manager Clarke and, after one devastating loss, poked his head inside the locker room and shouted with his high-pitched, German accent, "K-witters! Each one of you!" He emphasized the "K" to make a special point. Just to be certain that nobody could misinterpret his implication, Dreyfuss added, "And for you, Konetchy, that goes double!"

In reality, Konetchy's subpar performance was merely part of the problem. Reliable Honus Wagner hit only .252; Max Carey's average slumped to .243, although he led the league with triples (17); Mike Mowrey, the third baseman acquired from the Cardinals with Konetchy, was injured early in the year and played in only 79 games, hitting .254.

Even the Bucs' customary domination from the pitching mound fell flat. Babe Adams could do no better than a 13-15 record; O'Toole fell to 2-9.

In addition to these woes, the Pirates faced another threat right in their own neighborhood. A pseudo-major-league, the Federal League, fielded clubs in various cities including Pittsburgh. The "Pittsburgh Federals" chose to play their home games at old Exposition Park, thus offering a viable alternative for local baseball fans who yearned to see a winning team. In addition, the Federals team was backed by wealthy investors who were unafraid to offer an attractive salary to any player who wanted to don its uniform.

Immediately following the disastrous 1914 season, both

Just prior to the start of the 1909 World Series, a photographer asked Honus Wagner to shake hands with Detroit's Ty Cobb. The two were certainly not the best of friends, but agreed, at least, to touch fingers. This wood cut-out shows the timid attempt at demonstrating good sportsmanship.

Konetchy and Mowrey jumped ship to join the Pittsburgh Federals. A patched-up Pirate squad took the field in 1915 and fought its way to a fifth-place finish, only one-half game out of the first division.

Honus Wagner, now 41 years old, set a standard for aging players. He started every game that year, hitting .274, had 32 doubles, 17 triples and six four-baggers. Fred Clarke, on the other hand, played in only one game, got one hit — the 2,703rd of his career — and never again stepped to the plate in a major league contest.

Two surprises — one positive, the other negative — surfaced that year. On the plus side, Pitcher Al Mamaux, a local boy from Duquesne who had won only five games the year before, posted a remarkable 21-8 record. Unfortunately his colleagues, including Wilbur Cooper (5-16) and Babe Adams (14-14), were unable to match his performance.

The negative surprise was the dissolution of the 22-year relationship between Barney Dreyfuss and manager Fred Clarke. The frustration of consecutive losing seasons was too much of a test for the patience of the spunky German. He asked Clarke to stay put as manager but at a substantially reduced salary. That was unacceptable to Clarke. Both men shook hands and Clarke retired to his Kansas ranch to raise mules.

"After handling ball players for years, handling mules should be easy," joked Clarke.

Fred Clarke led his club to more than 1,400 victories during his 16 years at the helm. While he was manager, Clarke's teams did not finish in the second division until his last two years. In nine of those years,

his clubs won at least 90 games. Fred Clarke received his rightful place in Baseball's Hall of Fame in 1945.

Replacing Clarke as manager was James "Nixey" Callahan, a former manager of the White Sox who had earned a reputation for impatience with player miscues. Like John McGraw, his counterpart with the Giants, Callahan left no guess as to how he felt about a bad performance. On more than one occasion when a pitcher made a mistake, Callahan followed the pitcher from the mound, through the dugout into the clubhouse, yelling at him with a generous dose of expletives thrown in for emphasis.

That approach did little to motivate better performance. The Pirates in 1916 skidded to sixth place.

The first base position was still unproductive, so Honus Wagner — perhaps in an attempt to give his legs a rest — took over as first-sacker. Wagner, with his .287 average and 39 RBI, showed that he was not nearly as dominating as in years past. Instead, it was Max Carey with his league-leading 63 stolen bases who generated the most postgame talk.

Another player who enjoyed a banner year was outfielder Bill Hinchman who batted .315 and led the National League with a career-high 16 triples.

The Pirates picked up Frank "Wildfire" Schulte, an established right fielder from the Cubs. This aging veteran, however, played in only 55 games and did not bring with him the necessary spark to turn things around for the club.

Pitching, historically a strength of the Pirate ballclub, left no genuine impact, unless you count Al Mamaux' mark of issuing 136 walks to lead all pitchers in that department.

Baseball is a game dominated by superstitions, and Barney Dreyfuss fell victim to this legacy. Hoping to change the luck of his Pirates, Dreyfuss moved spring training from Hot Springs, Arkansas, to Columbus, Georgia. Alas, even that move did not help one bit.

Following the disappointing sixth-place finish in 1916 and after seeing his team languish in the league basement after the first 60 days of the 1917 season, Manager Callahan, mysteriously disappeared without warning, on June 30th.

By 1917, his aging legs limited the skills of the mighty Honus Wagner, and the game was no longer fun for him.

Several days later he was located in Philadelphia. According to police reports, he was found lying in a gutter, a slobbering drunk. Nixey Callahan never again managed a major league team.

The burden of managing the club fell temporarily upon the shoulders of Honus Wagner who led the Pirates to only one victory in five games. Finally, the club hired Hugo Francis Bezdek, a 240-lb. Czechoslovakian who had gained notoriety as a football player in college, to complete the dismal season and an eighth-place finish. The club won only 51 games in 1917 and finished an embarrassing 20½ games behind the seventh-place Dodgers.

Again offering the only genuine hint of glory for the Bucs that year was Max Carey who led the league in stolen bases with 46. Bill Hinchman — last year's sparkling outfielder — fell to a .189 average and played in only 69 games.

The 1917 Bucs did manage to set off an occasional firework. One of their pitchers was a barrel-chested spitballer from the north woods of Emerald, Wisconsin, named Burleigh "Ol' Stubblebeard" Grimes, whose rugged face always looked as though he had just returned from a week-long hunting trip in the

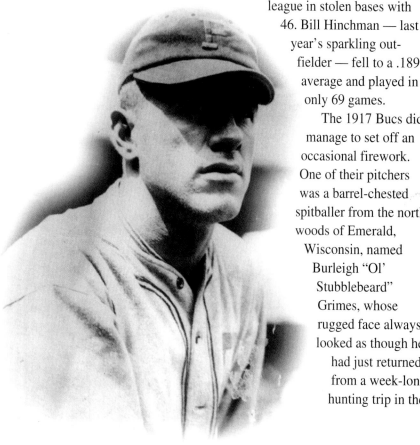

Pirate management believed that Charlie Grimm failed to take the game seriously because of his practical jokes and banjo playing in the clubhouse.

Alaskan wilderness. This 175-pounder was suffering through a horrible 3-16 record. During an 11-game losing streak toward the end of the season, Manager Bezdek commented on Grimes' lack of production. Burleigh took issue with the remark and, within seconds, the two of them got into a fight that left both combatants bloodied. His behavior should not have come as any surprise to the Pirates; after all, it was Grimes who once remarked that an intentional pass was four pitches toward the batter's head. Nonetheless, at the end of the season, Grimes was sent packing to the Brooklyn Dodgers.

This was the year, too, that John Peter "Honus" Wagner called his last. Now 43 years old, the Dutchman knew he could no longer perform up to his personal standards. He was now content to spend the rest of his life with his friends, especially those with whom he could have a cold Iron City Beer or Duquesne Pilsner at his favorite watering hole — the Elks Club in his home town of Carnegie.

Most baseball experts consider Honus Wagner the greatest shortstop who ever wore a major-league uniform; some, including John McGraw, Branch Rickey and Ed Barrow — all of whom saw both Ruth and Cobb play — even called him the greatest player of all time. "I name Wagner first on my list," said McGraw, "not only because he was a great batting champion and base-runner, and also baseball's foremost shortstop, but because Honus could have been first at any other position, with the possible exception of pitching. In all my career, I never saw such a versatile player."

If Honus Wagner was a painting, he'd be hanging in the Louvre. His statistics were incredible. He hit better than .300 in 15 consecutive seasons. Although he was built more like a catcher, this barrel-chested, bow-legged, awkward-looking shortstop had blazing speed on the basepaths and exceptional range in the field. Over his 21-year career (1897–1917), he stole 722 bases and compiled a .327 average — better than any shortstop in major-league history. He led the National League in batting eight times, in slugging six times, RBI five times, in doubles seven times and two times in runs scored. While playing in nearly 2,800 big-league games (all with Pittsburgh), the "Flying Dutchman" racked up 3,418 hits, 643 doubles, 252 triples, 101 home runs, 1,732 RBI, 1,735 runs scored and 963 walks. And, what many people never knew, Wagner even pitched in two games; in a total of eight innings he earned an ERA of 0.00.

The Pirates certainly could have used a new Honus Wagner in 1917. Not only did Pittsburgh have a bad ballclub that year, but, for the first time in his association with the club, owner Dreyfuss felt the sting of heavy criticism. Local media and fans alike questioned his ability to run the team. They felt the game had passed him by. Even the *Pittsburgh Press* that had supported Dreyfuss throughout his tenure, printed a front-page story blaming the owner for the present state of affairs. The conclusion drawn by the newspaper's editors was: "Dreyfuss must go."

The gloom of Pirate fans that year mirrored that of the nation for another reason. On August 6,

America declared war on Kaiser Wilhelm II and his German Army.

The next year, 1918, marked the nation's full-scale participation in what President Woodrow Wilson predicted would be a "war to end all wars." Baseball, like the rest of the country, felt the impact. In June, Provost Marshall General Crowder issued a "work or fight" order. By this he meant that each draft-age man had to serve in the military or work at an "essential job." Baseball was not considered "essential." Consequently, Labor Day marked the end of a war-shortened race for the pennant.

The Pittsburgh club ranked among the leaders of those who sacrificed players to the military service during the war. In spite of this, Bezdek improved the Pirates to a fourth-place finish. Max Carey was the shining light with 58 steals, good enough to lead the league one more time.

Germany signed an armistice on November 11, 1918. Americans could now concentrate on more pleasant things, including baseball. Major-league owners, unable to predict the war would end so abruptly, had reduced the number of scheduled games in the 1919 season from 154 to 140, yet fans flocked to their local ballparks, setting record numbers for season attendance. This rejuvenated support did little to change the fortune of the Bucs. They ended the 1919 campaign, again, in fourth place.

At the tail end of the '19 season, owner Dreyfuss called up from Little Rock a jovial, banjo-playing first baseman named Charlie Grimm. Although Grimm's lifestyle,

Not only did Pittsburgh have a bad ballclub in 1917, but, for the first time in his association with the club, owner Dreyfuss felt the sting of heavy criticism.

punctuated with fun and mischief, did not fit Dreyfuss' ideal image of a player, he demonstrated his uncanny ability to field his position and hit an eyebrow-raising .318 in 14 games.

The unpredictable antics of Grimm and the flashy play of Max Carey were not enough to instill a genuine team zeal for winning. Rightly or wrongly, the front office sensed a lack of enthusiasm by the Pirates' manager. As the season progressed, both Pirate executives and the media could see that Hugo Bezdek's first love was football. Those conclusions were confirmed when, shortly after the final out of the last game in 1919, the lovable native of Prague resigned as Pirate manager to coach football at Penn State University. It was a good move for both. The Pirates needed someone whose sole focus was on baseball, and Bezdek became a powerful coach; while at the campus in State College, Pennsylvania, Bezdek developed some of the strongest teams in the school's history.

The Pirates replaced a Czech with a Canadian when it appointed George "Moon" Gibson to lead the club in 1920. As a catcher for the Pirates for 12 years (1905-1916), Gibson had cultivated a solid reputation as a "thinking man's ballplayer." Some critics argued that the manager should

When Hall-of-Famer Rabbit Maranville played for the Bucs from 1921–1924, he generated plenty of excitement with his hitting and on-the-field pranks.

have concentrated more on the players' performance than on their thinking. Gibson's 1920 team finished just as they did the previous year — in fourth place.

The fans still had some things to cheer about that year. They witnessed Max Carey lead the league again in stolen bases (52). They watched a newcomer from Detroit, Fred Nicholson, hit .360 and place second in the league behind the immortal Rogers Hornsby. They marveled at Babe Adams, who led the senior circuit in shutouts with eight. But the consistent, solid hitting to which Pirate fans had grown accustomed was no longer present. With a sigh that showed his state of frustration, Gibson responded, "I guess you just have to get me another Honus Wagner."

Much of the baseball talk in 1920 was not about what happened on the field that year, but about what happened the previous year — in the World Series, to be exact. The nation was shocked by the revelation that the American League Champion Chicago White Sox purposely lost the series to the Cincinnati Reds. The "Black Sox Scandal," as it was labeled in the press, called for a stern solution. That was found in the person of a judge from Chicago. In a bold move to demonstrate that their intention was to keep a spotless image, the club owners appointed Kenesaw Mountain Landis as the game's first commissioner. Landis' rigid, no-nonsense approach to the game was just what baseball needed if it hoped to survive its biggest scandal. "The only thing in anybody's mind now is to make baseball what the millions of fans throughout the United States want it to be," he said. In the spirit of an Old West marshal who was hired to rid a town of outlaws, Landis issued unilateral decisions that included controversial suspensions for life for some Sox players.

Barney Dreyfuss was also not against bold moves if it meant improving his team. Since Honus Wagner's retirement, nine players attempted to fill his position with little if any success. He found, however, a near-perfect substitute in Boston's Walter "Rabbit" Maranville. To get him, Dreyfuss had to part with outfielder Billy Southworth, the promising youngster Fred Nicholson, infielder Walter "Dinty" Barbare, plus $15,000 cash.

The deal proved better than anyone had hoped. Maranville lit a fire under the Pirates as had no one else in the last few years. The diminutive 5'5" native of Springfield, Massachusetts, not only was an excellent hitter in 1921 (batting .294) and an expert glove man, but he was not afraid to play the role of a leprechaun and employ roguish antics to the delight of the crowd.

One time, for example, he caught a runner off second base by using the "hidden ball trick." Another time, when stealing second base, Maranville dove head-first to the bag . . . between the legs of Umpire Hank O'Day.

Other young stars developing that year were infielder James "Cotton" Tierney, who hit .299, and pitcher Charles "Whitey" Glazner with his 14-5 record and 2.77 ERA.

Not all of the action took place on the field during the 1921 campaign; some of the best scrapping took place in the stands. In one game, three fans were placed under arrest when they refused to throw back foul balls. When a city police officer wrestled one of the fans for the ball, the fan threatened to sue the officer and the city for damages. On July 9th, therefore, Robert J. Alderdice, Director of Public Safety, and the Pittsburgh Ball Club released the following announcement: "Fans who attend games at the National League baseball park here may keep balls knocked into the stands without fear of being molested by policemen."

Things were beginning to change for Pittsburgh, including greater opportunities for fans to attend ball games.

Prior to 1921, if a fan was unable to take off work and grab a seat at Forbes Field, the best for which he or she could hope was to read the box score in the morning *Gazette-Times*. Now, something new was available for the unfortunate fan who was forced to stay home or at the office — a play-by-play broadcast of the game on radio.

Pittsburgh's KDKA, the world's pioneer commercial station to schedule broadcasts on a regular basis, established another first on August 5, 1921, when it aired a major-league baseball game. Harold Arlin described the action between the Pirates and the Philadelphia Phillies, won by the Pirates 8-5.

Pirate management initially was skeptical about the broadcast of games; they thought fans would elect to tune in the games on their Zenith consoles in lieu of riding the streetcar to Schenley Park and fighting the crowds for a seat at the ballpark. Just the opposite happened. Exposure to

Manager Hugo Bezdek felt more at home wearing the sweatshirt of a football coach, much to the delight of Penn State fans during the early 1920s.

"Fans who attend games at the National League baseball park here may keep balls knocked into the stands without fear of being molested by policemen."

—ROBERT J. ALDERDICE
Director of Public Safety

PIE TRAYNOR

baseball via radio only created new fans. More Pirate faithful, including a marked increase in the number of women, flocked to the stadium to see, for themselves, the players about whom the announcers talked on radio. During 1921, in fact, 701,567 fans attended games at Forbes Field. That was an increase of nearly 300,000 from the year before.

Attendance at the games grew also because of the club's winning record. The scrappy Pirates finished in second place that year, only four games behind New York. Things were looking much better for the Pirates who, for too long, had not won a pennant. The fans and press were convinced the team was on a roll.

Unfortunately, that momentum did not propel the Bucs to a National League championship in 1922. Rather, it was a year that loyal Pirate fans of that era would like to forget.

Owner Dreyfuss was slowly taking more control of the day-to-day operations on the field. He expressed his opinions about the team's play to Manager Gibson much more than he ever did to Fred Clarke. He strongly urged Gibson to get rid of the "nice guy" image and to get tough with his players. When the club could earn no better than a fourth-place standing in the league after 52 games in 1922, Dreyfuss abruptly dismissed Gibson as manager and hired, instead, William Boyd "Deacon" McKechnie.

McKechnie was unlike his immediate predecessors. Not only was he a native-born American, but also a local boy, born in nearby Wilkinsburg. He also was an active member and an elder of the Presbyterian Church.

The Pirates in 1922 looked like championship material. Dependable veterans such as Max Carey (who led the league once again in stolen bases with 51 out of 53 attempts) continued to produce up to expectations. In addition, a bright, fresh talent appeared at third base. Playing his first full season at the hot corner was a man who many experts willingly admit is the greatest third-sacker of all time — Harold Joseph "Pie" Traynor. Traynor, who got his nickname as a boy in Framingham, Massachusetts, because of his fondness for the popular Yankee desert, hit a solid .282 that year and dazzled both the fans and the press with his sure hands and rifle-like arm.

The Bucs presented other fine hitters that year, including Ewell "Reb" Russell — an outfielder acquired from the White Sox — with a .368 average and 12 homers, Max Carey (.329, 10 home runs), Carson Bigbee (.350), Cotton Tierney (.345), second-year catcher Johnny Gooch (.329) and Clyde Barnhart (.330).

Veteran left-hander Wilbur Cooper led his team with a 23-14 record, and the National League with

27 complete games. Joining him in trips to the mound that year were Johnny Morrison (17-11) and Earl Hamilton (11-7). Babe Adams had a disappointing season with an 8-11 record.

With McKechnie's arrival, the Pirates began to click. However, they were unable to overcome their shaky start and had to be content to end 1922 in third place.

So close and yet . . . so close. That summarizes the Pirates' 1923 season. After traveling through several years of unpopular trades and emotional rivalries, the Bucs were ready to make more daring moves. One month after opening day, in an effort to bolster his pitching staff, Barney Dreyfuss completed yet another of his questionable swaps. He sent to the Phillies second baseman Cotton Tierney and pitcher Whitey Glazner, two of the club's rising stars, plus $50,000, in exchange for pitcher Lee Meadows and infielder Johnny Rawlings.

This trade worked out far better than even Dreyfuss could have imagined. Meadows won 16 games for Pittsburgh that year; Rawlings batted a healthy .284.

Dreyfuss also purchased the contract of Jim Bagby, a 31-game winner for Cleveland three years earlier. But the Pirates were quick to learn that a pitcher's arm has only so many victories; the crafty veteran could only post a modest 3-2 record.

First baseman Charlie "Jolly Cholly" Grimm was willing to set aside his banjo long enough to establish himself as a dependable player by hitting .345. Pie Traynor led the club with 12 home runs, hit .338 and fielded third base with the grace of a ballet dancer. Max Carey hit .308 and, once again, won the title as the National League's best base-stealer with 51. In 16 years with the Pirates, this former seminary student led the league in stolen bases 10 times. Another pleasant surprise was outfielder Walter Mueller who hit a steady .306.

Playing in the outfield alongside Carey at the end of the year was Hazen Shirley "Kiki" (pronounced "ky ky") Cuyler, who showed promise for stardom from the first day he set foot on a baseball diamond as a green rookie from Bay City, Michigan, three years earlier. Cuyler, called up from Nashville, played in only 11 games during the '23 campaign, but demonstrated that he had the raw material to make it in the big leagues.

The 1924 season became a testimony to why baseball owners and managers get old, fast. It was another heartbreaker of a season. The Bucs had the talent and, on paper, could be considered the best team in the National League.

One of the rays of hope for the Pirates that year was a young shortstop praised by Charles "Chilly" Doyle in the *Sun Telegraph* as: "The greatest since Honus Wagner." His name was Forest Glenn Wright from Archie, Missouri. With Rabbit Maranville moving to second, Pie Traynor at third and Charlie Grimm at first, the infield became a public relations bonanza. The only concern for owner Dreyfuss was that two of his infielders — Charlie Grimm and Rabbit Maranville — too often acted impish and appeared to be spending more energy planning practical jokes than winning ball games.

A Pittsburgh Pirates team jersey (circa 1920) was made of heavy wool. These uniforms became mighty uncomfortable for those whose schedule was limited to day games played under the grueling sun.

GLENN WRIGHT

To the surprise of no one, especially opposing pitchers and catchers, Max Carey — one of the finest base-stealers ever to lace on spikes — led the league with 49 steals and hit an impressive .297. His outfield mate, Kiki Cuyler, led the club in average (.354) and home runs (9).

Wilbur Cooper was the ace of the pitching staff with 20 victories, and two new pitchers — southpaw Emil Yde and Remy (Ray) Kremer — posted 16 and 18 wins respectively. Barney Dreyfuss felt he had not only a pennant contender, but was extremely confident he had finally gotten the best of his arch rival, John McGraw, and his Giants. Before their final three-game series that year, the Pirates had won 13 of their last 19 games. Winning only two of those final three games would guarantee Pittsburgh a berth in the World Series. "This time we ought to lick McGraw and make him like it," Barney crowed to Manager McKechnie.

The mischievous gods of baseball, however, were at work again, merely setting up Barney Dreyfuss for another monumental disappointment. The Giants won all three games, dashing every hope for a pennant in the Steel City.

The Pirates eventually ended the season in third place, three games behind the Giants. ■

Pitcher Burleigh "Ol Stubblefield" Grimes had a strong right arm and, as Pirate management would discover, a wicked right cross, as well.

BURLEIGH GRIMES

CHAPTER 5

TURNING THE CORNER

" *Pie Traynor would have played for nothing.*"

—"WHITEY" GLAZNER
Pirate pitcher 1920–1923

BARNEY **DREYFUSS VOWED** to endure no more disappointments. At the owners' annual meeting in December 1924, he pulled out all stops. He shocked the Pittsburgh faithful by trading away three of his key players — Charlie Grimm, Rabbit Maranville and Wilbur Cooper — to the Chicago Cubs for infielder George Grantham, rookie first baseman Al Niehaus and pitcher Vic Aldridge.

"I got rid of my banjo players," quipped Dreyfuss, with all the subtlety of a hurricane. He was referring, of course, to Charlie Grimm, who liked to plunk the banjo and to Maranville whom he called an "impish elf."

To say that Pirate fans were not exactly thrilled over the trade would be a gross understatement. Both they and the media appreciated the rebellious spirit of Grimm and Maranville. And the players they got in return were not exactly household names on which you could hang hopes for a pennant in 1925.

Aldridge had not been a consistent winner on the mound; Grantham established quite good records at the plate the past season hitting .316 and slamming 12 home runs, but he was erratic in the field and led the league in strikeouts (63); and nobody outside of his immediate family had ever heard of Niehaus.

At the end of '25, however, it was Barney Dreyfuss who could have said, "I told you so." For the first time in 16 years, the Pirates won the National League pennant. Chicago, to whom Dreyfuss

They called the Waner Brothers "Little Poison" (L) and "Big Poison" (R).

Wilbur Cooper was a mainstay for the Pirate pitching staff before heading to the Cubs in a controversial trade prior to the 1925 season.

traded those key players, ended up in the basement. But to even more satisfaction for the scrappy Pirate owner, McGraw and his New York Giants finished 8½ games behind the Bucs in second place.

Reasons aplenty accounted for the success of the club that year. Kiki Cuyler was steaming hot, slamming out 220 hits, 43 doubles, and a league-leading 26 triples; he also led the Senior Circuit with 144 runs scored and hit an eye-popping .357 He saved his best for September 18, 19 and 20, when the pennant was on the line; during that stretch, he pounded out 10 consecutive hits, tying a National League record. In the stolen base department, his 32 was second in the league to the 49 swipes by teammate Max Carey. Finally, as a testimonial to his athletic prowess, Cuyler hit 17 home runs that year; eight of them were inside the park — an all-time record for a major leaguer in one season.

Other players contributed to the Pirates' good fortune as well. Carey had his best season at the plate at .343; Grantham, one of the players picked up in the last trade, batted .326 and held his own in the field; Clyde Barnhart was close behind with .324; reliable Pie Traynor hit .320; catcher Earl Smith raised his average to .313; Glenn Wright impressed everyone with his .307 average and scored the first unassisted triple play in Pirate history; even reserve catcher Johnny Gooch hit .298.

Three players — Cuyler, Traynor and Wright — each scored and knocked-in over 100 runs.

As testimony to their power and speed, the '25 Pirates hit a modern record eight triples on May 29 against the Cardinals in a 15-5 win.

A secret weapon for the Pirates that year came not from players on the field, but from an addition to the dugout bench. Longtime manager Fred Clarke was called out of retirement at his ranch in Kansas to serve as McKechnie's head coach and "first lieutenant."

The World Series opened at Forbes Field against the reigning World Champion Washington Senators. Max Carey hit a blistering .458 during the Series, and Traynor .346. Nonetheless, the Pirates fell behind 3 games to 1.

In the opening game, Walter "Big Train" Johnson checked the Pirates with a five-hit, 4-1 victory before a solemn Forbes Field crowd.

Kiki Cuyler's long home run helped the Bucs pull off a 3-2 win in Game Two.

The Senators won Game Three in Washington by the score of 4-3, but not without controversy. With Washington leading by one run in the ninth, Pirate catcher Earl Smith hit a ball to deep center field. Washington outfielder Sam Rice ran back to the fence, leaped high, reached for the ball, but tumbled over the wall. When he reappeared, he was holding the ball in his glove for the most controversial "out" in World Series history.

Walter Johnson showed why he was the most dominating pitcher of the era in Game Four when he stifled the Bucs on a six-hit shutout, 4-0.

With the Pirates' backs to the wall, Cuyler and Barnhart rapped key RBI singles in a 6-3 victory for Pittsburgh in Game Five.

1925 WORLD CHAMPION PITTSBURGH PIRATES

Back at the friendly confines of Forbes Field, the Pirates won a squeaker, 3-2, with the help of second baseman Eddie Moore's home run in Game Six. With just one game left, they were facing no tomorrow.

The Senators once again called upon the mighty Walter Johnson to maintain their grip on the World Championship. In misty weather on that October 15, Washington hitters staked Johnson to a 4-0 lead in the first inning and it appeared to be all over but the shouting. But the persistent Bucs inched their way back and tied the game at seven runs apiece in the eighth inning.

In the same inning, with the bases full and two outs, the heavy mist turned into a light drizzle then a steady downpour. Cuyler fouled off a number of Walter Johnson fastballs until he got one he liked. He lined it sharply to right for a double. That made the score 9-7. It was the 15th Pirate hit off the "Big Train" that afternoon. The Bucs held the Senators scoreless in the top of the

ninth and won their second world crown before 42,856 screaming fans who braved the miserable weather. As they left Forbes Field, most of them didn't even notice that, for the first time all day, the sun was beginning to shine.

"You did it, Bill; you did it," said a weeping Barney Dreyfuss in a rare display of emotion. As a punctuation mark to his excitement, he hugged Manager McKechnie, then coach Fred Clarke. The players joined in the celebration, pouring bottles of Iron City Beer over their teammates' heads and openly talking about how they would spend their winners' checks totaling $5,332 each.

The ecstasy of the Pirate family was a stark contrast to the gloom in the visitors' clubhouse. Ban Johnson, president of the American League, was livid over the fact that young Bucky Walters, manager of the Senators, failed to lift Walter Johnson who had obviously run out of gas. Within minutes after the final out of the Series, Ban Johnson

(L–R) Front Row: Gooch, Spencer, Colloton, Ens, Cuyler, Kremer, and Sheehan.

Middle Row: Smith, Haas, Oldham, Thompson, McInnis, Carey, McKechnie, Clarke, Wright, Grantham, Bigbee, and Traynor.

Back Row: Fraser, Hinchman, Onslow, Barnhart, Moore, Yde, Watters, B. Dreyfus, S. Dreyfus, Rawlings, Aldridge, Adams, Morrison, Meadows, and Bill McKechnie Jr. (mascot).

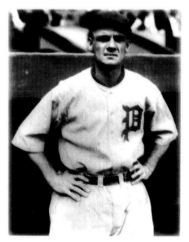

MAX CAREY

BILL MCKECHNIE

sent a blistering telegram to Harris that read: "You sacrificed a World Championship for our league to mawkish sentiment."

In 1926, the fans and the press expected Pittsburgh to dominate baseball and repeat as World Champions. They were quite startled, therefore, when their Pirates started off slowly and languished near the National League basement much of the first half of the year. They regained their optimistic enthusiasm as the club battled its way from seventh place to the league lead by mid-June. Even the prayers of "Deacon" McKechnie were not enough to sustain the drive. The Pirates lost four out of five games to the Cardinals in a critical series. Cheers turned to groans. Eventually the Bucs settled for their all-too-familiar third-place finish, 4½ games behind the National League Champion Cardinals.

Upsetting to the Pirate squad were not only the losses, but the arguments emanating from the bench as well. Fred Clarke, number one aide to Manager McKechnie, was never known for his discretion when it came to voicing opinions about baseball. If he saw something he didn't like, he let it be known.

Against Boston on August 7, with Max Carey, hitting a weak .222 and not having one of his better years, Clarke asked Manager McKechnie, "Why don't we get Carey out of there?"

"Who would I play in his place?" asked McKechnie.

"Anybody," said Clarke. "Put in the bat boy. He can't do any worse."

Carey didn't hear the insult, but his friend Carson Bigbee did. And he told Carey what was said.

Carey was crushed. When asked after the game about Clarke's remark made about Carey, Pitcher Babe Adams, who had admired Clarke for many years, sided with Carey and told a reporter, "I think the manager should manage and no one else should interfere."

Grumbling in the clubhouse included talk about a possible strike unless Fred Clarke was ordered to leave the bench during the games. In a secret ballot, the players voted 18-6 to keep Clarke right where he was. Clarke, in turn, demanded that the "mutineers" be disciplined. He got his wish. On August 13, Bigbee and Adams were released unconditionally; Max Carey was sold to Brooklyn.

On a brighter note, Kiki Cuyler led the league with 35 steals.

One other disaster hit the Pirates that year. Glenn Wright was accidentally beaned by a high, inside fastball thrown by the Cardinals' Vic Keen. He lay motionless at the plate for several minutes. Although he eventually recovered, Wright missed over 30 games. Keen, shaken by the incident, was never able to pitch with effectiveness again.

Pitcher Remy Kremer had another sensational year, leading the league with a 2.61 ERA, a .769 winning percentage and an 18-7 record.

A rookie who showed promise in 1926 was a second-sacker from the San Francisco area named Joe

Cronin. The young man, who had just turned 20 years old, played in 38 games that year and hit .265. The brightest star for the Pirates that year shown on a speed-demon rookie who could also hit with power. His name was John Paul Waner. The name "John" was dropped by the time he was a teenager in Harrah, Oklahoma. The young outfielder made heads turn with his .336 average and eight home runs. His 22 triples established a major-league record for rookies.

The future stardom of rookies notwithstanding, the turmoil of the 1926 season became too much, even for a man with Bill McKechnie's patience. The pressures of the job were finally getting the best of him. "You can't even celebrate a victory," he sighed. "If you win today, you must start worrying about tomorrow. If you win a pennant, you start worrying about the World Series. As soon as that's over, you start worrying about the next season." Without fanfare, at the end of the year, the "Deacon" asked for and got his release as manager of the ballclub.

Residents of Pittsburgh became more and more enthusiastic in their support of their beloved Bucs. If they were unable to get to the game, they could listen to Harold Arlin's broadcasts of home games on KDKA. In 1927, Pittsburgh *Gazette-Times* (it became the *Pittsburgh Post-Gazette* later that year) writer Chilly Doyle reported happenings of road games via telephone to his sports editor Chet Smith who set the story into print.

The timing for this continual coverage was excellent, since the 1927 Pirates introduced a team with a remarkable assembly of players,

including future Hall-of-Famers Pie Traynor, the two Waner brothers, and Joe Cronin (who played in only 12 games that year). According to the experts, they should have won the National League pennant with ease. However, standing in the way of an easy waltz to the World Series were some giant egos mixed with stubborn pride.

The new manager that year was Owen "Donie" Bush — the enthusiastic former Detroit Tiger — whose main goal was to transmit his positive attitude to his extremely talented players. The lineup included not just Paul Waner, but also his brother, rookie Lloyd. Paul batted and threw left, Lloyd batted left and threw right.

Paul and Lloyd were both rather small — 5'8½" tall. Lloyd was said to be a few pounds lighter than his brother. His official weight was listed at 150 lbs., but insiders say that his real playing weight was closer to 135 lbs. Paul was not only a bit heavier at 155 actual pounds, he was also gifted with strong wrists and forearms and possessed an uncanny ability to judge pitches. Joe Cronin claimed that Paul, who wore glasses toward the end of his career, "had the sharpest eyes of any player in the National League. I never saw him hit at a bad pitch."

Residents of Pittsburgh became more and more enthusiastic in their support of their beloved Bucs.

Fresco Thompson, Eddie Moore, and Glenn Wright

Brother Lloyd Waner set a major-league record for rookies with 223 hits in 1927.

Paul Waner — dubbed "Big Poison" (because he hit with more power) by opposing ball clubs — won the batting crown that year hitting a blistering .380; his 237 hits set the all-time Pirate record. His brother Lloyd — "Little Poison" — hit .355, an average that would have made any seasoned veteran proud. Of Lloyd's 223 hits that year (a major-league record for most hits as a rookie), 198 were singles. He also scored 133 runs, another record for a first-year player. Eyewitnesses claim that Lloyd, a slap hitter, was the fastest player they ever saw going from home to first.

Two stories were told about how the brothers got their lethal nicknames. The first was that they were both poison to opposing pitchers. The second was that one fan from the Bronx asked to see the big and little persons but, in typical New Yorkese, pronounced it "poisons."

Paul played right field, while brother Lloyd roamed in left. Between them was Kiki Cuyler, one of the most popular players ever to don a Buc uniform. This speedy outfielder stole 35 bases the previous year, enough to lead the league. But in the middle of the 1927 season, the three-year Pirate veteran from Harrisville, Michigan, suffered a rare slump.

Much to Manager Bush's dismay, the team had also demonstrated a perceived lack of enthusiasm for the game. In an effort to ignite some sort of fire in his players, Manager Bush shuffled the lineup and had Cuyler hitting second. Cuyler, however, did not like that place in the batting order. He was a straightaway, power hitter and felt that he would be of much more value to the team remaining in his familiar third slot. Cuyler went 0-for-5 in his first game as the number-two hitter.

In the clubhouse following the game, Cuyler complained to Bush that this move was not in the best interest of anyone, including himself. The manager listened, but simply responded, "You'll get used to it."

Cuyler had played quite well up to that point. In the first 85 games that year he batted .309 and stole 20 bases. But Cuyler believed there was a correlation between the new batting position and his performance. After what he felt was a particularly poor showing in Cincinnati, Cuyler stormed after Bush, yelling, "Take me out of that second slot before I become the worst player on the team."

Bush considered this outburst a challenge to his authority and shouted back, "You'll stay there until I'm ready to change you."

Following that pointed confrontation, Cuyler and Bush daily argued in the clubhouse. Tension between them continued to fester.

In a game against the New York Giants a few days later, Cuyler failed to slide into second base on a double play ground ball. Afterward, he claimed that by going into the bag standing up he provided a bigger distraction for the second baseman.

His argument did not convince Manager Bush, who slapped Cuyler with a $25 fine.

Several Pittsburgh newspaper reporters sided with Cuyler. This further irritated Bush who took this as another challenge to his authority. Consequently, he benched Cuyler and replaced him with Clyde Barnhart, a much slower outfielder. Barnhart covered left field; Lloyd Waner moved to center.

Pittsburgh sports writers ripped Bush for his decision, often turning their columns into editorials asking for Cuyler's return. Spectators held high signs demanding: "We want Kiki" and chanted the refrain from the stands.

The most vocal of the fans sat in the 50-cent seats of the left field bleachers. Several became too boisterous and had to be escorted from the game when they threw empty beer bottles at Manager Bush.

Barney Dreyfuss backed his manager. The criticism in the press and the vocal disdain by the fans only made the conservative German more stubborn in his support. "We're not going to let the fans, or even those fellows up in the press box, pick our lineup," he retorted.

The plea of fans and the press went for naught. Kiki Cuyler would never play another inning for the Pittsburgh Pirates. Other Pirate players did, and quite well. Pie Traynor hit .342. Joe "Moon" Harris, a first baseman acquired that year from Washington, hit .326. Clyde Barnhart batted .319, and George Grantham hit .305. Chief among the pitchers were Carmen Hill (22-11), Ray Kremer (19-8), Lee Meadows (19-10) and Vic Aldridge (15-10). Kremer led the National League with a 2.47 ERA.

The Pirates won the league championship that year, but it wasn't easy. They beat the Cardinals (World Champions just the year before) by only one-and-a-half games and Barney Dreyfuss'

nemesis, John McGraw and his Giants, by only two games.

One of the keys to winning the National League pennant in 1927 was young Pie Traynor. This slick fielder, eyewitnesses claim, could scoop up a ground ball, get it out of his glove and rifle it to first base faster than anyone who played the game before or since. And he was fleet. The rugged, rangy and handsome third-baseman could cover so much ground he was often dubbed: "the Pirates' second shortstop."

On Traynor's fielding, one writer remarked: "A batter hit a double down the left field line, and Traynor threw him out at first."

Traynor was just as accomplished on offense. Never a consistent power hitter (he hit only 58 home runs during his 17 years as a player), he sprayed line drives and, with speed and aggression, turned many singles into doubles.

Traynor was one of the classic ballplayers of old who counted it an honor just to wear a major league uniform and felt blessed just to play the game. "Pie Traynor would have played for nothing," said Charles "Whitey" Galzner, a Pirate pitcher from 1920–1923, "he loved baseball so much. We had several doubleheaders in a row. One day, when we had only a single game to play, Pie said, 'I'll get fat playing only one game.'"

Traynor was a superstar even before the term was popularized. He led the Bucs back to the World Series in 1927.

. . . the team had also demonstrated a perceived lack of enthusiasm for the game . . . in an effort to ignite some sort of fire in his players, Manager Bush shuffled the lineup.

Right-hander Remy Kremer spent his entire 10-year career with Pittsburgh, racking up an impressive 143-85 record.

But he and the Pirates were about to be humiliated by a vastly superior squad. A lineup that became known as "Murderer's Row," was led by arguably the most awesome, one-two punch in baseball history: Babe Ruth and Lou Gehrig.

Ruth had just completed the memorable season in which he led the American League with 60 home runs. Perhaps even more amazingly, Gehrig hit 47 homers, hit .373 and knocked in 175 runs. Those two combined to rap out an amazing 864 total bases (Gehrig had 447; Ruth, 417). With the other big guns in the Yankee arsenal — Tony Lazzeri, Bob Meusel and Earl Combs — thrown at them, the Pirates were, frankly, no match.

To the surprise of nearly every baseball enthusiast of that generation, the Pirates out hit the Bronx Bombers nine to six in the first game, and succeeded to knock from the box Waite Hoyt, New York's top pitcher. Nonetheless, Pittsburgh came out on the short end of a 5-4 score.

When Lloyd Waner led off with a booming triple in the first inning of game number two and later scored, the Pirate faithful envisioned possible revenge. Their enthusiasm was short lived, however, and the Yankees easily won the contest 6-2.

More than 60,000 fans filled Yankee Stadium for Game Three and might have sat through a ho-hum 8-1 Yankee win, except for one thing. Yankee pitcher Herb Pennock (19-8 for the regular season) chose the World Series to pitch the best game of his spectacular career. Pennock systematically retired the first 22 Pirate batters. He was en route to pitching a perfect no-hit, no-run game.

Broadcasting the game by radio, announcer Graham McNamee sensed history in the making. His chain-saw voice showed increased strains of tension with each Pirate out. Although sportscasters at that time were schooled to remain neutral, his enthusiasm matched the lustful cheering of the partisan crowd. After the first Pirate was retired in the eighth inning, McNamee, the announcer, became McNamee the fan. He shouted into the micro-phone to a nationwide audience for the first time all game that Pennock was tossing a no-hitter. Within seconds after his pronouncement, the Pirates' Pie Traynor lined a sharp single to left — the first of only three hits for the Pirates all after-noon. After the game, some Yankee fans blamed McNamee for causing the breakup of the no-hitter. They claimed that his mentioning it put a "curse" on the pitcher. To this day most broadcasters shy away from mentioning that a no-hitter is in progress for fear of causing the same result.

The Pirates vainly attempted to salvage something from the Series, but lost the fourth and final game by a score of 4-3.

The only bright spots in the Series for the Bucs came from the bats of the brothers Waner; Lloyd hit .400 and Paul clubbed a healthy .333.

Immediately following the Series, Barney Dreyfuss showed deep bitterness. For one thing, Yankee manager Miller Huggins had gotten the best of Dreyfuss in the infamous "five for three swap" as manager for the Cardinals in 1913. Another

1927 NATIONAL LEAGUE CHAMPION PIRATES

reason was that the Pirates acted like a defeated club throughout the entire World Series. "No team that is good enough to win the championship of a major league should lose four straight games to another team," he moaned.

Barney Dreyfuss was, once again, second-guessed by the press and the fans. Clyde Barnhart, who replaced Kiki Cuyler in left field, hit a respectable .313 in the Series. At the same time, more than a few of the disgruntled fans muttered: "If they would have played Kiki, at least we would not have lost four straight games."

Neither Dreyfuss nor anyone else of that era could know, however, that the Pirates were beaten by a group of players considered by many experts as the greatest baseball team ever assembled.

Some of those 41,567 fans who saw the first game at Forbes Field on October 5, claim the Series was actually won during batting practice.

Forbes Field was a spacious ballpark. Between the left field line and right-center field, no stands blocked the concert of colors generated each fall by the maple trees of Schenley Park. Two years earlier, the right field stands were moved in 65 feet so that the foul line stretched only 300 feet from home plate, but an 18-foot-tall mesh screen was added to the 9½-foot concrete wall. The roof over the two tiers of seats towered 86 feet above the grass. During the 18 years of major league baseball there, no one had ever hit a baseball into the second tier of seats.

Joe Cronin, years later, told the story of how Babe Ruth — a master at creating a psychological advantage — got an idea during batting practice. Just before he stepped into the batter's box for the pregame warm-up, Ruth asked the batting-practice pitcher to throw the ball at medium speed, right down the middle, belt-high. The pitcher did as Ruth wanted. On his very first swing, Ruth propelled the ball on a line drive deep into the second deck.

Pittsburgh players, some of whom were heading for the clubhouse to change uniforms for the game, heard

(L–R) Front Row: OF. Paul Waner, INF. George Grantham, INF. Harld Rhyne, Manager Donie Bush, Club Pres. Barney Dreyfuss, Treasurer Sam Dreyfuss, Secy. Sam Watters, Catcher Johnny Gooch, OF. Clyde Barnhart, OF. Loyd Waner, and 1B. Joe Harris.

Middle Row: P. Johnny Miljus, P. Remy Kremer, P. Vic Aldridge, INF. Heinie Groh, P. Carmen Hill, P. Michael Cvengros, 3B. Pie Traynor, SS. Glenn Wright, P. Lee Meadows, Catcher Earl Smith, P. Emil Yde, and Catcher Roy Spencer.

Back row: P. Otis "Doc" Crandall, Scout Chick Fraser, Scout Bill Hinchman, Coach Jewel Ens, OF. Adam Comorosky, OF. Fred Brickell, P. Walt Tauscher, OF. Kiki Cuyler, INF. Joe Cronin, P. Joe Dawson, and INF. Dick Bartell.

the ball rattling around the second-deck seats. They stopped in their tracks and watched with reverence.

The next pitch was also just where the Babe ordered it. Again, he smacked one into the lower decks. The Pirates still stood in awe.

The third pitch was lined into the second deck — even deeper than the first ball. On the fourth pitch, Ruth took a tumultuous swing, connected squarely and sent the ball high and deep, a prodigious shot that hit the facade of the roof. According to Cronin, it missed by 18 inches of going over the roof. Nobody on the Pirate squad had imagined anyone could ever hit a ball that far.

Ruth chuckled under his breath and, after only four swings of his bat, walked back to the dugout. He winked at the next batter — teammate Lou Gehrig. The "Iron Horse," as they called him, stepped into the batter's box and slammed the first pitch. The ball sailed over the screen into the lower deck of the right field stands.

"Good, but not excellent," chided Ruth in a voice loud enough to be heard throughout the ballpark. Ruth's remark was not meant for Gehrig; he and Gehrig had not spoken to each other for years. Instead Ruth aimed his comment at the Pittsburgh players.

Ruth's teammates roared with laughter. Paul Waner and the other Pirates stood silent . . . in shock. Some of the players later admitted that following the pregame display of power by Ruth and Gehrig they began the Series secretly wondering if they belonged in the same ballpark with such awesome hitters. Lloyd Waner was overwhelmed by the power of the Yankees. He turned to his brother and said, "Geeze, they're big, aren't they?" Just before the start of the game, Manager Donie Bush whispered to the elder Waner, "Let's go out on the ballfield and hope we don't all get killed."

Following the Series, Paul Waner was elected as the league's Most Valuable Player — an honor he richly deserved. Still, that was not enough to take away the sting of losing four straight games in the Series to the New York Yankees. ■

KIKI CUYLER

CHAPTER 6

MUTINY AND THE PASSING OF AN ERA

"Mr. Dreyfuss was one owner who refused to allow commercialism to interfere with his ideas of how to operate a club."

—WILLIAM HARRIDGE
President American League, 1932

DESPITE ITS PUMMELING by the New York Yankees in the '27 World Series, the Pirate club fielded what experts conceded was the team to beat in the National League in 1928.

The fate of Kiki Cuyler was a foregone conclusion. In the eyes of Pirate management, Cuyler was blatantly insubordinate. In one of baseball's most notorious trades (at least as far as Pittsburgh fans were concerned), owner Barney Dreyfuss negotiated a deal with Bill Veeck, president of the Chicago Cubs, in which the talented Cuyler would be sent to the Cubs in exchange for two comparatively average players — Earl "Sparky" Adams and Floyd "Pete" Scott.

Dreyfuss, for one of the few times in his life, allowed emotion to override logic. Adams, a 5'5" shortstop, played only one-and-a-half seasons for Pittsburgh before being shipped off to St. Louis. Scott played only 60 games for the Bucs that year and, while batting a respectable .311, abruptly ended his three-year baseball career when he suffered a severe concussion after colliding with the concrete right field wall at New York's Polo Grounds. Meanwhile, Kiki Cuyler began an outstanding seven-year record with Chicago, piling up Hall-of-Fame statistics.

Dreyfuss partially redeemed himself for the Cuyler "giveaway" (as the sports writers called it) when he unloaded pitcher Vic Aldridge for former Pirate and future Hall-of-Famer Burleigh

Many fans claimed that had Kiki Cuyler played in the 1927 World Series, the Bucs would not have been beaten four games to nothing.

the Bucs led the league in batting with a .309 team average. Certainly one of the reasons for Pittsburgh's tumble in the standings was the ailing arm of shortstop Glenn Wright. Despite valiant efforts by trainers and physicians, the once powerful throw of the classic infielder was mysteriously reduced to that of a mediocre sandlot player. Whispers around the press box suggested that Wright had failed to keep in shape during the off-season.

At the National League meetings in December that year, Dreyfuss traded fan-favorite Wright to Brooklyn for pitcher Jesse Petty and infielder Harry Riconda.

Many loyal Pirate followers felt that Dreyfuss had given up much too quickly on Wright. But Dreyfuss insisted that Wright's arm had gone lame and that his best playing days were over. Barney Dreyfuss' critics later acknowledged that he was correct; Wright was able to play in only 24 games in 1929.

Many years later baseball great Al Lopez praised Wright: "He was the best shortstop I ever saw. Before he hurt it, he had a tremendous throwing arm. And how many shortstops are powerful enough to hit fourth?"

The '29 Pirates came a bit closer to winning the pennant, but earned no cigar, finishing in second place, nine-and-a-half games behind the Cubs.

In view of the superb seasons enjoyed by key players, it's a wonder the Pirates didn't finish the year higher in the standings. Several Bucs hit over .300: Pie Traynor (.356), Lloyd Waner (.353 with a league-leading 20 triples), brother Paul (.336), outfielder Adam

Grimes. Grimes, that year, led the league in wins (25), games (48), complete games (28) and innings pitched (330.2). Aldridge, on the other hand, was a holdout for nearly half of the season and posted an unimpressive 4-7 mark.

The Pirates finished the 1928 season in fourth place, eight-and-a-half games behind former Pirate skipper Bill McKechnie's pennant-winning St. Louis Cardinals.

Both Paul Waner, with a .370 average (second in the league), 223 hits (another second), 50 doubles (league lead), 19 triples (second in the league) and 142 runs (league lead), and Pie Traynor, with his .337 average, had standout years. In fact

Comorosky (.321), George Grantham (.307) and Dickie Bartell (.302).

Burleigh Grimes ended the 1929 campaign with a 17-11 record and a respectable 3.13 ERA, in spite of the fact that he broke his thumb during a game with the Giants. Ray Kremer was 18-10 and Erv Brame was 16-11. One newcomer showing promise was Larry French, a 6'1", 195-lb. left-hander who batted from both sides of the plate.

Neither Barney Dreyfuss nor the Pittsburgh fans had much patience with losing ballclubs. A longtime baseball belief is: "If you want to make a change, it's easier to replace one manager than an entire team." The 1929 Pirates yielded to that line of reasoning. On August 29, just five weeks before the season's end, Barney Dreyfuss met privately with the Pirate manager. Less than one hour later, Dreyfuss issued a terse statement: "Owen Bush has tendered his resignation as manager of the Pirate club, and I accepted it. There is nothing further to say, except that Jewel Ens has been named to succeed Bush for the remainder of the season."

Ens, a former second baseman with the Bucs, was familiar with the problems of his club and had earned the respect of his players as an intelligent baseball man. His record during the final 35 games of the 1929 season was also striking, winning 21 games.

Pirate players, as well as the nation, were distracted from baseball shortly following the World Series. The stock market crashed and, as *Variety* magazine reported, Wall Street laid an egg. Americans, prior to that fateful October 29, 1929,

enjoyed the benefits of prosperity; now, during the Great Depression, they were forced to count every penny. Money formerly spent for luxurious outings — and that included baseball games — now had to be saved for essentials such as food, clothing and shelter.

The rather impressive finale of the Pirates in 1929, under the leadership of Jewel Ens, did not carry over into the next season. The Pirates of 1930 dropped to fifth place, 12 games behind first-place St. Louis.

What irritated loyal Pirate fans was that when they were able to scrape up enough money to buy a ticket for a game in 1930, no one could predict which team would show up to the ballpark. The Pittsburgh club was a study in inconsistency. The Pirates appeared to have a relatively good team that would be a viable contender for the National League title. In fact, solid performances were registered by Paul Waner (.368), George Grantham (.342) and Adam Comorosky (.313). But Lloyd Waner was ill with a mysterious disease that knocked him out of all but 68 games.

August Richard "Gus" Suhr, a rookie first baseman from San Francisco, impressed Pirate brass and Pittsburgh media with his .286 average and 17 home runs.

In the pitching department, Ray Kremer was a work horse as he tied for the league lead with 20 wins despite a horrible ERA of 5.02. He led all other pitchers with 276 innings. Ervin Brame and Larry French each had 17 wins.

To claim one man could have made the difference between

Americans were forced to count every penny during the Great Depression. Money formerly spent for luxurious outings — and that included baseball games — now had to be saved for essentials such as food, clothing and shelter.

finishing in fifth place or first place may seem like an overstatement. Consider, however, that Burleigh Grimes was a consistent winner for the Pittsburgh club. Because his number of wins dropped from 25 in 1928 to 17 in 1929, Owner Dreyfuss cut his salary. Grimes would not accept this and refused to sign a contract or appear at spring training. Just before the 1930 season, therefore, Dreyfuss shipped Grimes off to Boston in exchange for an ineffective pitcher named Percy Lee Jones. Boston immediately traded Grimes to St. Louis. It was Grimes' 13 wins in 1930 that helped put the Cardinals in first place.

In 1931, things remained much the same. Paul Waner had another stellar year, hitting .322; brother Lloyd pounded out a league-leading 214 hits, while compiling a .314 average. A surprise that season came from the right arm of Pitcher Henry "Heinie" Meine; in his third year with the club he tied for the National League lead with 19 wins and pitched more innings (284) than anyone else.

Probably the most consistent statistic for any Pirate was that begun by Gus Suhr on September 11, 1931. On this day, the big first-sacker started his streak of playing in 822 consecutive games — a National League record at that time which would last until 1957 when Donora's Stan Musial would break it. In spite of all this, the 1930 Pirate team demonstrated such an erratic behavior that Pirate management would have been wise to add a full-time psychologist to its staff.

In June, for example, the club was 8-18; in July it won 19 and lost 10.

In August they slumped to a 15-20 mark; during September they rebounded with a 16-9 record. The year-end total of a 75 wins and 79 losses marked the end of Ens' managerial career with the club.

The club's unpredictable behavior was not the only thing on owner Barney Dreyfuss' mind. He was nearing his 65th birthday and thinking seriously of retirement. Baseball had been his life for nearly a half century. Yet Mr. Dreyfuss anticipated that turning over the club leadership duties would be more rewarding than traumatic. For the past 14 years, he schooled his only son, Samuel, in the real world of running a baseball team.

Young "Sammy," as he was known to the office staff, and his father enjoyed an extremely close relationship. Since the day he graduated with honors from Princeton University, Sammy was heir-apparent to his father's throne. Insiders observed that Barney's primary joys in leading the club came when he did something that would build even a stronger organization, and legacy, for his only son.

During the early part of 1931, however, Sammy grew ill and was confined to bed with what the doctors diagnosed merely as a strong case of the flu. The sickness, however, refused to go away; instead it got worse and developed into pneumonia. On February 19, only four days before his father's 65th birthday, Sammy Dreyfuss died in his sleep.

For the next few weeks, Barney Dreyfuss walked the halls of the Pirate office in a daze. His primary purpose for life had vanished.

Lloyd "Little Poison" Waner (L), Paul "Big Poison" Waner (R).

National League president John Heydler and other club owners did what they could to give comfort to the grieving father. Nothing worked.

Frustrated and depressed, Barney Dreyfuss was a man without focus. The ballclub had lost its importance to him. Out of desperation he telephoned his son-in-law, William "Bill" Benswanger, who had married Barney's daughter, Eleanor Florence. Benswanger was a Pirate fan by osmosis, and a sound business man as demonstrated by the way he ran his successful insurance agency. But Bill Benswanger's passion was music, not baseball. The gifted pianist was a prominent board member of the Pittsburgh Symphony Orchestra. He was more familiar with Bach and Mozart than he was with Traynor and Waner.

Author Frederick Lieb reports Dreyfuss asking his son-in-law, "Will you come out to the ballpark and help me?"

"If you want me, I'll come," replied Bill.

"If I want you?" shouted Dreyfuss. "What do you think I called for, if I didn't want and need you?"

"All right. When do you want me?"

"No later than two weeks from now," shouted Dreyfuss.

Barney immediately turned over much of the day-to-day operation of the club to Benswanger. In turn, Benswanger gave up the lucrative insurance business he had nurtured for 18 years.

Barney Dreyfuss never recovered from the shock of his son's death. Gone was his contagious, high-pitched laughter. His eyes used to dance; now they lacked even a hint of sparkle. His own health showed signs of crumbling. Within months he was treated for glandular problems that required an operation at Mt. Sinai Hospital in New York. The surgery itself, was successful, although unexpected complications set in. On February 5, 1932, 65-year-old Barney Dreyfuss died of pneumonia.

Following her husband's death, Mrs. Florence Dreyfuss became chairperson of the board. Her first official duty was to meet with her son-in-law and convince this man who had less than one year's experience with baseball to assume the duties as president. ■

"Bensy" Benswanger responded to owner Dreyfuss' plea for help in 1931.

BILL "BENSY" BENSWANGER

CHAPTER 7

DECADES OF STRUGGLE AND GLORY

"All we have to do is win one of these three games and we'll be all right."

—MANAGER PIE TRAYNOR
1938

Hollis Studio, Cooperstown, NY

*T*HE BLISTERING OF THE PIRATES by the Yankees in the 1927 World Series signaled the beginning of a 33-year-long drought for the Pirates, at least in terms of participation in another World Series. At the same time, the Bucs produced their share of unforgettable characters who would become topics of conversations between parents and their children.

One of the Pirate legends came to the club as a result of a chance conflict of schedules.

Arthur Griggs, a scout for the Pirates who lived in Los Angeles, got a tip about a young catcher, Willard Hershberger, who was completing his senior year at the local high school. On the same team was a shortstop by the name of Floyd Vaughan; his teammates nicknamed him "Arky" because he was born in Arkansas. Vaughan was labeled a definite prospect by the New York Yankees and its scout, Vinegar Bill Essick. Both Griggs and Essick were scheduled to watch the Fullerton team on the same day. However, Essick decided to stop by nearby Long Beach to scout another player. Griggs, intent on wooing Hershberger into the Pirate camp, was mesmerized, instead, by the hustle of the hard-hitting shortstop. By the time Essick arrived on the Fullerton High School campus,

Mr. & Mrs. Ben Benswanger, standing next to Honus Wagner's locker at Baseball Hall of Fame.

Arky Vaughan had already signed with Pittsburgh. Not wanting to go back to New York empty handed, Essick quickly signed Hershberger. After only three years as a part-time player in the majors, however, Hersberger's career came to an abrupt end on August 3, 1940. In the privacy of his hotel room, in the pitfalls of a depression, he put a gun to his head and committed suicide.

George "Moose" Gibson, the husky Canadian catcher who had been part of the Pirates' 1909 World Championship team, was brought aboard once again by Barney Dreyfuss before his death in 1932, replacing Jewel Ens as manager. The decision proved to be wise, as Gibson guided the Bucs to a second-place finish. The 1932 Pirates actually led the league for 44 days during that year, but eventually lost to Charlie Grimm's Chicago Cubs by only four games.

Bensy Benswanger, like former Owner Dreyfuss, didn't enjoy finishing second, but he did congratulate George Gibson for putting up such a good fight. "And in this Depression period, the boys can use the second-place checks," he said.

One of Gibson's better decisions in 1932 was inserting the young Arky Vaughan, who had only one year's professional experience, at shortstop. Vaughan batted .318 that year. In fact, he didn't hit below .300 for 10 straight seasons.

Pie Traynor had another good year, batting .329. Paul Waner did even better as he hit .341 and led the league in doubles (62). Lloyd nearly matched his brother with his .333 average.

Larry French earned his pay in

1932 by pitching in a league-leading 47 games and winning 18 of them. Bill Swift won 15, while Heinie Meine had 12 victories.

League officials thought that because hitters were dominating baseball, the ball must be too lively. So, prior to the 1933 season, the ball was "deadened." Most batting averages took a dive, yet the Pirates hit well enough to lead the league in hitting with a team average of .285. But that was good enough only to earn them a second place finish, five games behind new manager Bill Terry and his New York Giants.

This was the year, also, that Arch Ward, sports editor for the *Chicago Tribune*, conceived of an idea of pitting the best players of the National League and the best of the American League, as voted by the fans of baseball, in a mid-season classic known as the "All-Star Game." Representing Pittsburgh on July 6, 1933, were Pie Traynor and Paul Waner. The game, held at Comiskey Park in Chicago, was won by the American League, 4-2.

Bill Benswanger, now much more comfortable as the Pirates' top gun, initiated a major trade with the Giants. Pittsburgh swapped Glenn Spencer and a chunk of money to the Giants in exchange for Freddy Lindstrom, a heavy-hitting (38 league-leading home runs the year before) third baseman.

He also acquired the services of veteran pitcher Waite "Schoolboy" Hoyt — the former Yankee star — who, after his release in 1930, wore the uniforms of the Tigers, Athletics, Dodgers and Giants. "We thought he would last only a short time," admitted Benswanger, "but he gave us five years and some outstanding performances."

Another smart move by Benswanger was to add the popular Honus Wagner to his coaching staff. Wagner, who left the ballclub in 1917, had owned a garage in Carnegie, but this business venture proved to be more challenging than any opposing pitcher. He ran as the Republican candidate for Sheriff of Allegheny County, yet even this popular sports hero could not combat the avalanche of Democrat votes. He did land a job as a sergeant at arms of the Pennsylvania State Legislature in Harrisburg, but he soon left because he felt there was nothing much to do.

Finally, he teamed with Pie Traynor to open a sporting goods store in Pittsburgh that bore Wagner's name. But, the Dutchman's timing in the batter's box was much better than that of his business timing. The new store struggled in face of the impact of the nation's Great Depression.

Honus Wagner's wife, Bessie, must be given credit for seeing things others could not. She took Honus by the hand, led him to the office of "Bensy" Benswanger and asked if there was a job for her husband in the organization.

"What kind of job?" asked Benswanger.

"One with a uniform," responded Honus.

With the approval of manager Gibson, Wagner was hired as a coach and assistant.

"His coaching of the young players was invaluable," recalled Benswanger. "In addition, he brought with him a wealth of good will."

Bensy Benswanger gradually grew impatient with manager George Gibson. On paper he should have the best team in baseball. Second place finishes two years in a row were unacceptable. In mid-season, 1934, when it became apparent to everyone that the Pirates would still not capture the National League flag (they were in fourth place with a 27-24 record), Mr. Benswanger asked for and received Gibson's resignation as manager. In his stead stepped the fan favorite, Pie Traynor, as player-manager.

This had all the appearances of an ideal transition. Pie Traynor loved the Pittsburgh Pirates, but his playing days were nearing an end. His once cannon-like arm lost its zip and accuracy. Nobody felt the agony of his miscues more than Pie, himself. He limited his play to 119 games, although he batted .309.

A few other bright spots were the fact that Paul Waner won his second batting title, whacking the ball at a .362 clip; Arky Vaughan hit .333, and catcher Tommy Padden hit .331.

The year also marked the first time the Pirates played ball on Sunday. For years, major-league baseball bowed to the so-called "blue laws" prohibiting Sunday games. On April 9, 1934, that all changed, at least in Pittsburgh. The team did make one concession. They would begin no inning of a Sunday game after 7 p.m., thus allowing their fans to attend evening church services. The Pirates defeated Cincinnati by a score of 9-5 on a blustery, cold afternoon that day.

The delay in offering Sunday baseball resulted not so much from pressure by the conservative

Arch Ward, sports editor for the Chicago Tribune, conceived of an idea of pitting the best players of the National League and the best of the American League, as voted by the fans of baseball, in a mid-season classic known as the "All-Star Game."

Outfielder Johnny Dickshot could be quite effective once he was
determined to catch a fly ball instead of chasing his hat.

Christian community, rather from financial concerns. Former Owner Barney Dreyfuss believed that Sunday ball would "kill our Saturday afternoon business." Dreyfuss was mistaken. Saturday attendance remained constant, and Pittsburgh became one of the most supportive cities in the National League for Sunday baseball.

The rest of the 1934 season was uneventful. Under Traynor, the club won only 47 of the remaining 99 games, slipping one more spot to fifth place at season's end. Yet, surprisingly, the Pittsburgh club won 13 of the 22 games played with the eventual World Champion Cardinals of that year. Unfortunately, that wasn't good enough; the Bucs finished the season two games under .500 and wound up in the second division (fifth place) for the first time in years.

The next year also produced a mixed blessing. The Bucs settled for a mediocre fourth-place finish in 1935, but that failed to diminish the enthusiasm of the Pirates talented Arky Vaughan. The kid from Arkansas batted a hefty .400 throughout much of the season, ending with an impressive .385 batting average to lead the National League. In addition, he whacked 34 doubles, 10 triples, 19 home runs and knocked in 99 runs, earning for him the league's slugging title (.607).

Pitching leaders on the club were Darrell Elijah "Cy" Blanton (2.59 ERA, 18-13 record) and Bill Swift (2.69 ERA, 15-8 record).

Frankly, the fans and management had hoped for a much better finish for their Pirates. A preseason trade brought to the Pirate lineup

pitchers Guy Bush and big (6'6", 230 lbs.) James Weaver to Pittsburgh, along with slugger Floyd "Babe" Herman, once a .393 hitter with 35 home runs playing for the Dodgers. Bush ended up with a far-less-than-spectacular 11-11 record and would be released halfway through the next season. Weaver enjoyed three fairly good seasons (14-8, 14-8 and 8-5) before being sold to the St. Louis Browns in 1938. Herman, never known for his fielding, was totally out of place in the spacious Forbes Field outfield grass; after only 26 games, both Traynor and Benswanger were convinced he just didn't belong and they sold him to Cincinnati.

Perhaps the most memorable moment of Pittsburgh's 1935 season — one that's still discussed among baseball buffs — came not from the performance of anyone wearing a Pirate uniform, but from an old American League hero who wore the uniform of a Boston Brave.

George Herman Ruth had signed a contract with the Braves (a nickname Boston had adopted in 1912). Ruth was to serve three positions: a part-time outfielder, a club vice president and an assistant manager to former Buc skipper Bill McKechnie. The legendary Ruth soon realized he had lost his prowess as the game's most dangerous hitter, and that his on-the-field appearances were more for drawing crowds than anything else. His anemic .181 batting average over 28 games was testimony to the fact that his days as a serious threat were gone.

However, the gods of baseball seemed to save one last miracle for the Babe's final game. On May 25, 1935, a 41-year-old, woefully out of

Arky Vaughan batted a hefty .400 throughout much of the 1935 season, ending with an impressive .385 batting average to lead the National League.

shape Babe Ruth, once again, was the "Sultan of Swat." During his first three times at bat at Forbes Field, he hit towering home runs — the last was the first one ever to clear the right field roof. The ball kept sailing until it landed on Joncaire Street. According to eyewitnesses, the closest anyone came to doing that was in 1927 when Ruth hit the facade in batting practice. After he lined a single to right field his last time at bat, Ruth called time-out, walked to the dugout and tipped his hat to an appreciative crowd of applauding fans.

A few days later, Babe Ruth officially retired from baseball, but not before he had put on one of the most impressive shows ever by a player at Forbes Field.

Things began to click for the 1936 Pirates and, for the first time in nine years, fans began to think pennant. Manager Traynor yielded his third base position to a University of California graduate by the name of Wilbur Lee "Bill" Brubaker. Arky Vaughan was on his way to leading the league in walks and an impressive .335 batting average. However, this was not good enough to win another batting crown. That honor went to teammate Paul Waner who slugged a .373 average. It was the third time Waner earned that coveted title.

Unfortunately, on July 10, hard-hitting outfielder Chuck Klein and his last-place Philadelphia Phillies clubbed the Pirates in a 10-inning, rain-dominated ball game at Forbes Field. Klein provided most of the offense in this 9-6 contest by sending four home runs into the right field stands. The weather was

miserable for the game which nearly was called with the score tied after nine-and-a-half innings.

Manager Pie Traynor took the loss harder than anyone else. He sat in the dressing room after the game, stared at the floor and shook his head. "Why would Chuck Klein do that to us when they were going nowhere and we need games so badly?" he asked.

Traynor's lament was a premonition of disaster; something strange happened to the Pirates after that game. In the year when England's King Edward VIII abdicated the throne for "the woman I love," the Pirates appeared to forsake all passion for winning. The Bucs could muster no more than a .500 pace for the remainder of the year, while the Giants' Carl Hubbell went on a 16-game winning rampage and led his club to the National League pennant.

Pittsburgh ended the year in fourth place, eight-and-a-half games behind the Giants, despite the fact that outfielder J. Owen "Chief" Wilson batted .300 and hit 36 triples — more than any other major leaguer in the history of the game. Oddly enough, this is the only significant single season batting record that has not been broken since 1936 in the minor leagues.

In spite of this crushing disappointment, one thing happened in 1936 that, forever, would bring another measure of pride to Pittsburgh and its Pirates. A special committee appointed by Commissioner Landis elected to baseball immortality the first inductees into the Hall of Fame. The five pioneers were: Babe Ruth, Ty Cobb, Christy Mathewson, Walter Johnson and the Pirates' Honus Wagner.

The new infield of Brubaker, Vaughan, Jeep Handley and Gus Suhr led the Pirates to a third-place finish in 1937. Once again, the Bucs demonstrated their prowess at the plate with Paul Waner hitting a healthy .353, brother Lloyd hitting .330 and Arky Vaughan hitting .322. But weak pitching was Traynor's downfall. Defensive play also left a lot to be desired.

Fans of that era remember the antics of one Pirate outfielder, Johnny Dickshot. Owner Benswanger didn't know whether to laugh or cry when he recalled one incident: "Dickshot came in for a short fly, and when he did so, his cap flew off. Instead of chasing the ball, Johnny chased his cap, as two runners circled the bases."

Prior to the 1938 season, following years of frustration, Bill Benswanger, Pie Traynor and the rest of the Pirate family said among themselves: "This is our year, finally."

Several pleasant surprises flamed the fires of enthusiasm. A young slugger named Johnny Rizzo, an outfielder bought from the Cardinals' farm team in Columbus, clubbed 23 home runs — more than any other Pirate at that time. In fact, the rookie Rizzo hit home runs in all nine National League parks that year. The reason there were nine parks was that Philadelphia changed venues from old Baker Bowl to Shibe Park halfway through the season.

Pitching was still a weakness for the '38 Pirates. Absent from the roster was a dominating Babe-Adams-like pitcher, although right-hander Mace Brown led his squad with a 15-9 mark.

Along with the home-run heroics of Johnny Rizzo, other batters rolled up impressive statistics. Lloyd Waner hit .313 in '38 and out-slugged his older brother who hit only .280. Reliable Arky Vaughan again led the club with a .321 average.

With these outstanding performances, the Bucs regained their positive attitude. Winning 40 out of 54 games in June and July, Pittsburgh broke out in front of the pack and, by September 1, enjoyed a seven-game lead on Chicago and Cincinnati who were tied for second.

September is "crunch time" in baseball, and a superior team cannot take any other club for granted. But that's exactly what happened when, one month earlier, Chicago fired its manager, the banjo-playing Charlie Grimm, and named former catcher Charles

Handsome Frankie Gustine, slick-fielding third baseman, lived in suburban Greentree during and after his playing days with the Pirates.

"Gabby" Hartnett as his successor. It was the shot in the arm needed by the heretofore lowly Cubs who flexed their muscles and, nearly unnoticed by the media, started a steady climb in the standings.

During their last swing through the eastern states that season, the Pirates were knocked around not only by opposing teams, but by the weather. A hurricane lashed its force against several East Coast cities, leaving the club idle for several days at a time the team was hot.

Once the winds died down and the fields were again made playable, the Pirate ballclub lost four games from its schedule against the last-place Phillies and seventh-place Dodgers. The Cubs, meanwhile, kept on winning. By the last week of the season, the Pirates lead had shrunk to only a game-and-a-half. Now it was time for a critical three-game series at Wrigley Field in Chicago beginning on September 27.

"All we have to do is win just one of these three games," Traynor reminded his club in the locker room prior to the first game of the series, "and we'll be all right."

Pie Traynor's attempt at motivating the club fell short. His team lost all three.

In Game One of the series, former Cardinal legend Dizzy Dean, who had won only seven games for the Cubs that season, reached deep inside himself and pitched a masterful 2-1 victory for his team and the more than 42,000 Chicago partisans in the stands.

Player-manager Gabby Hartnett slammed a ninth-inning home run to break a 5-5 tie in the second game. The home run was barely seen by the fans and umpires, as Wrigley Field (a ballpark with no lights at the time) was engulfed in darkness. Had Pirate pitcher Mace Brown retired Hartnett, the game would have been called and would have gone into the books as a tie.

With the Cubs now a half game in first place, the Pirates were on the defensive. Obviously they needed much more defense; they were pummeled by Chicago, 10-1, in the third contest.

Chicago won the pennant that year by two-and-a-half games.

Bensy Benswanger, to his dying day, blamed the Pirates' demise not so much on Gabby Hartnett's home run, but on a hurricane. "The pennant was lost *before* the Cubs series," he said. "The hurricane prevented us from winning. We went East good and hot. Everybody knows that when a club is hot, it can make wrong plays and still win; when it is cold, nothing turns out right.

"We were unable to play in Brooklyn and Philadelphia just when we needed every game. To lose a pennant by losing ball games is one thing; to lose by idleness is another."

Perhaps the most regrettable event of 1938 involved nobody on the Pittsburgh roster. Instead, it was about one player the Bucs let get away. From nearby Donora, Pennsylvania, a Polish-bred lefty named Stanislaus Musial had a tryout as a pitcher at Forbes Field and impressed Scout Pie Traynor and his assistants; unfortunately the Pittsburgh organization failed to act fast enough or hard enough. Musial had already signed a contract with the Cardinal organization, and the

Manager Pie Traynor (center) goes over some of the fine points of the game with Johnny Rizzo (left) and Arky Vaughan (right).

Pirates made no genuine effort to obtain his rights from St. Louis.

The Pirates were still reeling over their collapse in the final weeks of the 1938 season; that was obvious from the first pitch at the 1939 spring training camp in San Bernardino, California. The eagerness, enthusiasm and spark normally associated with the start of a new season were sapped from the 1939 Pirate ball club. Paul Waner hit .328 that year and Arky Vaughan a solid .306, but the lack of both consistent hitting and solid pitching resulted in an inglorious sixth-place finish.

Mr. Benswanger realized that the club needed revamping long before the start of the '39 season. However, one "keeper" was a tall, sandy-haired pitcher from Alabama named Truett B. "Rip" Sewell. His 10 wins in 1938 spelled future success. He would later become a fan favorite with his unorthodox "eephus" pitch or "blooper ball."

At the December 1938, National League meeting, Benswanger traded catcher Al Todd and Johnny Dickshot (who turned many a routine fly ball in the outfield into a contest) to the Braves for catcher Ray Mueller. Gus Suhr, the iron-man first baseman, had slowed. Benswanger, consequently, acquired Elbie Fletcher, a slick-fielding first baseman from the "Bees" (Boston's nickname from 1936–1940) in June; Fletcher hit .303, and Suhr was sent to the Phillies on waivers.

Even the Waner brothers could not expect to remain young and energetic much longer. To bring more power into its lineup, the club brought up two young outfielders — Bob Elliott and Maurice Van Robays. Both were impressive. Elliott hit .333 in 32 games; Robays hit .314.

Players were not burning National League basepaths with blazing speed in 1939 as evidenced by Lee Handley, Pirate third baseman, who tied the Cubs' Stan Hack for the stolen base crown with only 17.

The most popular trade acquisition made by Benswanger was at the end of the season when he signed a 19-year-old, handsome third baseman named Frankie Gustine.

Frankie Gustine could play any infield position (he would even be brought in to catch a game later in his career), but preferred third base. While Gustine could have benefited from daily observations of his boyhood hero Pie Traynor, such was not to be the case. Traynor was dismissed as manager following the ho-hum 1939 season. Traynor, however, remained faithful to the Pirate organization. He continued to serve the club as a scout, as farm director and as a sportscaster. ■

GUS SUHR

CHAPTER 8

THE WAR YEARS

“ *Major league baseball should continue for the best of the country.”*

—PRESIDENT FRANKLIN D. ROOSEVELT
1942

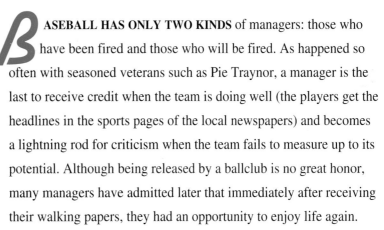

ASEBALL HAS ONLY TWO KINDS of managers: those who have been fired and those who will be fired. As happened so often with seasoned veterans such as Pie Traynor, a manager is the last to receive credit when the team is doing well (the players get the headlines in the sports pages of the local newspapers) and becomes a lightning rod for criticism when the team fails to measure up to its potential. Although being released by a ballclub is no great honor, many managers have admitted later that immediately after receiving their walking papers, they had an opportunity to enjoy life again.

Frankie Frisch was one of those people.

On New Years Day, 1940, Frisch was basking in that rewarding moment of peace and tranquillity. Frisch had earned some fine accolades as a hard-nosed second baseman for both the Cardinals and the Giants. From 1933 to 1938 he was manager of the famous Gas House Gang and led them to the 1934 World Championship. When the Cardinals slipped to sixth place in '38, Frisch was dismissed as manager. His only contact with baseball came from an announcer's booth as he called the play-by-play in Boston.

According to Frisch, he was now "sleeping better than any time in 15 years."

It is a testimony to the persuasive power of Bensy Benswanger that Frisch allowed himself to

Frankie Frisch was the Pirate's manager 1940–46.

be talked into leaving his new-found paradise to accept the challenge of managing the 1940 Pirates.

Frisch was dubbed by the media as "The Fordham Flash." Not only was he one of the few college graduates in major-league baseball in that era, he had captained three sports — football, baseball and basketball — while at Fordham. He was an all-around athlete who jumped directly from the college campus to the big leagues in 1919.

As a manager, Frisch was not the model of a sophisticated college graduate. He was a throwback to the managerial style of the feisty John McGraw, for whom he had played during eight full seasons. Frisch was known to walk onto the field with fists clenched, ready to fight the opposing team, the umpires, even his own players, if it would help win a game. His autocratic rule ruffled the feathers of some of his players, but that did not seem to bother the tranquil Mr. Benswanger.

The pugnacious Frisch got his 1940 Pirates off to a rousing start; the Bucs won their first five games. But sweet dreams of a World Series championship quickly yielded to sour reality, as Pittsburgh lost 11 of its next 12.

Former Pirate immortals showed they were all too human. Bat swings were not quite as fast. Young stars-to-be now pushed them out of the sports columns.

Arky Vaughan barely missed hitting .300 with a .2996 average. Paul Waner played in only 89 games, brother Lloyd in 17 less. In fact, Paul, a man who was as much a fixture in Pittsburgh as the Liberty Tubes, was given his unconditional release at the end of the season and eventually signed with Brooklyn.

Paul Waner had an incredible career with Pittsburgh. His Hall-of-Fame credentials include the fact that he hit .300 or better 14 times and won three batting titles. The front office was often concerned about Paul Waner's drinking habits during the season, yet nobody ever claimed that his alleged bouts with the bottle affected his play on the diamond.

Johnny Rizzo was swapped to Cincinnati for Vince DiMaggio, oldest member of baseball's "royal family." Vince had a healthy swing. Unfortunately, he too often caused only a breeze at home plate. In four seasons he led the league in strikeouts.

Some bright spots in the Pirate lineup in 1940 included pitcher Rip Sewell with his 16-5 record and 2.79 earned run average (third best in the league). Another hurler, Mace Brown, tied for the league leadership in saves (7). Third-baseman Bob Elliott hit .292, which included 34 doubles, 11 triples and 5 home runs.

Debs Garms, a recent acquisition from the Red Sox, won a controversial batting crown. The third baseman-outfielder hit .355 in 358 times at bat during 103 games. National League President Ford Frick deemed these figures sufficient to grant him the batting title. Spud Davis was another new addition to the roster. This former Phillies catcher hit a lusty .326 in 99 games. In his first full season with the club, Frankie Gustine hit .281 while playing second base and an occasional outfield position.

In June of that year, Frisch and Benswanger traded Catcher Ray

Berres for one of the games' most celebrated backstops — Alfanso Lopez. "Señor Al" played some of his greatest ball for the next five seasons with the Bucs. His best year would be 1946 when he hit .307.

Also, a new era began in 1940 when the Pirates played their first night game at Forbes Field on June 4. Before more than 20,000 fans, Pittsburgh clobbered the Boston Bees, 14-2.

Frankie Frisch was able to lead the struggling Pirates to a fourth-place finish, which helped owner Benswanger regain his pride. "Frankie has us back in the first division," he said. "I think we're on our way up."

Although the team had shown definite improvement, Frisch took losing ball games in a way that fostered a breeding ground for ulcers. Once, following a spectacular stretch of 17 wins in 20 games, he told author Frederick Lieb: "We should have won the entire 20." Instead of talking about the 17 he won, the brooding Frisch could only concentrate on the three that were lost.

At the start of the 1941 season, even the most astute baseball fan kept only one eye on the sports pages of the local newspaper; the other was glued to the headlines telling of military aggression by the Germans in Europe and the Japanese in the Pacific. Perhaps in an effort to relieve some of the anxiety of the day, major league cities showed even more enthusiasm for their representative teams. Pittsburgh was no exception.

Pirate fans attended games with regularity. Baseball offered them a welcomed distraction. That relief for Pittsburghers came from following a struggle for the pennant and from watching antics on the field by some of the more colorful characters on their club.

One of the Pirates most outlandish in his behavior was Manager Frankie Frisch. Often a thorn in the flesh of umpires, Frisch left no doubt when he thought an arbiter made a poor decision. Once, for example, when he felt the umpires did not call a game soon enough during a rain storm, Frisch strolled out of the dugout wearing rubber boots and holding an umbrella. That gesture earned him nothing more than an early exit.

Nagging umpires, even by a seasoned pro such as Frisch, did little to win ball games, however. In 1941, the Pirates, again, finished fourth.

Arky Vaughan showed his steady play by hitting .316, although his playing time was limited to 106 games.

Frisch brought aboard the Pirate ship some of his old cronies in an attempt to patch weak spots in the Pirate lineup. Stu Martin, a former Cardinal, batted .304 but played in only 88 games. Jim "Rip" Collins, a native of Altoona and former first baseman with the old Gas House Gang, was supposed to add punch at the plate, but he hit a disappointing .210.

Lloyd Waner played only three games before being shipped off to the Braves (Boston's nickname from '41 until their departure to Milwaukee in '52) for pitcher Nick Strincevich. Van Robays and Bob Elliott were now vying for team leadership.

At the start of the 1941 season, even the most astute baseball fan kept only one eye on the sports pages of the local newspaper; the other was glued to the headlines telling of military aggression in Europe and the Pacific.

The peaceful, relaxed picture of manager Frankie Frisch is a stark contrast to his blistering attacks on umpires.

Although Vince DiMaggio hit .267 and slammed 21 home runs, his 100 strikeouts became a chief concern of the manager. "If a batter hits a ball — even a weak ground out — there is a chance of something happening that will allow the batter to reach first or to advance runners," said Frisch. "But when he strikes out, absolutely nothing positive can result."

Major league baseball came close to folding a few months after the "Subway World Series" between the Dodgers and their crosstown rivals, the New York Yankees. The "Day of Infamy," December 7, 1941, ushered America into World War II, and stars of our national pastime did not

escape a call to duty. From December 1941 through August 1945, baseball would send 428 major league players into wartime service. Bob Feller, Hank Greenberg, Ted Williams, and Johnny Mize, were just some of the household names who left baseball fields for military training fields.

In this era, huge lighted areas were considered potential targets were an enemy bomber to cross America's borders. Not just major cities, but also smaller towns and villages practiced "lights out" drills during which volunteer "wardens" walked the streets to insure that their neighbors abided by the law. Keeping with this practice, nearly all of baseball's schedule for 1942 consisted of day games. Significant numbers of citizens were concerned not so much about night games vs. day games but whether or not major league baseball should continue at all. They asked: "Why should we in the United States have fun at a ballpark while our sons, husbands and fathers are laying down their lives for our freedom?"

President Franklin D. Roosevelt put much of this anxiety to rest when he wrote a letter to Commissioner Landis on January 15, 1942, in which he expressed his desire that major-league baseball continue, as he put it: "for the best of the country." In that same letter, the President even urged that the number of night games be increased in order to give people who worked the day shifts more of an opportunity to see a game.

At the winter baseball meeting shortly after the attack on Pearl Harbor, Bensy Benswanger made a tough call in an effort to revitalize his team. On December 12 he traded Pirate fan favorite, Arky Vaughan, to the Dodgers for several players — Babe Phelps, Pete Coscarart, Jim Wasdell and Luke (called "Hot Potato" because of his temper) Hamlin — none of whom were headliners. The Pirate front office tried to rationalize the decision, but the sports writers and the faithful fans of Pittsburgh had a difficult time accepting the move.

The armed forces of World War II called-up few of the Pittsburgh Pirates at the beginning of the conflict. One promising player sent to the front was Billy Cox, an acrobatic shortstop who was brought up from a Class B Harrisburg team to the club the previous fall and played 10 games in Pittsburgh. Pie Traynor, now a scout for the club, strongly endorsed this youngster and convinced the Pirates to invest $20,000 to add him to their roster. That was one of the highest figures ever paid for a Class B player. Another hot prospect drafted into the military was Vincent Smith, who later became Bob Feller's catcher in the Navy.

At its last spring training camp in San Bernardino, the 1942 Pirates were more concerned than ever with their spotty infield. "Jeep" Handley had been the team's steady third baseman for five years, but an off-season, nearly fatal automobile accident left him with a dead arm. He was released to the minors and given an opportunity to work himself back into shape.

Frankie Frisch asked outfielder Bob Elliott to play third base. Pete Coscarart and Alf Anderson split the shortstop duties. Fan-favorite Frankie Gustine shared second base with Stu Martin.

Pitching, however, remained the club's weak link. Only Rip Sewell was able to complete 10 games. Frankie Frisch wore a path trotting out of the dugout and waving in relief pitchers Hank Gornicki, Max Butcher, Bob Klinger, Johnny Lanning, Luke Hamlin, Aldon Wilke, Kenny Hentzelman and Lloyd Dietz from the bullpen.

Two rookie outfielders showing promise were rapid Johnny Barrett and long-ball-hitting Jim Russell, who thrilled fans with his shoe-top catches of sinking line drives.

The raw talent was there, yet the Bucs of 1942 could do no better than land a fifth-place finish.

A poor finish was certainly not the only concern for Pirate management. Although President Roosevelt had given a "green light" to continue major league baseball, the shortage of quality players left its impact, or lack of it, at the gate. Only 8.8 million attended all of the big league games that year. Pittsburgh's attendance, for example, dropped to 448,897. Bill Benswanger, for one of the rare times in his professional career, showed signs of losing patience.

When the Pirates had to settle for a fourth-place finish in 1943, Benswanger openly expressed his frustration. "Can't we do better than wind up in fourth all the time?" he asked a reporter from the Pittsburgh *Sun-Telegraph*. Neither the reporter nor any of his colleagues had an answer.

Bob Elliott became a fixture at third base, missing only one game

Although President Roosevelt had given a "green light" to continue major league baseball, the shortage of quality players left its impact, or lack of it, at the gate.

all year, while hitting a healthy .315. Frankie Gustine was consistent in the field and hit .290. Elbie Fletcher showed his usual steadiness at first base.

A few other bright spots in 1943 included Rip Sewell whose 21-9 record demonstrated why he was selected for the All-Star Game in Philadelphia. Vince DiMaggio (.248 average and club-leading 15 homers) was also selected to represent the National League, but his league-leading 126 strikeouts drew the wrath of Pirate management.

Leading the league in hitting that year with a sizzling .357 average was Stan Musial — the young man from Donora who tried out for the Pirates just five years earlier.

Frankie Frisch enjoyed his best year as manager in 1944 when he led the club to a strong second-place finish behind the World Champion St. Louis Cardinals. Big Jim Elliott hit a lusty .298 that year and pounded out 28 doubles, 16 triples and 10 home runs. Jim Russell hit .315, while Johnny Barrett led the league with triples (19) and stolen bases (28).

Replacing Elbie Fletcher (who was called up to the Navy) at first was Babe Dahlgren who had been acquired in a trade with Philadelphia for Catcher Babe Phelps. Dahlgren hit a respectable .289 and drove in 101 runs.

Shortstop Frankie Zak tore up the league at the beginning of the season and ended the year at .300 across 87 games. Harry Keck, sports editor for the *Sun-Telegraph*, described the youthful Zak as "a lucky piece for the team," since he was able to manufacture runs with his speed on the basepaths.

The interest of the nation, however, continued to drift away from baseball statistics, focusing more on movements by the Allies in Europe and Japan. Attendance in all of major league baseball dropped even more than the year before to 7.7 million. Cross-state rivals, the Philadelphia Phillies, in fact, declared bankruptcy. Bensy Benswanger and Frankie Frisch pledged to do everything possible to prevent that from happening to Pittsburgh. In an effort to win, and needing increased fan support, Frisch called back Jeep Handley from the minors and Lloyd Waner from Brooklyn in June.

Other additions to the Pirates brought with them a few new "twists." One was the method of delivering a pitch by 37-year-old Fritz Ostermueller from Joliet, Illinois, who was acquired from the Dodgers. The left-hand pitcher delighted both fans and reporters with his unique "windmill" windup. Bending deep at the waist, Ostermueller almost touched the ground with his glove and pitching hand as he rocked back and forth before delivering a fast ball or curve to home plate.

Rip Sewell, the Pirates' top pitcher with another 21-game winning season, introduced his "blooper pitch." Outfielder Maurice Van Robays preferred to call it an "eephus" pitch. "An eephus ain't

Truett B. "Rip" Sewell (left and below) delighted fans and frustrated hitters with his patented "blooper pitch."

nothin'," he said, "and that's what that ball is." Instead of overpowering a hitter with a fast ball or sharp-breaking curve, Sewell tossed the ball toward the batter as if he were on the mound in a slow-pitch softball game.

The ball at times reached 20 to 25 feet in the air before coming down across the strike zone. Hitters, often not believing what they were seeing come at them, swung with gusto at the ball that seemed to float up to the plate. Most of the time they con-tacted nothing but the air, much to the delight of Pittsburgh fans. It was one of the few pitches ever to extract a display of anger from mild-mannered Stan Musial who once threw his bat to the ground in frustration after striking out against the pitch.

Battling Frankie Frisch continued to have shouting matches with umpires. In one instance, when that yelling included some expletives unacceptable even on a baseball diamond, Frisch was tossed as were two of his players. The next day, the two players received a telegram from League President Ford Frick telling them they were fined $50 each. "Nothing happened to me," said Frisch. "I was quite pleased that I had escaped. Two days later I received a wire from Mr. Frick: 'I'm sorry I overlooked you. You're fined $75.'"

A fine for misbehavior was an accepted part of the game. However, two "back stage" decisions in 1943 paved the way for future movements that would impact the game.

Renegade baseball man Bill Veeck, early in the year, made a bid to buy the bankrupt Phillies in order to stock the team with black players. The owners flatly rejected his plan and demonstrated how determined they were to keep baseball an "all white" sport.

The second decision was made outside the baseball arena, within the halls of the United States Congress. In an effort to keep wages from getting out of hand on the home front during the war years, the federal government imposed a wage freeze that kept players' salaries to a $6,400 average. Angry players, especially those from industrial cities such as Pittsburgh, voiced their resentment. They were more open than ever to forming a players' union.

Pittsburgh finished the 1944 season in second place, but the Bucs did not put up much of a fight against the eventual World Series Champion St. Louis Cardinals.

Rip Sewell topped the Pirate pitching staff with 21 victories. Nick Strincevich won 14; Elwin Charles "Preacher" Roe, in his first full season in the majors, won 13 as did veteran Albert "Max" Butcher.

Outfielder Johnny Barrett led the league with triples (19) and stolen bases (28). No regular player that year hit .300 or better.

Although he displayed some home run power, something which the Pirates desperately needed, Vince DiMaggio was too inconsis-tent at the plate. He led the league in strikeouts three years in a row. But the biggest gulf between DiMaggio and the team's management was created off the field.

Following a night game in Philadelphia, Vince claimed that the regular dining room at the hotel was

In an effort to keep wages from getting out of hand on the home front during the war years, the federal government imposed a wage freeze that kept players' salaries to a $6,400 average.

closed, so he ate dinner at the Hotel Ben Franklin's swank night club. The bill far exceeded the team's meal allowance. Sam Watters, the club's treasurer and road secretary, challenged DiMaggio's check. Both of them aired their disagreements to the press. It proved to be a mighty expensive dinner for DiMaggio. The following winter, he was traded to the Phillies for left-hand pitcher Al Gerheauser.

At 4:15 in the morning on June 6, 1944, the chimes of downtown's Trinity Cathedral rang out "America" at the announcement of the D-Day invasion of Europe. For the first time in nearly three years, Americans breathed a long sigh of relief; this was a positive sign that the end of the War may not be far off. That notwithstanding, the *Sun-Telegraph* carried two related items: One announced that the Pirates would face Cincinnati's Ed Heusser at Forbes Field that evening; the second was that Heusser had just received his orders to report for his Army physical.

Midway in the 1944 season, the All-Star Game, won by the National League 7-1, was played at Forbes Field. It was the last baseball game ever seen by baseball's first commissioner, Judge Kenesaw Mountain Landis.

While nobody wished bad luck on the World Champion Cardinals, the 1945 Pirates could not help but be pleased with the fact that St. Louis roster was trimmed by a call to the armed services of some of its key players. Stan Musial, Walker Cooper, Max Lanier and Danny

Litwhiler were among those who changed uniforms. As a contrast, the only regular player from Pittsburgh called up that year was the aging Ostermueller who was sent to the Navy in May and was returned to the club three months later.

The Pirates had 35 players in the military over the course of the War; most were youngsters who had yet to prove themselves in the big leagues. One of them was a rookie outfielder named Ralph McPherran Kiner who would later become a club legend. Kiner served his country as a Navy pilot and, while

Fritz Ostermueller was famous for his "windmill wind-up."

Vince DiMaggio never shared the spotlight with his two brothers, unless you want to count the number of years he led the National League in strikeouts and his dinner tab in Philadelphia.

in the service, developed some muscles that later helped him lead the league in home runs for seven straight years.

New faces were added to the Pirate roster in 1945. One was an outfielder from Dysart, Pennsylvania, Al Gionfriddo. The 5'6" Italian was a handsome young man and quickly became a favorite of the female bobby soxers who saw the same charisma in him as crooner Frank Sinatra. Gionfriddo electrified the crowd as he, according to a *Pittsburgh Press* reporter, "scampered around the bases like a jack rabbit." He also hit .284 that year.

Another bonus for Pirate fans was the performance of catcher Bill Salkeld. Back in 1934, Salkeld was a promising player in the Coast League. But a knee injury, followed by extensive surgery, spelled the end to his baseball career — at least that's what the doctors said. Salkeld, however, was determined. He worked his way back to a tryout with the Pirates as a backup to the veteran Al Lopez. "Salkeld's not likely to hit much, but he has some solid minor league experience as a catcher," concluded manager Frisch. To the surprise of Frisch and the entire Pirate squad, Salkeld was the club's only .300 hitter in 1945, hitting .311. He also slammed 15 home runs — many of them "game-winners."

Ace of the mound staff was Elwin "Preacher" Roe (14-13) who led the National League with 148 strikeouts.

Pirate fans envisioned a pennant, but it was the Chicago club that dominated the National League and the Pirates ended the campaign in their all-too-familiar fourth spot. ■

ARKY VAUGHAN

CHAPTER 9

THE KINER CRAZE

" *Ralph Kiner was my hero. I was in awe of him. And we were teammates.* "

—TONY BARTIROME
former Pirate first baseman

*P*RIOR TO THE END OF THE **1945** SEASON, the nation and the world ushered in the atomic age when Col. Paul Tibbets and his crew of the *Enola Gay* dropped the first A-bomb on Hiroshima on August 6. A few weeks later, America and its allies celebrated V-J Day. But that was the only "championship" in the 1940s for Pittsburgh Pirate fans.

The Pittsburgh front office was at a low ebb following the '45 campaign. Mrs. Dreyfuss had lost her zest for baseball. Insiders agreed that repeated fourth-place finishes did nothing to add to her encouragement.

The next year, however, would not feature another fourth-place finish. The Bucs struggled, instead, just to stay out of the National League cellar. Their eventual seventh-place finish — just two games out of last place and 34 games behind league-leading St. Louis — in 1946 was the team's worst record since 1918.

In 1946, team regulars had mediocre years. Big guns such as Jim Russell (.277), Bob Elliott (.263), Elbie Fletcher (.256) and Frankie Gustine (.259) did not post spectacular numbers. The only player to hit for a solid average was Billy Cox. He lived up to all the accolades given him by scout Pie Traynor. Following four years of military service and a bout with a tropical fever that knocked him down to 135 lbs., the acrobatic Cox hit .290 and learned the fine points of the game from Honus Wagner.

Ralph Kiner powered his way to lead the National League in home runs for a record seven straight years (1946–1952).

The traditional bad pitching of the club was worse. Fritz Ostermueller (now called "Old Folks" because he was 39 years old) led the Bucs with a 13-11 record. Rip Sewell slipped to 8-12, although he did appear in the All-Star game where Ted Williams proved that someone actually could hit a home run off Sewell's famed "blooper" pitch.

One of the bright spots for management in 1946 was the amazing loyalty of the Pittsburgh fans. More than 759,000 of them crossed the turnstiles.

One of the reasons for the impressive attendance was the young man from Santa Rita, New Mexico, Ralph Kiner. Kiner, now back from a near three-year stint with the Navy Air Corps, hit a modest .247, but smacked 23 home runs to tie Johnny Rizzo as the single-season Pirate home run hitter. It was good enough to earn the coveted title as the National League home run king.

According to Charles "Chilly" Doyle — popular sports columnist for the Pittsburgh *Sun Telegraph* — the young slugger had hit 21 home runs, but came down with a horrible cold in late September. Kiner was tempted to sit out the rest of the season. But Doyle pointed out to him that he was close to tying or establishing a club record. With a high fever and running nose, Kiner agreed to play the last few games. He hit two more home runs. That year, in fact, he hit one in every ballpark of the league.

Ralph Kiner was different from any ballplayer the Pirates had seen for decades. He demonstrated consistent power that had outfielders playing near the fences and short-

stops positioning themselves on the edge of the outfield grass. He employed a unique batting stance: feet wide apart, standing perfectly still, eyes glued on the pitcher, while holding his bat far back, perpendicular to the ground, allowing him to get even more snap in his wrists when he swung his 42-ounce Louisville Slugger. He also possessed a charisma that charmed both the veteran baseball fan as well as a newcomer visiting Forbes Field for the first time.

The Pirates started looking at this talented youngster when he was only 14 years old. Pittsburgh scout Hollis "Sloppy" Thurston was extremely impressed when he saw the young Kiner play at Alhambra High School as an infielder and pitcher.

Mr. Benswanger agreed with Hollis' assessment and offered Kiner a contract with a $3,000 signing bonus to play Class "A" baseball at Albany, New York, for $150 a month during the 1941 season. To Ralph Kiner, or anyone else for that matter, in 1940 this was a lot of money. It was a move that would change the focus of the Pirates for the next seven years.

The Pirates experienced a preview of other coming attractions during that '46 season. Baseball, until this time, was a unilaterally run sport. Club management decided who would play when and where. Players were traded, bought and sold. Few, if any, had input as to where they would play. One Boston attorney, Robert Murphy, organized what he called "The American Baseball Guild." The concept was to create a union of ballplayers that would allow them to have a voice in their futures. Because Pittsburgh, with its vast steel-manufacturing empire, was a union-dominated city, Murphy targeted the Pirates as his team for a litmus test. Murphy was led to believe that he had 95 percent approval from the players to form the union.

At first, Owner Benswanger refused to recognize Murphy as a player representative. Vice President Sam Watters was even more outspoken. "What is this," he asked, "some kind of new racket?"

Murphy was not impressed. Murphy finally met face-to-face with Watters and Seward French — the Pirate attorney — and said, "I understand you're not in favor of these new rackets. I get it. You're in favor of the old ones."

Battle lines were drawn. Tempers grew short. Prior to a night game with Brooklyn on June 5, for the first time in 12 years, Bensy Benswanger met with the players in the clubhouse. He spoke to them like a father would to his children. While more than 20,000 people waited in the stands, Murphy called for a strike. The players, by a show of hands, rejected the motion, then ran onto the field to play the game.

Two nights later, Murphy called for another strike vote. This time all non-players, including Manager Frisch, were excluded from the locker room while the team voted in secret. The result: 20 voted yes; 16 voted no. However, a three-fourths majority was needed to call the strike, and the vote lost.

"We did not strike because we hold President Bill Benswanger in high regard," said Lee Handley, who spoke for the team. Rip Sewell was another leader of the anti-strike faction. He later stated that although the call for a strike was defeated, the players did believe it was high time to create a plan for representation.

Another setback for the Pirate front office that year involved a "free day" for 500 *Pittsburgh Post-Gazette* newspaper carriers. The game, however, was rained out. When the carriers showed up the next day, Sam Watters ordered that they be turned away. The next morning, the *Post Gazette* ran a blistering editorial. Mrs. Dreyfuss was shocked and hurt. Shortly thereafter, Mrs. Dreyfuss informed Bill Benswanger that she intended to sell the club. On August 8, came the official announcement. Mrs. Dreyfuss had sold the Pirates for $2.5 million to a group of new owners: Frank McKinney, a banker from Indianapolis; John W. Galbreath, a Columbus realtor; Tom Johnson, an executive with Standard Steel Spring Company; and Harry L. "Bing" Crosby—America's beloved popular singer and movie star.

H. Roy Hamey, president of the American Association, was named general manager.

Billy Cox was a fan-favorite in Pittsburgh because of his energetic play.

HANK GREENBERG

Ray Kennedy, formerly with the Yankee organization, was new farm director. Bob Rice was named road secretary. Finally, the popular radio broadcaster, Albert Kennedy "Rosey" Rowswell, became director of public relations.

Both manager Frisch and the new Pirate front office agreed that a fresh approach was needed in all aspects of management. With but three games remaining in the season, and with the Pirates out of the league basement by only two games, Frisch ended his employment with the Bucs and was replaced by Virgil "Spud" Davis, who led the club to one victory. That was good enough to enable the Pirates to finish in seventh place, two games ahead of the cellar-dwelling Giants.

Opening day, 1947, marked a turning point for the major leagues. Prior to that date, big-league baseball was played only by whites. Blacks (more commonly called "Negroes" at that time) were relegated to the so-called Negro Leagues. Star players of these teams such as Leroy "Satchel" Paige, "Cool Papa" Bell and Josh Gibson would probably have developed into all-time greats in the majors were it not for a ban on non-whites endorsed by Judge Landis, baseball's first commissioner. But the Brooklyn Dodgers, spear-

headed by its flamboyant general manager and part owner, Branch Rickey, offered to a superb black athlete and graduate of UCLA, 28-year-old Jack Roosevelt Robinson, a major league contract. Whether Rickey's motives were primarily humanitarian or sound business is debatable. One thing was certain — when Jackie Robinson stepped onto Ebbets Field on April 15 and took his position at first base against Johnny Sain and the Boston Braves, he initiated a new era for baseball.

Not everyone, however, welcomed the change.

Robinson became the target of racial slurs. He could not always stay at the same hotels as his teammates. Fans openly heckled him from the stands. Opposing ballplayers shouted vicious obscenities from their dugouts. Even several of Robinson's own teammates let it be known in no uncertain terms that they did not welcome the idea that they would have to share the same uniform and locker room with, as they put it, "a person of color." During spring training, some of the players even passed around an anti-Robinson petition in the clubhouse. That was soon quashed by Dodger management.

Most outspoken of the Dodgers was Fred "Dixie" Walker, from Birmingham, Alabama, who, by his own admission, could not rid himself of his racial prejudice. Walker stuck with the team for the full '47 season, even hit .306. At the end of the year, however, he demanded to be traded. And he was . . . to the Pittsburgh Pirates.

The 1947 Pittsburgh team had all the raw material for a fresh start as well. Vice President Sam Watters (the man who ordered the newsboys turned away from Forbes Field the year before) exited with Manager Frisch. Named as new manager of the Bucs was William Jennings Bryant "Billy" Herman, an infielder for the Boston Braves.

Knowing that the Pirates wanted the popular Herman, Lou Perini, Braves president, agreed to let Herman go, but for a price — a steep price. He demanded Bob Elliott and catcher Hank Camelli. Pittsburgh also received the services of reserve infielder William "Whitey" Wietelmann, right-hand pitcher Elmer Singleton and reserve outfielder Sam Wentzel.

The deal cannot be listed as one of the Pirates' better transactions. Herman was slated to be a player-manager, but his arm went bad in spring training and he played in only a few games during the '47 campaign. Bob Elliott, on the other hand, batted .317 for the Braves and was voted that year as the National League's Most Valuable Player.

In a desperate move to get better pitching, the Bucs picked up a slew of discards from other clubs, including the Red Sox' Jim Bagby, Jr., Ernie Bonham and Mel Queen from the Yankees, plus Kirby Higbe and Cal McLish from Brooklyn. The last acquisitions cost the Pirates the popular Al Gionfriddo who would go on to star for the Dodgers in the '47 World Series.

The biggest move that year was the purchase of future Hall-of-Famer Henry "Hank" Greenberg. Greenberg, a constant home run threat, led the American League the previous season with 44 home runs and knocked in 127 runs. Teaming this Detroit legend with Ralph Kiner caused an overload on the switchboard at the Pirate ticket office. Preseason sales escalated beyond all anticipation.

Many of those preseason sales may have been scuttled had Manager Billy Herman gotten his way. When the Pirates landed Hank Greenberg, Herman recommended that Kiner be traded, since the Bucs now had an established cleanup hitter in Greenberg. Roy Hamey and the rest of the Pirate front-office disagreed, feeling that Kiner and Greenberg would offer an ideal "one-two punch."

Treasurer John Galbreath orchestrated the Greenberg deal. The Pirates offered "Hammering Hank" an impressive salary of $80,000 and paid Walter Briggs of the Tigers $40,000 for the rights to the big, 36-year-old slugger.

To accommodate the right-hand pulling power of Greenberg, the Pirate ballclub built a new, 30-foot-wide bullpen in left field. This shortened the distance from home plate to the left field fence to 335 feet. A three-foot wooden wall served as the front of the bullpen. On top of that was five feet of chicken-coop wire. The new fence stretched 200 feet from the left field foul line toward center field. The area was baptized the "Greenberg Gardens."

During the season, Greenberg did not take full advantage of the shortened field. Nagged by bone chips in his left elbow and back pain, Greenberg hit only .251 in 125 games, although he did club 25 round-trippers. The one who profited

Hall-of-Fame infielder Billy Herman served as Pirate skipper during the 1947 season.

most by the "Greenberg Gardens" was Ralph Kiner.

Kiner went on a tear, banging out 51 home runs, good enough to tie him with big John Mize of the New York Giants for the league lead and was the sole leader in the majors with a slugging average of .639. Toward the end of the season, when he hit seven homers in just four games, Kiner even threatened to break Babe Ruth's mark of 60.

Most of the Pittsburgh slugger's home runs were not lazy fly balls that just cleared the fence. They were towering line-drives ("Kiner Liners" as sports reporters and fans dubbed them) that seemed to defy gravity and were still rising as they cleared ballparks. Talk around the league was that young Kiner could hit a ball out of any park — including Yellowstone. John Sciulli, currently an usher at Three Rivers Stadium, never missed a home game at Forbes Field for eight years. He saw plenty of Kiner's powerful blasts. "I think he broke every tree branch in Schenley Park," said Sciulli.

Part of the reason behind Kiner's success was the coaching he received from his teammate, Hank Greenberg. Greenberg sensed the raw potential in Kiner (nicknamed "Ozark Ike" after a famous comic strip character) and advised him to stand closer to the plate and to be more aggressive.

"Hank put me in a better position in the batter's box," recalls Kiner. "This enabled me to pull outside pitches. He changed my stance and my whole approach to hitting."

Obviously the counsel worked.

Greenberg also appreciated Ralph Kiner's "work ethic." Following a

home game, after his teammates had left the stadium, Kiner often took extra batting practice while some fortunate local teenagers were stationed in the outfield to retrieve batted balls.

Kiner's home run rampage remained the primary draw for Pirate fans. Although the Bucs languished in or near the basement most of the season, attendance swelled to an incredible 1,283,611 — the first time the Bucs drew over one-million fans in a single season. That was more than a 400,000 increase in attendance compared to any previous year. During the final game in 1947, Forbes Field was jammed with 33,704 fans — many of whom were there to see if Kiner would break his tie with Johnny Mize.

Ralph Kiner quickly gained the attention of the national media. Sports writers wrote about his major-league-leading 51 homers plus his 127 RBI. One observant writer commented that Kiner was often unfairly criticized in the press as being a mediocre defensive player; he pointed to the fact that the young left fielder led the league in put-outs (390) that season.

Adding to fan excitement over Kiner's home runs in 1947 were the flamboyant descriptions by Rosey Rowswell, Pirate radio broadcaster since 1936. The 5'6", 120-pounder was the Pirates first announcer and was not afraid to create unique descriptions of events taking place on the field. When he announced a Pirate home run, he belted out his trademark call: "Raise the window, Aunt Minnie, here she comes . . . right into your petunia patch." It was a call he had made back in 1938 when Pirate Gus Suhr hit a four-bagger. The expression became so popular, the fans demanded he continue to use it.

When the Pirates were on the road, Rowswell refused to leave home to travel with the team. As a result, he and sidekick Bob "The Gunner" Prince recreated the games from a studio at radio station WWSW. Based on messages sent them via a Western Union relay

Albert K. "Rosey" Rowswell — "I'm proud of my Bucs."

Veteran outfielder "Dixie" Walker came to the Pirates one year after Jackie Robinson joined the Brooklyn Dodgers.

station, the announcers described the play-by-play as if they were viewing the action. This gave Rowswell an even greater opportunity to dramatize a Pittsburgh home run. As soon as Kiner or any of the other Pirates slammed one out of the park, Rowswell shouted his familiar: "Raise the window, Aunt Minnie, here she comes." He paused for a second, then pointed to an assistant who dropped a tray loaded with bolts, nuts, broken glass . . . anything that simulated the sound of a window breaking. Rowswell would sigh: "She never made it."

Rowswell coined other unique phrases. When an opposing batter struck out, it was the "old dipsy doodle." If a Pirate slammed an extra-base hit, it was a "doozey marooney." If the Pirates had the bases loaded, Rowswell remarked: "They're FOB" (translation: the bases are Full Of Bucs"). When the Pirates lost, Rowswell simply moaned, "Oh, my achin' back." Out-of-towners who heard Rowswell broadcast a game for the first time often sought an interpreter; they simply did not know what he was describing.

Rowswell had a unique gift. He not only described the details of the game, he became a member of the family. He seemed to be broadcasting directly into the living rooms and kitchens of listeners' homes, until homemakers and others who had never seen him, thought of him as kin. He was a delightful human being who devoted hours each week visiting hospitals and nursing homes with a word of cheer for his never-forgotten shut-ins.

Aunt Minnie's favorite nephew died on February 6, 1955, at age 71 in his Fox Chapel home. The front-page news contained an editorial in the *Pittsburgh Press* that read, in part: "To the hundreds of thousands of district baseball fans, he was the symbol of the Pirates."

Those who attended Pirate games during 1947 were not all full-paid admissions. The front office knew they had to generate a larger base of fans for the future. On Saturdays, children under 12 years of age were admitted free to the right-field stands at Forbes Field. Thursdays were "Ladies' Day," and the feminine gender of Pittsburgh could attend Pirate games for only 50 cents. While this last gesture may, by today's standards, be deemed "sexist," at the same time it went a long way to cultivate interest in baseball for those who had previously allowed themselves to be shielded from the game because of babies and household chores.

"Old Folks" Fritz Ostermueller led the club with a 12-11 record, while his mound partner, Ernie "Tiny" Bonham was 11-8.

When Pittsburgh management realized that the team would finish no higher than seventh place in 1947, they announced that Manager Billy Herman, who had come to Pittsburgh with all the promise of a superlative leader, was released with one game remaining. He was replaced by Bill Burwell, a native of Jarbalo, Kansas, who managed the club to one final victory against Cincinnati, which was enough to win a tie with the Phillies for seventh place.

On October 2, 1947, the Pirate front office issued two bulletins. The first was that the new manager for 1948 would be Bill Meyer — a manager in the Yankee farm system. The second was that Hank Greenberg would no longer be a Pittsburgh Pirate. Greenberg, an American Leaguer at heart, had requested his unconditional release. The Pirates agreed.

A few of the media criticized Pirate management for their signing of Greenberg during the '47 season, calling it an "expensive experiment that failed." Although Greenberg's statistics with Pittsburgh may not have reflected his superstar credentials, at the same time his instruction and inspiration given to the younger players (especially Ralph Kiner) resulted in dividends for the Bucs that would be enjoyed for many years.

Prior to the '48 campaign, once again the Pirates dug into the well of players put on waivers by other clubs. From the Braves the Bucs got first baseman Johnny Hopp and utility second sacker Danny Murtaugh; from Brooklyn the team acquired Stan Rojek, a shortstop who backed-up Pee Wee Reese, and slick-fielding first baseman Eddie Stevens. Another former Dodger was Romanus "Monte" Basgall who was penciled in to start at second base for the Pirates. From the Reds organization the Bucs picked up Elmer Riddle. Two other players added a youthful enthusiasm to the roster — Eddie Fitzgerald, a tall, thin catcher from Sacramento and pitcher Bob Chesnes, who not only had a wicked fastball but could also swing a bat for average.

In a daring move, Pittsburgh traded the popular Billy Cox and pitcher Preacher Roe to Brooklyn for one of the legends of the game — Fred Dixie Walker — along with pitchers Vic Lombardi and Hal Gregg.

Walker was the key ingredient. Dubbed the "People's Churce (Brooklynese for 'choice')" by the Brooklyn faithful, this easygoing outfielder from Alabama knew that his tenure with the Dodgers was over when he openly opposed Branch Rickey's signing of Jackie Robinson.

The 1948 Pittsburgh club surprised everybody — even the most optimistic Pirate fans. For several weeks during the early part of the season, the Bucs actually led the National League. Elmer Riddle could not seem to lose. Bob Chesnes not only baffled hitters, he also hit with consistency and was used sometimes as a pinch hitter.

By season's end, Danny Murtaugh, who beat out Monte Basgall as the starting second baseman, and Stan Rojek, each hit a respectable .290. In addition, they were acrobatic on the field, turning a club record 150 double plays. First baseman Ed Stevens (.254, 10 home runs) gave the Pirates some power from the left side of the plate — something they lacked the year before. These players were hungry and played as if every game was important.

Ralph Kiner's 40 home runs once again tied him with the Giants' Johnny Mize for the National League and major league lead. Kiner's home run output, coupled with the retirement of Hank Greenberg, was

Bob "The Gunner" Prince

Ernie "Tiny" Bonham pitched for 10 major-league seasons before his untimely death during the 1949 season.

enough reason to rename Greenberg Gardens as "Kiner's Korner."

The Pirates eventually ended up in fourth place, only eight-and-a-half games behind front-running Boston. It was a record worth celebrating, especially in light of so many disappointing finishes over the previous few years. Since the 1948 club won 21 more games in Meyer's first year than they had the year before, and since they ended the season only two games behind the second-place Cardinals, both the media and the fans wondered: "Could a World Series be far away?"

Enthusiasm for the Pirates turned up a few notches as Pittsburgh fans continued to fill Forbes Field during the 1949 season. This was supposed to be a breakthrough year. The Pirates, instead, took a couple of steps backward and slipped to sixth place in the standings.

The Pirate family were shocked during the season when Ernie "Tiny" Bonham (7-4) was rushed to the hospital for an emergency appendectomy. The 36-year-old rotund pitcher didn't survive the surgery.

Two of the other key pitchers — Kirby Higbe (0-2 before being traded to the Giants) and Hugh Casey (4 wins) — were no longer able to play up to their prewar standards. Others such as Dixie Walker (.282 with only one home run) and Walt Judnich (.229 in just 10 games) also felt the impact of age.

The faithful support by Buc fans

in 1949 was not because their Pirates demonstrated championship ability. It was solely a testimony to the amazing drawing power of slugger, Ralph Kiner.

"Pirates keep slipping, but Kiner keeps climbing" read a headline in one edition of *The Sporting News*. And Kiner's success was enough to unite the entire city. "Ozark Ike" appeared to be unstoppable that year and the fans followed his every at-bat.

Anyone who says that Ralph Kiner was the real draw for the Pirates has earned a Ph.D. in the obvious. Even if the score was 9-0 against Pittsburgh, fans remained until Kiner's last at-bat. If he hit a home run, they went home happy. Conversation around the water coolers at work the next morning did not begin with: "How did the Pirates do last night?" Instead, most people asked: "How did Kiner do?"

On the last day of the 1949 season, for example, with the team hopelessly out of first division, the Pirates played a doubleheader at home against Cincinnati. Kiner had already hit 54 home runs (actually 55, but one of his round-trippers was discounted due to a rain-out earlier that year) and had the chance to tie or even surpass the National League record of 56 four-baggers for one year clubbed by the Chicago Cubs' Lewis "Hack" Wilson in 1930.

More than 40,000 fans packed Forbes Field that day. The seating capacity of the park was only a bit over 33,000. Some of the paid admissions, therefore, agreed to sit on the outfield grass in right field. A special ground rule for that day said that any ball hit into this crowd was an automatic double.

Danny Litwhiler, left fielder for the Reds that afternoon, still tells the story of how all 40,000 plus fans screamed for Kiner to hit one out of the park. Unfortunately, the best he could produce was a single in each of the two games. After Kiner's final at-bat during the second game, "it seemed as though the entire ball park emptied out," says Litwhiler. "I would guess that not even 1,000 people remained in the stands to see the last out."

Kiner not only led all major league players with his 54 homers — the first National Leaguer ever to hit 50 two times — but also with a slugging average of a whopping .658. He led the National League in RBI with 127.

The strapping, sandy-haired bachelor, was a favorite not only with traditional Pirate fans, but with a new kind of fan — young women. He elevated his stature as Pittsburgh's teenage heart-throb each time he circled the bases with his patented loping stride after walloping a home run. His image became even more enhanced when the name of Pittsburgh's most eligible bachelor appeared in Hollywood gossip columns as a result of his dates with popular movie stars such as Elizabeth Taylor and later, Janet Leigh — who starred in the 1951 movie *Angels in the Outfield* that featured some of the Pirate players. Each appearance at the plate by Kiner brought screams of excitement from vocal females.

Kiner also reached out to the community through plenty of personal appearances at charitable functions. He was one of the first major league ballplayers to host his own local television show. All of this helped swell attendance at the park and devotion to him as a local hero.

Other notable performers that year included center fielder Tom Saffell, a rookie from Etowah, Tennessee, who hit .322, and veteran Johnny Hopp who hit .318 in 105 games before being sent to the Dodgers. Most effective on the pitching staff was Cliff Chambers (13-7), a 6'3" left-hander obtained from the Cubs before the season, and 42-year-old Rip Sewell.

Sewell actually started spring training that year as a coach. Just two days before the season opened, Manager Bill Meyer took a hard look at his staff and decided that few could pitch as well as the old blooper-ball specialist. Sewell was quickly activated.

In spite of this, Bill Meyer was unable to motivate his players as he did just one year earlier. *Sport* magazine reported that during one game in the middle of the year, Meyer gave a hit-and-run sign, but the runner was an easy out at second following a pitchout. After the game, Meyer left the impression with reporters that the runner ran on his own. From that moment on, Billy Meyer had lost the respect of most members of the squad.

Because of the turnaround by the Pirates in 1948, Meyer was named "Manager of the Year" by the Baseball Writers Association of America. He was soon to discover

Kiner not only led all major league players with his 54 homers — the first National Leaguer ever to hit 50 two times — but also with a slugging average of a whopping .658. He led the National League in RBI with 127.

BILLY MEYER

Dino Restelli had one glorious streak during his 1949 debut in the majors, giving joy to every Pittsburgher — especially Italian-Americans.

that success is a fickle companion. Shortly following the disastrous 1949 season, Meyer ran into Casey Stengel, manager of the New York Yankees who had just been named "Manager of the Year" for '49. The "Old Professor" greeted the Pirate skipper with another one of his patented quotes: "Ain't it funny, Bill, how all of a sudden I got so smart and you got so dumb."

The 1949 season would not be complete without a mention of Dino Restelli. This powerfully built Italian-American outfielder came to the Pirates in mid-season and, for a brief spell, was the talk of big-league baseball. In slightly more than two weeks after his contract was purchased from the San Francisco Seals, Restelli hit nine home runs. Even *Life* magazine featured him on its cover. Restelli seemed to counter every fastball with an even swifter swing of his bat. He was on fire. For the first time in four years, fans talked about someone other than Ralph Kiner.

He even added a bit of "down-home color" when he would pull a large, red handkerchief from his hip pocket to wipe his brow before stepping up to the plate.

Finally, pitchers discovered his weakness. Restelli, who wore thick eyeglasses and looked more like a scholar than a ballplayer, had difficulty hitting a curve ball. He saw little else from every pitcher for the remainder of the season. He ended the '49 campaign with a grand total of 12 homers and a .250 average. Dino Restelli had exhausted his 15 minutes of fame. He could not make the Pirate roster the next year.

Pitching posed a real problem again for the 1950 Pirate team. Rip Sewell finally called it quits after the '49 season after a respectable 6-1 record. From the statistics of the mound staff during the '50 season, one might argue that all the Pirate pitchers came close to quitting. Not one hurler posted better than a .500 average. Cliff Chambers led the team with 12 wins, but had 15 losses and an ERA of 4.30.

One bright addition to the ranks was 20-year-old Vernon Law from Meridian, Idaho. Although Law's 7-9 record and 4.92 ERA that year were not enough to earmark him for future greatness, he showed the sort of mound savvy that would carry him through 17 productive years with the Bucs.

Vernon Law and his family were faithful members of the Church of Jesus Christ of Latter Day Saints (the Mormons). When other major league scouts went to the Law home to talk with young Vern, they were smoking cigars. This upset Vernon's parents who opposed smoking for both health and religious reasons. "You can come inside," they said, "but leave your cigars outside."

In sharp contrast, two Pirate scouts — Babe Herman and Herman Welker — came to the house bearing a box of candy for Mrs. Law. That created a much better impression. As if to add icing to the cake, while the scouts were inside talking with the pitcher's mother and father, the telephone rang. It was a call for Mrs. Law from Bing Crosby. "She almost fainted on the spot," remembers Vernon.

What neither young Vernon nor his parents realized at the time was that being a baseball scout required skullduggery similar to that used by corporate executives. Both Babe Herman and Herman Welker gave cigars to scouts from other teams telling them that Mr. Law loved them and would really appreciate these as gifts.

Tom Saffell, rookie sensation of a year before, slipped to a .203 average and hit only two home runs. In his stead came another promising youngster — rookie outfielder David Russell "Gus" Bell. This strong left-hand hitter stroked 11 home runs. Along with Ralph Kiner (and his league-leading 47 homers) and Wally Westlake (15 round trippers), the Pirates finally had an established outfield that could hit with power.

All that power, unfortunately, was not able to keep the team out of last place for the second year in a row. The Bucs finished the season 33½ games behind the "Whiz Kids" of Philadelphia.

John Galbreath, a successful businessman, assumed the duties as new president of the club. He was not afraid to spend money and make changes, nor, if it happened, to make a mistake here and there.

One of the moves he never liked to remember was the signing of a high-school pitching sensation from Southern California named Paul Pettit. The Pirates, in a desperate attempt to add talent and fan support, signed the youngster to an unprecedented sum of $100,000, plus an all-expense-paid honeymoon to Hawaii. The left-hander lasted parts of only two seasons, pitched in a total of 12 games and compiled a career record of 1-2 with a 7.34 ERA.

The 1951 season had its share of excitement and controversy. South-paw Pitcher Cliff Chambers threw a no-hitter in the first game of a doubleheader against Boston on May 6. He and the Bucs won 3-0 despite his giving up eight walks.

Galbreath also brought to the Pirates as general manager one of his former fraternity brothers at Ohio Wesleyan University, the Dodgers' Branch "Mahatma" Rickey.

In his first year with the Pirates, Rickey upset many fans when he traded, in mid-season, the popular outfielder-slugger Wally Westlake and pitcher Cliff Chambers (who had pitched a no-hitter just six weeks earlier) to St. Louis for catcher Joe Garagiola, pitchers Howie Pollet and Ted Wilks, plus two other players. When one reporter reminded him that his decision to trade these popular players would create problems, Mr. Rickey responded: "Problems are the price you pay for programs." Mr. Rickey added that he was embarking on a five-year plan to bring a National League pennant to Pittsburgh.

The 70-year-old Rickey was determined to make his plan work. "It will be highly embarrassing if

Branch Rickey came to the Pirates as general manager in 1951 with a "five-year plan."

I die before the culmination of this program," he said.

Baseball in 1951 was not so much concerned about five-year plans as what was happening at the moment. This was the year in which America's pastime became conscious of the media — particular television.

The popularity of television skyrocketed in 1951. Many baseball fans, for the first time, could follow their favorite teams via 10-inch, black and white sets from the comfort and convenience of their living rooms.

Enthusiasm for baseball in Pittsburgh may have been alive, but scarcely breathing. Pirate management, in an effort to generate excitement, even recalled the flash-in-the-pan sensation of '49, Dino Restelli. That experiment lasted only 21 games as the lovable Italian could muster only one home run and a .184 average.

Manager Meyer moved Ralph Kiner to first base for a third of the season, yet that change did not hamper the big slugger's consistency at the plate. He again led the league in home runs (42), tied for runs scored (124) and batted .309. He was the only Pirate to hit over .300. Gus Bell tied the Cardinals' Stan Musial with 12 triples. Relief Pitcher Ted Wilks led the league in games pitched (65) and saves (13), and Murry Dickson got on the plus side of .500 with a record of 20-16. Outside of these glimpses of glory, Pittsburgh fans had little to cheer about. Their disappointment was demonstrated by attendance, rather, by lack of attendance. For the first time in five years, paid attendance at Pirate home games in 1951

(980,590) dipped below one million.

Pirate management, media and fans waited patiently for something to turn the club around.

The club did make a turn in 1952, but for the worse. The Pirates won only 42 games that year and lost 112, securing their rightful position in last place with a .273 winning percentage. Mr. Rickey's five-year plan was slow in developing.

To say that most of the Pirates' play during the 1952 season was wooden is an insult to trees. Few rewards were given the 686,673 Pirate fans who paid to see a ball game that year. They continued to cheer Ralph Kiner, now a local idol, who again led the league, this time with 37 home runs, tying him with Hank Sauer of the Cubs. It was the seventh year in a row in which Pittsburgh's number-one hero held or shared the Senior Circuit lead in four-baggers.

No other player in the history of baseball has accomplished that feat — even more remarkable, considering the teams for which Kiner played. On most baseball clubs, the most powerful hitting player is followed in the lineup by another who is also a long-ball threat. Ruth, for example, was followed by Gehrig, and Maris by Mantle. Kiner, on the other hand, was the only consistent long-ball hitter on the team for most of these years. Consequently, opposing teams knew to "pitch around" Kiner — i.e. give him nothing good at which to swing. It's not surprising, then, to realize that Kiner led the league in walks three of those seven years.

In spite of this handicap, the young slugger still powdered the ball and kept his name atop the list of home run hitters. Many astute baseball fans, still to this day, argue that had Kiner played for the Yankees or Dodgers, he would have, indeed, established an all-time home run record for one season.

Playing his only year in the majors in 1952 was 5'10" Tony Bartirome, a homegrown youngster just out of high school. Bartirome was one of the slickest-fielding first basemen who ever donned a glove. But his .220 average and no home runs were not the sort of statistics a club wants from a first sacker. Tony realized this as well and, following a stint in the armed services and several years in the minors, pursued another trade becoming an outstanding trainer. He was, in fact, the Pirates' trainer from 1967 to 1985.

Another Pittsburgh 19-year-old who had just received his high-school diploma, was outfielder Bobby Del Greco, who posted a .217 average in 99 games that year.

A diamond in the rough that year was a young shortstop from Duke University named Richard Morrow Groat, who was born in Wilkinsburg and showed his talent as an athlete at Swissvale High. This former baseball and All-American basketball star for Duke University showed confidence during the 95 games he played hitting .284.

Youth and enthusiasm, unfortunately, were not enough to compete with the experience and depth of other National League teams.

Leading the pitching staff with 14 wins in 1952 was Murry Dickson. He also led the National League with losses — 21. Perhaps the only memorable result of that dismal year

was that it gave Catcher Joe Garagiola — now a popular sports announcer — plenty of material for after-dinner speeches that launched his television career. He jokingly describes the '52 team as a group of players sitting in the clubhouse before the game dreaming of new ways to lose. "When we had a rain-out," he claims, "we had a victory dance." Describing the '52 Pirates, he said, "We were so bad we deserved to end up ninth in an eight-team league."

The Pirates made Garagiola a prophet when they managed to lose 112 games that year. Tension on the club was in overdrive, enough to test the patience of any manager. Billy Meyer proved that when he addressed the team with a lava-spewing, locker room-trashing, tirade: "You clowns can go on *What's My Line* in full uniforms and stump the panel."

Perhaps no one summed up the year any better than the club's president, Branch Rickey, who said, "They finished last — on merit."

No one was happy as a result of the 1952 season, especially Ralph Kiner when he met with Executive Vice President and General Manager Branch Rickey and was offered a contract with a 25 percent cut from his $90,000 salary the previous year.

"Why do I get a cut?" asked the usually mild-mannered Kiner. "I led the league last year in home runs."

Vernon Law, a loyal Morman, was not afraid of brushing back batters who crowded the plate.

Rickey, who may have been more of a business man than a baseball man, raised one of his bushy eyebrows, looked Kiner in the eye and asked, "Where did we finish last year?"

"In last place, Mr. Rickey," answered Kiner.

"Hummmmm," responded Rickey. "Well, let me tell you something. Son, we could have finished last without you."

Kiner had to sign the contract. It was either that or not play baseball.

Former major leaguer turned Hollywood actor, Chuck "The Rifleman" Connors, observed: "It's easy to figure out Mr. Rickey's thinking about contracts. He had both players and money — and just didn't like to see the two of them mix."

Fred Haney came over from the Cardinals to manage the Pirates beginning in 1953. He was joined by some other new faces. Haplessly, they were not veterans of a baseball environment. Two of the players were twin infielders — Johnny and Eddie O'Brien — All-American basketball players from Seattle University. Another was Vic Janowicz, an athlete who had earned his reputation in football as the Heisman Trophy winner during his junior year at Ohio State.

Janowicz was a catcher in 42 games for the Pirates that year. His main drawback was that he had a habit of throwing side-arm, which caused a lot of problems when he attempted to throw out a runner stealing second while a left-hand batter was at the plate. After being with the Bucs for part of two seasons, Janowicz traded his chest

protector for shoulder pads and played in the NFL for the Washington Redskins.

From opening day of 1953, it became obvious that the club was going nowhere. Everyone knew that something had to be done, but few expected the bombshell that was about to hit. Midway through the season, on June 4, Art McKennan, the Pirates' public-address announcer, made a startling revelation to the 3,182 fans entering Forbes Field prior to a game with the Chicago Cubs. McKennan announced that their number-one hero, Ralph Kiner, had just been traded to the Cubs along with catcher Joe Garagiola, pitcher Howie Pollet and reserve

Ralph Kiner and the Giants' Johnny Mize tied for the league home-run leadership in 1947 and 1948. Both eventually were inducted into the Hall of Fame.

infielder George Metkovich. In exchange, the Bucs received Toby Atwell, Bob Schultz, Preston Ward, George Freese, Bob Addis, and Gene Hermanski, plus $150,000.

When Rosey Rowswell and Bob Prince repeated the news on KDKA radio, Pirate fans throughout the Tri-State area still could not believe the report. It was only when Ralph Kiner walked out of the Cubs dugout wearing a Chicago uniform that fans

realized the unthinkable actually happened.

Pirate fans were truly saddened by the trade. Ralph Kiner had become the focal point of their loyalty. Most felt that the slugger still had some good years left in him. Mr. Rickey's response to this last observation was his often-cited quote: "It is far better to trade a player a year too early than a year too late."

The day following the shocking trade, Pirate officials attempted to dismantle the shortened left field fence that marked "Kiner's Korner," however, the National League office ordered them to wait until the end of the season.

With no Pirate regular batting better than third baseman Danny O'Connell's .294, and without Kiner's home run power (although Frank Thomas hit 30 four-baggers), the Bucs still managed to win eight more games that year than they did in '52. Nonetheless, they ended the season in last place again, a distant 15 games behind the seventh-place Cubs.

Murry Dickson led the league in losses for another year with 19, and no Pirate pitcher that year had a .500 season or better.

Ralph Kiner would play only three more years. A bad back forced him to retire after only 10 years as a player. But in that one decade, he hit 369 home runs, drove in 1,015 runs and walked 1,011 times. Kiner hit a home run every 14.11 times at bat; of all the major league players who

A spunky Joe Garagiola honed his keen wit with stories of the infamous 1952 Pirates.

have completed their careers, he ranks second in that department only to Babe Ruth. He received the highest honor given to any player when, in 1975, he was elected to Baseball's Hall of Fame in Cooperstown. In 1995, famed slugger Ted Williams named him one of the original inductees to his Hitters Hall of Fame.

Kiner later became a broadcaster with the New York Mets. He lives in Palm Desert, California, with his wife, DiAnn, and plays a wicked game of golf at every opportunity.

The Pirates retired Kiner's number 4 jersey on September 9, 1987. "It was a wonderful day for me," he said. "I shall always cherish my memories of Pittsburgh as a city with loyal Pirate fans and a true love for baseball." ■

At Forbes Field in 1951, Ralph Kiner and Boston slugger Ted Williams met during an exhibition game. Later, Williams would name Kiner as one of his 25 original inductees to his Hitters Hall of Fame.

**Ralph Kiner hit 369 home runs in an abbreviated 10-year career.
"He hit them like he had a bus to catch," said Ted Williams.**

CHAPTER 10

GROWING PAINS

> "*Somehow, Roy always found a way to get people out.*"

—VERNON LAW
on relief pitcher ElRoy Face

$\mathcal{P}$ROBABLY THE ONLY PERSON IN PITTSBURGH who actually felt good about Ralph Kiner's departure from the Pirates in 1953 was left fielder Frank Thomas. "That trade was the best thing that happened to me," he admits. "I had been only a reserve outfielder. On the day he was traded, I began to play regularly."

Frank Thomas demonstrated that he deserved to be an everyday player. In 1954 he hit .298, led the club with 23 homers and, as a pleasant surprise, topped the league with 14 assists. He rightfully represented Pittsburgh in the All-Star contest.

Rookie first baseman Bob Skinner showed promise and a lot of courage. He demonstrated potential when he hit .249 and belted eight home runs. He showed courage by wearing Ralph Kiner's old number 4 jersey; a lot of Pirate fans considered this number a sacred icon.

In 1954, seven years after Jackie Robinson broke the color barrier, the Pirates got their first black ballplayer. He was Curt Roberts, a slick-fielding, light-hitting 24-year-old second baseman.

The *Pittsburgh Courier,* a newspaper published for blacks, ran a headline on April 17 of that year: "Record Group of Negroes in Majors on Opening Day." Roberts, the paper noted, was the

The 1957 Pirates were not without power. Taking aim at opposing pitchers were: (L–R) Roberto Clemente, Bill Mazeroski, Dick Groat, Hank Foiles and Frank Thomas.

FRED HANEY

Curtis Roberts became the first black player to don a Pirate uniform in 1954. He filled the second-base slot for two years until the arrival of a rookie name Mazeroski.

"37th player of color" now drawing a major-league salary.

Unlike Robinson, Roberts never had to endure an onslaught of boisterous taunts by grandstand bigots. Much of the credit for the more humane treatment goes to the Pittsburgh fans who accepted Curt Roberts as they would any player who might give them some added infield defense. "We didn't think of him as a black guy," said pitcher Nellie King, who later became a Pirate broadcaster. "He was just a player. He could be a pain in the rear at times and a real nice kid at others, just like everyone else."

But Nellie King also remembered that Roberts still had to endure some consequences of prejudice: "Black players couldn't stay at the same hotel as the team when we were in St. Louis." Vernon Law said the same policy existed in Philadelphia. Some restaurants even refused to serve Roberts when the Pirates were on the road.

Roberts had a magnificent glove. It was his hitting, or lack of it, that spelled his demise. "All Curtis needs is a little wood," proclaimed the *Courier*. Unfortunately, that "wood" never arrived. Following a .232 average in his rookie year, young Roberts appeared in only 37 games during the next two years. His fate was sealed in 1956 when the Pirates called up from their Hollywood farm team a 19-year-old rookie second baseman named William Stanley Mazeroski. Curt Roberts would never play another major-league game.

Without much hitting support in 1954, starting pitcher Murry Dickson

again had the dubious distinction of leading the Pirates with only 10 wins and the entire National League with 19 losses. Dickson did, however, take the opportunity to pass along sage advice about pitching to other young hurlers on the squad. One of his pupils was 5'8" right-hander ElRoy Leon "Roy" Face. Roy's 6-8 record that year may not have been outstanding, but he would later become one of the game's greatest relief pitchers and win the hearts of Pirate fans everywhere.

Sid Gordon, acquired in a trade with Milwaukee prior to the season, hit .306, and catcher Jack Shepard hit (.304). They were the only Pirates to bat over .300.

For the third year in a row, the Pirates seemed to be stuck in neutral as they finished the season in the National League basement,

22½ games behind seventh-place Boston, and 54½ games behind the pennant-winning Dodgers.

The poor record of the team in 1954, coupled with the loss of Ralph Kiner, the Pirates' number-one drawing card since 1946, left little to attract fans to Forbes Field. Only 475,494 paying customers marched through its turnstiles that year, marking the lowest attendance of any National League club.

The fifth in Branch Rickey's five-year plan, 1955, produced little change. The Bucs ended the season eight games behind seventh-place St. Louis and 38½ games behind the league-leading Dodgers. The hodgepodge of personnel on the playing field was a recipe for disaster. A running joke in Pittsburgh that year was that five minutes into the opening-day game, the Pirates were already eliminated from the National League pennant.

All jokes aside, this was an extremely frustrating year for Pittsburgh fans. The steel industry — the backbone of the city's economy — was no longer controlled by Western Pennsylvania. Using advanced technology, other countries — especially Japan made great strides. For the first time since anyone could remember, steel companies were laying-off employees. Add to this the demise of their Pirates and the patience of the fans was tested as never before.

Attendance fell to 469,397 — again the lowest in the National League. Johnny O'Brien (.299) came closest to hitting .300.

The 1955 club initiated the season on a positive note with a lasting memo-rial to one of its all-time greats. On April 27, with an ailing 81-year-old Honus Wagner in attendance, the Pirates unveiled a statue of him in Schenley Park, just outside of Forbes Field. Less than nine months later, Honus Wagner died at his home in Carnegie.

Stationed in right field that year was a glimmer of hope in the person of a flashy, 20-year-old rookie from Carolina, Puerto Rico, named Roberto Clemente. His real name was Roberto Clemente Walker, but someone had gotten his name mixed up in the translation during his early years playing baseball and Roberto did nothing to correct it.

Brooklyn Dodger great Duke Snider recalls that Clemente had started his professional career with the Dodgers who signed him for a $10,000 bonus. A rule at that time required that any player who signed for more than $4,000 had to be put onto the big league roster after a year in the minors, else his contract could be purchased by any other club. Brooklyn tried to hide Clemente after one year, but Branch Rickey remembered the flashy outfielder. As soon as Clemente's contract with the Dodgers had expired, Rickey quickly put him into a Pirate uniform.

Clemente immediately caught the attention of some of the media not because of his overwhelming batting average (.255), but because of his unique way of playing baseball. He shagged fly balls, for example, using a "basket catch," as did Willie Mays. On the rare occasion when Clemente dropped a ball, some Pirate fans hooted, claiming he was a "showoff."

During the 1955 season came to the Pirates a glimmer of hope for the future. His name was Clemente. Roberto Clemente.

Clemente also was unorthodox in his approach to hitting. When he stepped to the plate, he moved his shoulders around in tiny circles and twisted his body like a person who had spent the night on a bad mattress. Constantly moving while in the batters' box, the slender Puerto Rican often swung at pitches that were 10 inches outside the strike zone — and laced them to right field for hits.

Pirate broadcaster Bob Prince became one of the few media personalities who saw what most others missed — the raw material for a brilliant career. Prince, in fact, was chiefly responsible for creating a special rallying cry for Clemente. Over the air, he encouraged Pirate fans to holler: "Arriba! Arriba!" — a native cheer akin to the Spanish "Ole!" or the Italian "Bravo!" — whenever Clemente came to the plate or performed one of his spectacular catches in right field.

The only other rays of sunshine penetrating this otherwise overcast season were the performances of two pitchers — Bob Friend and Vernon Law. Friend, showing signs of maturity, not only topped his club with 14 wins, but also made a dramatic improvement in his ERA (2.83), good enough to lead all pitchers in the National League in 1955. Law exhibited his prowess as an "iron man" on July 19 when he pitched 18 innings for a no-decision 4-3 victory over the Braves.

In the meantime, Branch Rickey's former team, the Dodgers, following years of heartbreak, finally beat their crosstown rival New York Yankees in the World Series.

So much for five-year plans.

In 1956, the Pirates hoped a change in managers would prove a cure-all for the problems vexing the team across the past few decades. Fan apathy was on the increase; attendance on the decline. Gone were any hopes of a pennant; no new Ralph Kiners emerged for whom to cheer.

The latest to enter the revolving door of managers was 39-year-old Bobby Bragan, former shortstop and catcher for Philadelphia and Brooklyn. Bragan was known to possess a rare mixture of spunk and patience. He looked like a natural to inspire and nurture a young team with soon-to-be-distinguished young talent that included Dick Groat and the to-bacco-chewing Ohio coal miner's son named Bill Mazeroski. Other "Baby Bucs" (as some of the media labeled them) who showed promise were pitchers Vernon Law, Roy Face and Bob Friend.

Roberto Clemente was another who continued to blossom. His .311 average showed he belonged in the majors. Veteran sports writers, including Chilly Doyle, felt that Clemente embodied more raw talent than any Pirate to don a uniform in years. At the same time, insiders discovered that Clemente was unpredictable. One day he came to

Dale Long provided the year's greatest highlight for Pirates fans when he smacked home runs in eight consecutive games in 1956.

Pirate Coach and former gunnery sergeant Len Levy acts as drill sergeant for Pirates who served in the Marine Corps. (L–R): Cpl. Bob Skinner, Pvt. Johnny Powers, Sgt. Danny Kravitz and Pvt. Roberto Clemente.

the park fired up, jovial and eager to play. The next day he would sit quietly in the dugout, staring into space. If anyone approached him and began talking, the Puerto Rican would snap back with a blistering retort. Once in a while, he even refused to play although nothing appeared to be physically wrong.

When faced with Clemente's perceived erratic behavior, Manager Bragan was willing to play the role of psychologist, priest, nurse or whatever was needed to keep his young right fielder relatively happy. Meanwhile, he was challenged to keep the rest of the team from feeling that Clemente was receiving special treatment. Bragan was a

successful peacekeeper, unfortunately, he could not play the role of a winning manager. The Bucs still ended up in last place.

One moment of exultation for Pittsburgh that year came on May 28 from the bat of first baseman Dale Long, when he established a major league record (since then tied by Don Mattingly and Ken Griffey, Jr.) by hitting a home run in eight consecutive games. After he circled the bases and went into the dugout, fans at Forbes Field continued to yell out his name, holding up the game for 10 minutes until he finally emerged from the dugout and took a well-deserved bow.

Alas, moments of glory such as

this were rare as the Pirates did little to lift themselves out of the doldrums of the National League basement.

The only genuine improvement in 1957 was shown by outfielder Bob Skinner who hit .305 (an increase of 103 points from the year before) and slammed 13 home runs. Frank Thomas again led the club in four-baggers (23) and RBI (89).

Ace of the mound staff, Bob Friend, led the league with 277 innings pitched, but could do no better than compile a 14-18 record.

After sleepwalking through 104 games in the 1957 season, Bragan's Pirates were still hopelessly entrenched in last place. General Manager Joe Brown thought he had no other choice. He called Bobby Bragan into his office and informed him that he was being replaced that day by former Pirate second baseman, Daniel Edward Murtaugh.

The managerial debut of the likable Irishman from Chester, Pennsylvania, was impressive. He left a wake-up call for the struggling Pirates and came out on the winning side in 26 of the 51 games he managed. It was good enough to tie Chicago for seventh place.

Was this a glimmer of hope for the Pirate faithful? The fans certainly thought so.

Murtaugh's winning pattern picked up steam in 1958. His club clawed its way up the ladder to a second-place finish by winning 22 more games than it did the year before.

A steady influence on the 1958 club was the recently acquired Ted Kluzewski. The former Cincinnati Reds first baseman, whose trademark blacksmith-like arms hung from the cutoff sleeves of his uniform, was a gentle giant who assisted in bringing focus to the club. In a season when he was plagued with injuries, "Big Klu" batted .292 and hit only four home runs.

Frank Thomas hit a club-leading 35 homers. Dick Groat hit an even .300 and Bob Skinner led his team with his .321 average.

Bob Friend (22-11) regained his winning ways by tying the Braves' Warren Spahn for the league lead in victories, and ElRoy Face topped all National League relievers with 20 saves. Ron Kline (13-16), unfortunately, led the league in losses.

The success of the 1958 Bucs was impressive enough for *The Sporting News* to name as its Major League Executive-of-the-Year, General Manager Joe L. Brown — the first Pirate executive to receive the award given annually since 1936.

In 1959, loyal Pittsburgh fans struggled through another mediocre year (78-76), especially in light of the previous season's performance. They endured pitching problems that had plagued the Bucs for years. Although Vernon Law came into his own with an 18-9 record and a healthy 2.98 ERA, Bob Friend had an ERA of 4.11 and an 8-19 season to lead the National League in losses — a dubious honor held by Pirate

Harvey Haddix tries to look cheerful when congratulating Joe Adcock who broke up his masterful no-hitter in 1959.

pitchers in three of the past seven years.

Added to the club's pitching woes was the fact that no Pirate regular hit .300 or more. Catcher Forrest "Smoky" Burgess (11 homers) and first-sacker Dick Stuart (27 home runs) tied for the team lead by batting .297.

Big (6'4", 212 lbs.) Dick Stuart had set a minor league record by clubbing 66 homers for Lincoln, Nebraska, a few years earlier. He also thrilled Pittsburgh fans when he laced some tape-measure blows over the 457-foot mark painted on the left-center field wall.

Nobody could question Stuart's ability to hit major-league pitching. It was his fielding that gave managers and coaches grey hair. The media saddled him with the nicknames: "Dr. Strangeglove," "Stonefingers," and "Clank." Dick Stuart remains candid about his strengths and weaknesses on the field. He even ordered a special vanity plate for his car that read: "E-3."

"One night in Pittsburgh, 30,000 fans gave me a standing ovation when I caught a hot dog wrapper on the fly," he admits.

For seven straight years (1958-1964), Stuart either led or tied for the major-league lead in errors for a first baseman. It's a record nobody else has come close to equaling. But Stuart has few regrets for that streak. "I know I was close to being the world's worst fielder, but who gets paid for fielding?" he asks. "There wasn't a great fielder in baseball getting the kind of dough I got for hitting."

Dick Groat defended Stuart: "His biggest problem defensively was his lack of concentration. He was constantly thinking about hitting instead of playing defense. Dick just wanted to hit the ball; he didn't want to be catching it or fighting ground balls. To Dick, fielding was a necessary evil."

The front-page headline of the May 27 *Sun-Telegraph* read: "Haddix Hurls Greatest Game of All Time." By the time that evening edition hit the newsstands, however, everybody in town knew what had happened. The evening before, in Milwaukee, the Pirates' Harvey Haddix tossed a perfect game for 12 innings. Unfortunately, his teammates could not score any runs. In the top of the 13th, the Braves' Felix Mantilla reached first base on a throwing error by Don Hoak. After Mantilla was sacrificed to second and Hank Aaron was intentionally walked, Joe Adcock slugged one over the right-center field fence. It would have been a home run except for the fact that, in his excitement, Adcock passed a base runner and was awarded only a double. The Bucs and Haddix lost by a score of 1-0.

Making other headlines throughout that 1959 season was the relief work of Roy Face. The right-handed relief specialist dazzled hitters with his fork ball — a pitch he learned from

Team captain Dick Groat was a local boy who made good. His leadership was a key ingredient in the rebuilding of the Bucs during the late '50s.

HARVEY HADDIX

General Manager Joe L. Brown shows concern that Pirate Dick Groat might not sign his 1957 contract. Groat, did, of course, and hit .315 that year.

former outstanding Yankee reliever, Joe Page. Face's fork ball approached the plate much like a fast ball, but, at the last second, darted sharply down, like the outlawed "spitter." Roy Face sometimes faced near impossible situations — bases loaded, no one out — and proceed to retire the side without allowing one run. It's no wonder he was selected as an All-Star Game participant.

"He made me look like a genius," admitted Manager Murtaugh.

"Somehow Roy always found a way to get people out," said fellow pitcher Vernon Law. "If the bases were loaded and nobody was out, there was no one better to come into the game than Roy Face."

Roy Face won an amazing 18 straight games in relief that year.

The ingredients were now in place. It was time for something big to happen. ■

ELROY FACE

CHAPTER 11

THE SEASON, THE GAME, THE HIT

"*We have seen and shared in one of baseball's great moments.*"

—BROADCASTER CHUCK THOMPSON
as he described Hal Smith's eighth inning
home run in the 1960 World Series

HEN CAME *THE* SEASON . . . 1960. It was a year distinguished by significant changes in American history. A young Roman Catholic Senator named Kennedy was elected as the nation's president, and the so-called "establishment" was compelled to follow the torch passed to a new generation. It was the start of the "Age of Aquarius." But for Pirate fans throughout the world, 1960 would be a year remembered for something different — their beloved Pirates. Today, parents and grandparents pass along to their offspring, with unbridled enthusiasm, stories about the magical moments of the 1960 Bucs.

Some who celebrated that season relive in infinite detail the Bucs' climb to the National League pennant and the subsequent World Series triumph that made nearly everyone in the nation a Pirate fan.

From the minute the Pirate club set foot on the diamond for the opening game on April 12 in Milwaukee, an aura of hope engulfed its players, coaches and manager. That hope turned into genuine anticipation only five days later, on Easter Sunday. During the second game of a doubleheader against Cincinnati, following a masterful pitching performance by Bob Friend who blanked the Reds in the first game, the Buccos seemed to be headed for a split. They were losing by the score of 5-0 going into the ninth inning. However, Pittsburgh "rose from the dead" to score six runs, high-lighted by reserve catcher Hal Smith's three-run homer and Bob Skinner's game-winning, two-run shot into the right field stands.

Prior to Game 1 of the '60 World Series, Manager Murtaugh reviews his line-up with Pirate Captain Dick Groat (L) and soon-to-be Series hero Bill Mazeroski.

The opening game of the 1960 World Series against the New York Yankees brought a standing-room-only crowd to Forbes Field.

Two themes emerged from that glorious season. The first was a pep-song, so to speak, that had a simple chorus: "The Bucs are going all the way." Even announcers Bob Prince and Jim Woods, never to be confused with the Everly Brothers, led the city in singing the song during Pirate broadcasts.

The second theme came in three short words: "Beat 'em Bucs!" It was a rallying cry. The words appeared on automobile bumper stickers, on buttons worn by men in business suits, and on pennants waved by enthusiastic school children. Those two expressions of hope united teacher and student,

Award from the Baseball Writers Association of America.

Roberto Clemente, clearly the most exciting player in baseball that year, hit a sizzling .314 with 16 home runs and a club-leading 94 RBI. Baseball writers and broadcasters agreed that Clemente wrote the book on how to play right field. Not only was he gifted with sure hands and gazelle-like quickness that reduced certain extra-base hits into outs, he possessed a powerful throwing arm that gunned-down many runners who attempted to advance from first to third on a single.

Others played key roles in the Pirates' enchanted season, including first-string catcher Smoky Burgess (.294 average, seven home runs) and backup Hal Smith (.295 average, 11 four-baggers). Both gave consistent performances behind and at the plate. Another pleasant surprise was Glenn Richard "Rocky" Nelson, used mostly as a pinch-hitter and backup first baseman, who hit an impressive .300. Finally, Dick Stuart, always the long-ball threat, led his team with 23 round-trippers.

In line with a pattern established years before, the Bucs' pitching was the principal factor in its drive for the pennant. Vernon Law, now a deacon in the Mormon Church, scared the Devil out of opposing batters with his blistering fastball, biting curve and Solomon-like mound savvy. He led the league with 18 complete games while posting a 20-9 record. His outstanding performance won him the coveted Cy Young Award as the year's outstanding pitcher.

While dining at Poli's Restaurant,

FORREST "SMOKY" BURGESS

DICK STUART

parent and child, CEO and custodian. All of Pittsburgh, it seemed, became one family.

Shortstop Dick Groat established himself as both an on-and off-the-field leader. The Pirate Captain reigned as league batting champion with a .325 average and won the coveted Most Valuable Player

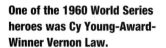

One of the 1960 World Series heroes was Cy Young-Award-Winner Vernon Law.

a popular hangout for Pirate players, shortstop Stan Rojek told this author that when he was with Vernon Law, he had the privilege of sharing the company of one of the finest human beings ever to walk this earth. According to Rojek, Vernon Law's love for his fellow man did not take away from his aggression on the field. If a batter stood too close to the plate, Law had no qualms about pitching him high and inside. If a batter had to duck out of the way of a brush-back pitch (nothing that would be considered dangerous), Vernon often shouted: "Bless you, Brother."

After one of the Pirate batters was struck by a pitched ball, Manager Murtaugh told Vernon to knock down the first hitter for the other team "just to send a message."

"Skip, it's against my religion," said Law. "After all, the Bible says: 'Turn the other cheek.'"

Murtaugh replied, "It will cost you $500 if you don't knock him down."

Vernon Law paused for a second, then said, "The Bible also says: 'an eye for an eye.'"

Law's mound companion, Bob Friend (18-12) was voted "Comeback Player of the Year" by the United Press International. Roy Face, although unable

to equal his once-in-a-lifetime stats of a year before, had a respectable 10-8 record and led the league by pitching in 68 games. Finally, Wilbur David "Vinegar Bend" Mizell, an acquisition from St. Louis in May, won 13 games for the Pirates, including three shutouts. Mizell enjoyed talking about the 1960 Pirates even after he was elected to the United States Congress in 1969.

The Pirates finished seven games ahead of Milwaukee in 1960 and they prepared to meet the powerful New York Yankees.

The Yankees, managed by Charles Dillon "Casey" Stengel, fielded one of baseball's most feared lineups. Perennial All-Stars Mickey Mantle, Roger Maris, Yogi Berra, Tony Kubek, Bobby Richardson, Bill Skowron and Elston Howard were compared by the press with the 1927 Yankee "Murderer's Row" — Ruth, Gehrig, Lazzeri, Combs and Meusel. Ironically, 1927 was the last year the Pirates had won a pennant.

Still hovering over Pittsburgh in 1960 was the 33-year-old ghost of '27 when the Bucs were humiliated by the Bronx Bombers losing four straight games in the World Series. But no one dared jinx the outcome by saying the wrong thing. The city's focus was on winning the Series. Even the Federal Court downtown took a holiday when Judge Wallace Gormley announced that courts would be open from 9:30 a.m. until 11:30 a.m. on game days. Insiders speculated the real reason for the abbreviated schedule was that most of the judges had tickets for the games.

The 1960 World Series was rife

with offense. The first contest was played in Pittsburgh, and the Pirates, behind solid pitching by Vern Law and Roy Face, plus timely hitting by Bill Mazeroski, astounded baseball experts by winning 6-4. In games two and three, the Yankees rolled up their sleeves, played like the experts predicted, and devastated the Pirates by scores of 16-3 and 10-0.

Starting pitcher Vern Law, reliever Roy Face and center-fielder Bill Virdon pooled their talents to lead the Pirates to a 3-2 victory at Yankee Stadium in Game Four. Together, Law and Face limited the mighty Yankees to eight hits. But the most memorable sight took place in the outfield. Those who watched the game from the stands or on television still talk about the game-saving, leaping catch by Virdon in deep center that snagged a sure double away from Yankee slugger Bob Cerv.

Pitchers Harvey Haddix and Roy Face combined to tame the Yankees in Game Five, allowing only five hits, winning by a score of 5-2.

In Game Six, as if to say: "You've had your fun, now let's get on with it," the Yankees, behind Whitey Ford, whitewashed the Pirates 12-0. It was Ford's second shutout of the Bucs in the Series.

That was the overture for THE game — and THE hit — about which faithful Pirate fans continue to talk with awe and reverence.

The early sun peeking over the horizon on the morning of October 13, 1960, shown on the trees of Schenley Park just beyond the outfield walls of Forbes Field. A dazzling kaleidoscope of scarlet, lemon and gold leaves left the impression that even some of nature's finery wanted to

linger long enough to witness what was about to happen.

If everyone who claims to have attended Game Seven of the '60 World Series actually had been there, Forbes Field would have overflowed with a quarter of a million people. In reality, 36,683 people saw the game in person. Those fortunate to be there on that unforgettable day, plus the rest of us who listened to the excitement via radio or were glued to television sets, are blessed with a montage of magnificent memories.

The Pirates surged to an early 4-0 lead highlighted by a Rocky Nelson home run. The Yankees roughed up Vern Law, Roy Face and Bob Friend to take a 7-5 lead. In the bottom half of the eighth inning, with Gino Cimoli on first and one out, Bill Virdon hit a sharp ground ball to short that looked like an easy double play. Not so. The ball hit a stone on the infield, bounced straight up and hit Tony Kubek in the throat,

New York Yankees Manager Casey Stengel visits Pirate Manager Danny Murtaugh after Game One of the 1960 World Series.

Pitcher Elroy Face is "baptized" with champagne following the final game of the 1960 World Series.

knocking him out of the game. Both runners were safe. "Maybe God could have done something about that play; man could not," remembered Casey Stengel.

Groat followed with a single, scoring Cimoli. After Nelson flied out, Roberto Clemente beat out an infield hit. Catcher Hal Smith, a former Yankee, instantly won the hearts of Pittsburghers when he lined a home run over the left-center field fence. The stadium erupted. Broadcaster Chuck Thompson exclaimed: "Pittsburgh has just become an insane asylum. We have seen and shared in one of baseball's great moments."

The score was now 9-7 in favor of the Bucs.

In the top half of the ninth, the Yankees tied the game. Then came the most dramatic scene in Pirate history. At precisely 3:36 in the afternoon, with the score knotted 9-9, second baseman Bill Mazeroski guaranteed his spot in baseball immortality. Leading off in the bottom of the ninth, he took the first pitch by reliever Ralph Terry, normally a starter for Manager Stengel, high and outside for a ball. Terry's second pitch was a slider that failed to break low in the strike zone. Instead, it hung letter-high. Maz swung. The ball soared high and deep. Yankee left fielder Yogi Berra, with his back to the infield, in stunned disbelief, watched the 400-foot blast sail over the wall.

Fans erupted with gusto. A jubilant Mazeroski ran, skipped and hopped around the bases, waving his hat high above his head.

Forbes Field was turned upside down.

People poured onto the field grabbing at Mazeroski or any of the other World Champion Pittsburgh Pirates. They ran onto the streets surrounding the stadium. Office workers were given the rest of the afternoon off. School children who had earlier that morning called in "sick" and who watched the game on television, joined neighbors outside their homes, yelling and screaming.

If it is true that baseball is life with the volume turned up, then all of Pittsburgh that night was living life to its fullest. It was, for Pirate fans, a moment frozen in time.

In downtown Pittsburgh, the gala continued until the wee hours of the morning. Complete strangers hugged one another. Fans stood atop street

Danny Murtaugh congratulates Bill Mazeroski after the 1960 World Series victory.

cars waving "Beat 'em Bucs" banners. Others danced, sang and just shouted. Streams of paper showered down on Penn and Stanwix Street. It was New Year's Eve, the Fourth of July and V-E Day all rolled into one. "There was no destruction of property on that day," remembers Mazeroski, "only joy and true celebration."

The headlines of the *Pittsburgh Post-Gazette* the next morning told the story: "Bucs are Champs." That said it all.

For one of the rare times in its colorful history, the Steel City was the focus of attention for the entire nation.

What did Maz do following the game? While many of his champagne-soaked teammates joined in the hoopla in the streets of Pittsburgh, this son of a coal miner from Wheeling, West Virginia, and his wife, Milene, got into their old, black Lincoln, went to Gustine's Restaurant for a quick dinner, then retreated to Schenley Park to get

Bill Mazeroski hits his World Series home run and the celebration begins.

1960 WORLD CHAMPION PIRATES

Reserve catcher Hal Smith's dramatic eighth-inning home run in Game 7 of the 1960 World Series was, for Pirate fans, a moment frozen in time.

away from it all. "Nobody was there," recalls Maz. "No cars. Even the squirrels had disappeared. Maybe they were all out celebrating."

Both Maz and his wife talked about how the Pirates were now the champions of baseball. They didn't discuss the home run. They didn't have to. For most of the time they just sat there, quietly, admiring the beautiful autumn leaves, their fiery show of color now enhanced by the setting sun.

Privately, Bill and Milene Mazeroski tried to comprehend what this day would mean to them for the rest of their lives. ■

HAL SMITH

CHAPTER 12

AFTERGLOW

"*I was born twice. I was born in 1934 and again in 1955 when I came to Pittsburgh. I am thankful I can say I had two lives.*"

—ROBERTO CLEMENTE
1970

SHORTLY AFTER THE **W**ORLD **S**ERIES **L**OSS to the Pirates, the Yankees fired manager Casey Stengel. The Yankees said the reason was because he was 71 years old. Baseball fans knew better.

Bill Mazeroski's home run not only ended the World Series, it also marked the end of a tradition that was a part of baseball for nearly 60 years. This was the last season in which baseball would have eight teams per league; in 1961, America's pastime began a series of expansions. A new Washington Senators team (the 1960 squad moved to Minnesota) and the Los Angeles Angels were added to the American League that year; two teams would join the National League the following year.

The mischievous gods of baseball donned devilish uniforms in 1961, and insisted upon playing a cruel joke on Pittsburgh. The '61 Pirates were 180 degrees out of sync with the heroic team of the previous year. Everything seemed to go just right for the 1960 Pirates. Lazy, short fly balls fell in for singles just out of reach of outfielders. Ground balls seemed to have "eyes" as they dribbled just beyond the reach of outstretched arms of infielders. After one full season filled with such good fortune, the fans and media got used to dramatic, come-from-behind miracle finishes.

Even the astute base running of Willie Mays was unable to elude the defensive prowess of Bill Mazeroski, who had a skill of blocking the base with his left leg, giving the runner an even smaller target for which to aim.

Harry "The Hat" Walker was Pirate manager for 2½ years, beginning in 1965.

In 1961, that luck went south. Pirate shots down the line during the previous year fell in for extra bases; now they landed inches into foul territory. Late-inning rallies too often fell one run short. And, in the cruelest twist of providence, ElRoy Face, although managing 17 saves, proved to be vulnerable with a 6-12 record and a disappointing 3.82 ERA. So, instead of the City of Champs celebrating another Series victory, Pittsburgh watched in shocked amazement as their beloved Buccos imploded to a 75-79 record and a sixth-place finish.

Roberto Clemente won the 1961 National League batting championship (.351), and Bill Mazeroski was undoubtedly the best fielding second baseman in all of baseball, yet far too many other Pirate players failed to perform as expected.

Vernon Law's ailing arm limited the 1960 Cy Young-Award winner to 11 games and a 3-4 record. Bob Friend won 14 games, but led the league with 19 losses. Reliable Dick Groat hit 50 points lower in average than he did that marvelous year before.

The National League in 1962 followed a route previously taken by the Junior Circuit, as it expanded from eight to 10 teams. Added to the fold were the Houston "Colt-45s"; a replacement team in New York for the departed Giants was called the "Mets" and managed by former Yankee skipper, Casey Stengel.

The San Francisco Giants and Los Angeles Dodgers, both displaced New York teams, battled for first place that year and ended the season in a tie. A three-game playoff gave the pennant to San Francisco. The Pirates offered a mild threat to both clubs, but ended the year in the all-too-familiar fourth spot, eight games behind the leader.

Heading the Pirate "hit parade" that year was old reliable Smoky Burgess. When the rather rotund catcher came onto the field, he resembled a favorite uncle ready to play in a softball game at a company picnic. His appearance notwithstanding, behind the plate Burgess was a master at handling pitchers, and he was able to swing the bat good enough to hit .328 with 13 round-trippers over 103 games.

Captain Dick Groat flirted with .300 by hitting .294, first baseman Donn Clendenon hit .302 in 80 games, and Bob Skinner enjoyed a banner year with a .302 average and a club-leading 20 home runs.

Sharing the outfield with Bob Skinner was a newcomer to the Pirates that year — rookie Wilver Dornel "Willie" Stargell. He played in only 10 games, but those games marked the beginning of a fan-pleasing 21 years in a Buc uniform.

Pitcher Bob Friend (18-14) proved, again, he was the mainstay of the staff. Roy Face (8-7) led the league with 28 saves.

Pittsburgh's prowess fell several more notches in 1963 when the club could post only a 74-88 record and an eighth-place finish ahead of just Houston and New York — the two expansion teams from a year before.

Early in the campaign, the Pirates traded Bob Skinner to Cincinnati for pinch-hit specialist Jerry Lynch.

Skinner, who had been with Pittsburgh since 1956, was one of the few men ever to hit a ball out of Forbes Field over the right field roof, a feat he accomplished twice.

Mound ace Bob Friend struggled with a 17-16 record although he had a respectable 2.34 ERA. Sophomore lefty Bob Veale's fastball carried him to a 5-2 mark and a 1.04 ERA, while Al McBean's record was 13-3. Others, even ElRoy Face (3-9), were unable to register winning seasons. Pitching coach Don Osborn summarized the frustration of the year: "The only thing wrong with our pitchers is that they all have to pitch in each game."

Leading the Bucs at the plate in 1963 was a consistent Roberto Clemente. His .320 average with power (17 team-leading homers) distinguished him as the only Pirate to hit over .300 for the season. Second-sacker Bill Mazeroski added another year to his league-leading assists and double plays.

Clemente was brilliant in 1964. He led the National League in hitting for the second time in his career with a .339 average. He became baseball's premier right fielder. Most experts today agree that had Clemente played in a major market and received the media attention that accompanies such venues, he would have received a lot more national attention.

Roberto's heroics, however, did little to elevate the Pirates in the standings. Posting a lukewarm 80-82 record, the best the club could do was settle for a sixth-place tie with Los Angeles, 13 games behind the front-running Cardinals.

Big (6'6") Bob Veale, now in his third year with the club, finally developed his potential as a hard-throwing southpaw by winning 18 games that year and leading the National League with 250 strikeouts. Two key pitchers, Bob Friend (13-18) and Vern Law (12-13), slipped below the .500 mark. Supreme reliever Roy Face was only 3-3, with a disappointing 5.18 ERA.

Exit the popular Danny Murtaugh who wanted a break from the tension of baseball; enter Harry William "The Hat" Walker as the new Buc skipper in 1965. Harry Walker came to Pittsburgh with a popular reputation. His unusual nickname came from his habit of removing his hat between each pitch while in the batter's box during his playing days with the Cardinals. His brother, Dixie, played two years with the Pirates (1948-49), which made his name even more familiar. Some sportswriters, however,

BOB FRIEND

challenged Pittsburgh's choice of Walker who had only one year of experience managing in the big leagues — that was with St. Louis a decade earlier. The Cardinals' record that year was an unimpressive 51-67 for a seventh-place finish.

However, the congenial Alabaman clicked with Pirate players and fans. More importantly, he got positive results when he led the team to 90 victories in '65 and a third-place finish.

Roberto Clemente maintained his crown as National League batting champ with a .329 average. First baseman Donn Clendenon chimed in with a .301 mark, while Willie Stargell led the club with 27 homers and 107 RBI. In the field, still nobody was better than Bill Mazeroski who topped the Senior Circuit with 113 double plays and a .988 fielding average.

Vernon Law rebounded with a 17-9 record. He shared the lead in

club wins with fast-balling Bob Veale (17-12). Don Cardwell (13-10) also added strength to the pitching staff.

The following year, 1966, was even more satisfying, as the Pirates registered 92 wins.

One of the reasons for this impressive record was the hitting of center fielder Matty Alou. Joining the Bucs' roster through a trade with San Francisco before the start of the season, this 5'9" native of the Dominican Republic sprayed the ball to all fields as he led the league with a .342 average.

This was the year in which Roberto Clemente finally received the sort of national recognition he so richly deserved. His .317 average, 29 home runs, and club-leading 119 RBI won for him the National League's Most Valuable Player Award.

Clemente again sparkled in the field. Not only did he win (for the sixth year in a row) the coveted Gold Glove Award, he also led all league outfielders by cutting down 17 runners.

Other notable performances during the 1966 season were turned in by Willie Stargell (.315 and 33 home runs), Donn Clendenon (.299 and 28 home runs), outfielder-pinch hitter Manny Mota (.332), and shortstop Gene Alley (.299).

Bill Mazeroski, still a magician at second base, led all National League second basemen in putouts and assists. Nobody was quicker in turning the double play. With slick-fielding Gene Alley at shortstop most of the season, Mazeroski participated in 161 twin-killings in 1966 — more than

Harry "The Hat" Walker (R) took the managerial reins from Danny Murtaugh (L) in 1965. Less than three years later, Murtaugh was called back to replace Walker as Pirate Skipper.

any other second baseman in the history of major-league baseball.

Bullet Bob Veale topped the mound staff with a 16-12 mark, and a pleasant surprise was rookie pitcher Woodie Fryman who posted a 12-9 record.

Pirate announcer Bob Prince was open for anything that would generate fan excitement. For example, whenever the opposition began to score runs in 1966, Prince devised a method of cutting short the potential rally. From the broadcast booth, he stuck out an eight-foot long piece of cardboard shaped like a hot dog. But it didn't look like a typical hot dog. It was painted a bright, kelly green. Prince pointed the strange green figure at an opposing batter standing at the plate as a way of putting a "curse" on the visiting team. During a home game, when the opposition began to score runs, fans looked toward the KDKA booth and hollered: "Get the Green Weenie!" When Prince responded, the crowd let out a hearty cheer. Strange as it may seem, most of the time the gimmick worked. In fact, a *Time* magazine story on the contending Pirates that year featured two photos — one showing the players, the other of Prince demonstrating the proper use of the "Green Weenie."

Those sterling individual performances and promotional gimmicks, however, were able to produce three less wins than the pennant-winning Los Angeles Dodgers, good enough only to glean another third-place finish.

To add speed to the Pirates' offense in the 1967 campaign, the club traded third baseman Bob Bailey and utility infielder Gene

Michael to Los Angeles for Maury Wills. Wills' name was prominent in the record book on base-stealing; he led the league in that department six years. In 1962, he had swiped 104 bases. That was more than the total for most teams in any given year. Age finally outran Wills' enthusiasm for the game during '67. He batted .302, but was able to steal only 29 bases for the Pirates.

Making his debut behind the plate in 1967 was Manuel De Jesus "Manny" Sanguillen. Hitting .271 in just 30 games, the native Panamanian showed offensive punch, although he was known to swing at any pitch that came within a foot of the plate. General Manager Joe Brown quipped, "When Manny takes a pitch, either it's a wild pitch or paralysis has set in."

Matty Alou showed that his previous year's batting title was no fluke as he hit .338, and Manny Mota chimed in with a .321 average. Unfortunately, Wills (3 home runs), Alou (2 home runs) and Mota (4 home runs) were not legitimate threats to knock the ball out of the park.

It was another sensational season for Roberto Clemente who racked up a league-leading 209 base hits. His .357 average won the league batting title and, for the seventh year in a row, he won the Gold Glove Award. He also led his team with 23 homers and 110 RBI.

But the name of the game is winning. As baseball insiders know, you can't win without pitching, and that was still the Bucs' weakest dimension in '67. Bob Veale won another 16 games, but Woodie Fryman slipped to a 3-8 record.

Making his debut behind the plate in 1967 was Manny Sanguillen, who was known to swing at any pitch that came within a foot of the plate.

MANNY SANGUILLEN

Manager Harry Walker could orchestrate no more than a .500 record and sixth-place standing during the first 84 games of 1967. That, simply, was unacceptable to Pirate management. Hence, "Harry the Hat" walked the plank and was replaced by the man he succeeded nearly three years earlier — Danny Murtaugh. The popular Irishman, however, was unable to find the elusive magic wand that had turned him into a "genius" in 1960. The Bucs ended the season with an 81-81 record, in sixth place, 20½ games behind first-place St. Louis.

Pirate brass were shaken by the sixth-place humiliation of '67. In an attempt to add strength to their pitching staff, they traded Woodie Fryman and some minor leaguers to the Phils for veteran Jim Bunning in December 1967. They gambled on the inexperienced Larry Shepard to serve as manager and bring back the winning tradition to the "Burgh."

That tradition didn't resurface in 1968. The Bucs settled for another sixth-place finish with an 80-82 record, 17 games behind pitcher Bob Gibson and his first-place St. Louis Cardinals.

Dominating headlines in 1968 were stories about anti-Vietnam demonstrations, riots at the Chicago Democratic Convention, assassinations of Sen. Robert Kennedy and Dr. Martin Luther King, Jr., and increased racial tensions.

If any serious racial concerns existed in Pittsburgh, they never affected the fans' support of four black stars of the '68 Bucs. Willie Stargell led his team with 24 homers. Roberto Clemente missed hitting .300 by nine points, but hit 18 balls out of the park. Donn Clendenon chimed in with 17, and the only Pirate to bat over .300 that year was Matty Alou, whose .322 average fell only three points shy of league-leader Pete Rose of Cincinnati.

While the Pirates may have lacked punch at the plate, their pitching was noteworthy. Steve Blass (18-6) gained increased respect as he led the league in winning percentage (.750) and posted a 2.12 ERA. Pittsburgh's lack of run production is best demonstrated by the fact that Bob Veale could do no better than earn a 13-14 record, although he still compiled a fine 2.05 ERA.

In 1969, baseball expanded again and each league was separated into two divisions. Added to the American League were the Kansas City Royals and the Seattle Pilots. The National League also grew to 12 teams with the addition of the San Diego Padres and Montreal Expos.

Pittsburgh became part of the National League East, along with New York, Chicago, St. Louis, Philadelphia and Montreal.

At the conclusion of a 162-game season, the division leaders would have a best-of-five playoff series; the winners of these contests would head for the World Series.

In an exhilarating reversal, the 1969 Pittsburgh squad fought its way toward a third-place finish. Several Pirates showed muscle at the plate. Roberto Clemente looked like the Roberto of old, hitting .345 and pounding out 19 home runs. Others cracking the .300 mark were Matty Alou (.331), Willie Stargell (.307), catcher Manny Sanguillen (.303) and third baseman Richie Hebner (.301). Stargell, again, led the Bucs with homers (29) and 92 RBI, while Alou collected a league-leading 231 hits.

On the winning side of pitching percentage were 6-foot, 200-lb. Bob Moose (14-3), Steve Blass (16-10), Joe Gibbon (5-1), Bruce Dal Canton (8-2), Chuck Hartenstein (5-4), and Jim Bunning (10-9). Highlighting the pitching performances was the no-hit game tossed by Bob Moose against the Mets at Shea Stadium on September 20.

A third-place finish was not enough for Pirate brass; five games before the end of the season Manager Larry Shepard was replaced by Alexander Grammas.

During the winter following the '69 season, one player made a decision that eventually would leave a lasting impact on the game. Curt Flood, an outfielder with the St. Louis Cardinals, was traded to the Phillies. Flood rebelled and refused to report, claiming that he should have the right to sign with any team.

Club owners and Commissioner Bowie Kuhn disagreed. They argued that under the so-called "reserve clause," Flood was bound, by law, to the Cardinals. Flood claimed the reserve clause made him nothing more than a "slave." He filed suit in court challenging baseball's reserve clause. Curt Flood lost the suit in local court, but elected to exercise his right of appeal. He also lost the appeal. Nonetheless, the very fact that he was willing to challenge something as sacred as the reserve clause, inspired other players to take up the cause.

Alex Grammas, a 10-year veteran as a shortstop for several National League teams, guided the Bucs to four wins in the five games he managed at the tail end of the 1969 campaign. That was not enough, however, to earn him a spot as permanent manager. Instead, returning for his third stint as field leader in 1970, was Danny Murtaugh.

This time, the luck of the Irish suddenly reappeared. In addition, Murtaugh exhibited another dimension of maturity as a manager. Although he was not blessed with a team full of superstars, he got the best out of his players. "The more patient you are, the better manager you'll be," he said. "When I first came up as a manager I was too demanding. I had to learn never to expect a man to do something that he is not capable of doing. Now I try to analyze and find out their capabilities and then never ask them to exceed them." His patience reaped rewards. Murtaugh's Pirates won the East Division that year with an 89-73 record.

A rapidly maturing Manny Sanguillen developed into a second manager behind the plate. This

Bob Moose was part of the "Pirate Butcher Shop" pitching staff in 1970.

keenly aware catcher not only learned to handle pitchers, but also orchestrate the tempo of a game in a way that would make Leonard Bernstein proud. His baseball savvy and .325 average made him a valuable part of the Pirates. Others who contributed to Murtaugh's winning record were Matty Alou, who hit .297; Willie Stargell, once again the club leader in home runs (31) and RBI (85); and first baseman Bob Robertson, who added to the power department with his 27 four-baggers.

Pirate pitching in 1970 provided no eye-popping stars, but had a balanced attack featuring Bob Veale (10-15), Dock Ellis (13-10), Steve Blass (10-12), Bob Moose (11-10), Luke Walker (15-6), Dave Giusti (9-3), and Bruce Dal Canton (9-4).

Outfielder Matty Alou led the league in 1966 with a .342 average.

In the "good news/bad news" department, Dock Ellis no-hit the Padres in San Diego and won 2-0 with the help of Willie Stargell's two home runs. Subsequently, Ellis would admit that he pitched the game under the influence of drugs. "I was psyched," he recalled. "I had the feeling of euphoria. I remember hitting a couple of batters."

Some baseball writers noted that the '70 Pirates' pitching roster could be mistaken for a butcher shop with a staff of Moose, Veale and rookie John Lamb (0-1).

The brightest jewel in the Pirates' crown that year was Roberto Clemente who continued to dazzle those who saw him play right field. He played without a net, often forsaking potential harm to himself when he dove at low line drives or ran into a wall when chasing a long fly ball. On the offensive side of the ledger, he hit a strong .352 with 14 home runs.

Despite the fact that Clemente proved year after year he was the game's premier right fielder, the national media seldom featured this flashy Puerto Rican who was the embodiment of a complete ball player. Clemente had several things against him in addition to playing in a relatively small market. He was Puerto Rican and spoke with a strange accent. He also appeared to be cocky. Sports writers still called attention to those basket catches; they argued that by employing such "showboat tactics," Clemente increased his chances of dropping a routine fly ball. In addition, Roberto's underhanded throws back to the infield following a single left the impression that he was lazy; those who knew him, however, realized that this was a habit picked up from his playing days as a little boy in Puerto Rico.

In one outburst during spring training in Florida, the negative publicity finally riled the scrappy Clemente. Inside the clubhouse, he tore into reporters. "I win four batting titles," he shouted. "I kill myself in the outfield. I try to catch everything that stays in the park. I play when I am hurt. What more do you writers want from me?"

"He was misunderstood," insisted General Manager Joe L. Brown. "He was such a fine, warm, human being, and yet I don't think he always came across that way." Brown later commented that although Clemente was the highest paid player on the Pirate squad, Roberto never wanted that fact to be made public and never mentioned it to his teammates.

Pirate fans who knew baseball accepted Clemente for who he was. They also knew that he was one of the greatest who ever played the game. Clemente truly appreciated that. On July 25, 1970, when Clemente was honored in special ceremonies before a home game, the famed right fielder showed how much he welcomed the support of loyal fans. "In a way, I was born twice," he told the crowd. "I was born in 1934, and again in 1955 when I came to Pittsburgh. I am thankful I can say that I live two lives."

Roberto Jr. echoed his father's warm affection for the city of Pittsburgh. "My father was born a Pirate," he said. "Destiny brought him and the great city of Pittsburgh together."

As testimony to his value as a hitter, on both August 22 and 23, Clemente collected five hits in games against Los Angeles.

After capturing the East Division flag, the Bucs lost to Cincinnati in a three-game sweep during the League Championship Series. The games were close: 3-0, 3-1, and 3-2, but the Pirates were overmatched by the "Big Red Machine," featuring the likes of Pete Rose, Tony Perez and Johnny Bench.

This was the year remembered by Pirate faithful to this day not so much because of the Bucs' Eastern Division flag, but because June 28, 1970, marked the last game ever played at spacious Forbes Field. The 62-year-old steel was rusting into dust; sheets of concrete were falling away from its walls. With the University of Pittsburgh hungry for land, the Pirates left Forbes Field for a newer, bigger home — Three Rivers Stadium — on the shores of the Allegheny River. Ironically, the new stadium was built on the site of old Exposition Park — the little wooden bandbox the franchise had left in 1909.

Those who were there can testify that Forbes Field was not the ideal venue at which to see a ball game. Often part of the action was blocked by huge steel pillars that supported the roof. In the left field bleachers, most of the fans had to lean forward and turn halfway to the right on the crude wooden planks just to see home plate. In spite of its shortcomings and deteriorating condition, Forbes Field maintained the look of a classic ballpark. Fans still talk about the old fashioned Longines clock that stood above the scoreboard in left field. They tell their children and grandchildren about how scoreboard numbers were dropped by hand. They describe the rock-hard surface of the infield (you won't have to remind Tony Kubek),

The Pirates left Forbes Field for a newer, bigger home — Three Rivers Stadium — on the shores of the Allegheny River.

**Owners "Bing" Crosby and
John Galbreath.**

and how groundskeepers burned gasoline on the mound to dry it off. They remember the "baseball purity" of the park that allowed no advertisements or other signs on the outfield walls except for a 32-foot-high wooden cutout of a U.S. Marine placed next to the left field scoreboard during the summer of 1943. It was the perfect setting about which longtime Pirate P.A. Announcer Art McKennan observed: "There wasn't much flubdubbery. You just got a ballgame. If you didn't like it, you could stay home."

Because of its spaciousness, Forbes Field earned a reputation as a "pitcher-friendly field." Yet, over a stretch of 62 seasons and more than 4,000 major league games, not one no-hitter was ever tossed there.

Part of the red-brick, left field wall may be seen today in the Allegheny Club at Three Rivers Stadium, and a portion of the left-center field wall, with "457 ft." still painted on it, remains outside the University of Pittsburgh library. Every October 13, Pirate fans from yesteryear gather there to celebrate Bill Mazeroski's home run which won Game Seven of the 1960 World Series against the Yankees.

When the Pirates moved from Forbes Field to Three Rivers Stadium, they also donned a new look in playing attire. They were the first team in major-league baseball to sport double-knit uniforms. ■

ROBERTO CLEMENTE

CHAPTER 13

RAISED FLAGS AND FALLEN STARS

" *We had 'em all the way.*"

—BOB PRINCE, 1982
Pirate broadcaster from 1948–1975

*T*HE NEXT YEAR, ONE REMEMBERED WITH FONDNESS by Pirate fans, another World Championship flag would fly above their stadium.

The 1971 Pirates won 97 games. They were champions of the East Division, finishing the season seven games ahead of second-place St. Louis. Willie Stargell led his club and both major leagues in home runs (48) — some of them towering blasts into the upper decks of Three Rivers Stadium.

Roberto Clemente displayed his Hall-of-Fame form by hitting .341 and making defensive play a work of art.

He was the first player in Pirate history to draw fans to the ballpark just to watch him play right field. He had the speed of Willie Mays, the arm of Carl Furillo and the sure hands of Joe DiMaggio.

Catcher Manny Sanguillen showed why he was probably the greatest Pirate ever to wear a catcher's mask. The impact of this native Panamanian's .319 average was surpassed only by his league-leading 72 assists — most of which came from throwing out attempted base-stealers — and his leadership behind the plate. Before he closed out his career in 1980, Sanguillen compiled a .296 batting average — better than any catcher of the post-World War II era.

Outfielder Gene Clines hit .308; many of his hits were timely and were instrumental in earning Pirate victories. Another consistent

The 1971 Series was dubbed, for just cause, "The Clemente Series."

1971 PITTSBURGH PIRATES

(L–R) Front Row: Vic Davalillo, José Pagan, Coach Bill Virdon, Coach Don Leppert, Coach Frank Oceak, Manager Danny Murtaugh, Coach Don Osborn, Coach Dave Ricketts, Steve Blass and Manny Sanguillen.

Middle Row: Team Physicisn Dr. Joseph Finegold, Trainer Tony Bartirome, Bill Mazeroski, Jackie Hernandez, Dave Cash, Gene Alley, Gene Clines, Willie Stargell, Dave Giusti, Al Oliver, Luke Walker, Charlie Sands, Traveling Secretary John Fitzpatrick and Equipment Manager John Hallahan.

Top Row: Jim Nelson, Milt May, Bob Moose, Nelson Briles, Jim "Mudcat" Grant, Bob Veale, Bob Johnson, Dock Ellis, Bob Robertson, Rich Hebner, and Roberto Clemente.

contributor to the offense was Bob Robertson with 26 home runs.

Steve Blass (15-8, 2.85 ERA), Dock Ellis (19-9), Bob Moose (11-7) and Dave Giusti (5-6 but with a league-leading 30 saves) headed a healthy pitching crew.

On September 1, 1971, the Pirates announced their starting lineup:

> Rennie Stennett — second base
> Gene Clines — center field
> Roberto Clemente — right field
> Willie Stargell — left field
> Manny Sanguillen — catcher
> Dave Cash — second base
> Al Oliver — first base
> Jackie Hernandez — shortstop
> Dock Ellis — pitcher

It was the first time a major-league team filled its starting lineup with all minority players.

In the League Championship Series against the San Francisco Giants, the Pirates got off to a slow start, losing the first game 5-4. In

Game Two, first baseman Bob Robertson came out swinging. He clubbed three home runs that turned the tide. The Pirates won the game 9-4, and went on to win the next two by scores of 2-1 and 9-5 to take the best-of-five series.

The 1971 World Series between the Pirates and the Baltimore Orioles is still known as the "Roberto Clemente Series." The beloved Puerto Rican hit an astounding .414 during the seven games, slugged two doubles, a triple and two homers. He also played a flawless right field. Through national telecasts of the '71 Series, many baseball fans, for the first time, were compelled to acknowledge Clemente as baseball's premier right fielder. Dick Groat said, "He had the greatest God-given talent I ever saw. There was nothing in the game he couldn't do if he wanted to."

Still, Clemente felt neglected by the media. "They call Peter Rose

'Charlie Hustle,'" he once said. "I hustle just like Pete Rose, and they don't call me nothing."

Others agreed. Jerry Izenberg, a writer for the *Newark Star-Ledger* observed that "after 17 major-league seasons, Roberto Clemente is an overnight sensation."

Jim Murray of the *Los Angeles Times* felt that the media and some fans just expected too much from the talented right fielder. "The thing about Clemente," he once wrote, "is that he's the only guy to receive get-well cards after going five for five, throwing two runners out at the plate, and stealing second standing up."

Most of the pre-World Series hype focused on the Orioles. After all, Manager Earl Weaver's team had four 20-game winners: Dave McNally (20-5), Jim Palmer (20-9), Mike Cuellar (20-9) and Pat Dobson (20-8). According to the vast majority of baseball writers and broadcasters, Baltimore would win the Series in a cakewalk.

The first two games at Baltimore gave credence to their prophecies. After falling behind 3-0, Dave McNally shut out the Pirates on just two hits the rest of the way, while the Orioles got to pitcher Dock Ellis. The Birds won the first contest 5-3.

In Game Two, the Orioles slapped out 14 hits, and Brooks Robinson made onlookers shake their heads in disbelief with his miracle stops of sharp ground balls at third. Baltimore shelled six Pirate pitchers for an 11-3 win.

Once back on home turf, Pittsburgh regained its League Championship form behind the masterful three-hit pitching of Steve Blass. His pinpoint accuracy limited the mighty Orioles to only three hits as the Bucs won Game Three by a score of 5-1. Manny Sanguillen claimed that Blass could divide home plate into thirds. "That made my job much easier," said Sanguillen. "Both of us knew exactly where the ball would be pitched. He was so precise, I felt I could catch Steve Blass while sitting in a rocking chair."

Admittedly, the Pirates got some unexpected breaks during the contest. First baseman Bob Robertson was at the plate with two runners aboard in the bottom of the seventh. He was flashed the bunt sign by third base coach Frank Oceak. Robertson missed the sign, however, took a healthy cut and propelled the ball into the seats for a three-run homer that iced the win for the surprising Bucs.

The next evening, October 13, two messages flashed across the scoreboard at Three Rivers. The first read: "First Night Game in the History of the World Series." The second was a carry-over from the championship season of 1960; it read, simply: "Beat 'em Bucs!"

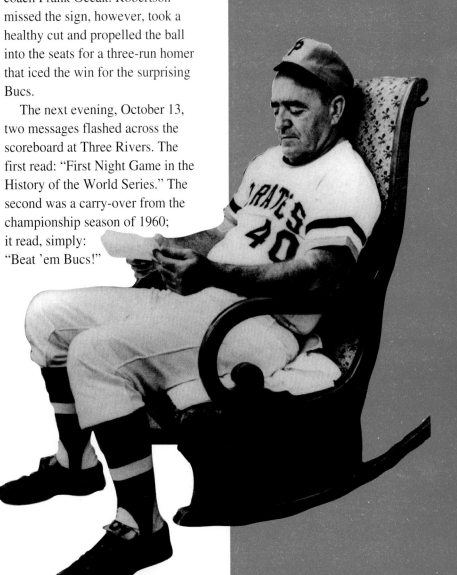

In his last season with the Pirates, the tobacco-chewing Manager Murtaugh had his office equipped with a rocking chair and, of course, a spittoon.

Four-time Pirate Skipper Danny Murtaugh was a master at handling players.

Danny Murtaugh

announced that he

was stepping down as

manager. Pirate fans,

sad to see him leave,

took satisfaction in

realizing that the popu-

lar Irishman could

leave while riding the

crest of a wave.

Baltimore chalked-up an early 3-0 lead in Game Four, but was held in check by the gritty pitching of Bruce Kison and Dave Giusti. Meanwhile, Buc batters kept pecking away until they eked out a 4-3 victory.

In Game Five, Nelson Briles (8-4 during the year) shutout the Orioles and 20-game winner Dave McNally on just two hits. Bob Robertson gave the Pirates all the offense needed when he slugged a 410-foot home run in the second inning. The final score was 4-0; the battling Bucs had a 3-2 Series lead.

Back in Baltimore for Game Six, Roberto Clemente hit a home run, but it was not enough. In the tenth inning, Baltimore scored on a sacrifice fly off the bat of Brooks Robinson, winning the game 3-2.

Steve Blass, mixing his 90-plus mph fastball and his legendary "slop drop" (a slow curve that kept sluggers Boog Powell, Marv Rettenmund and Frank Robinson off stride), out-dueled Mike Cuellar in Game Seven. The "slop drop" became the most famous new pitch in baseball since Rip Sewell's "blooper ball." Blass' masterful pitching, coupled with Roberto Clemente's second home run of the Series, spelled the difference when the Pirates won the decisive game by a score of 2-1 before a disappointed Baltimore crowd.

Roberto Clemente won the MVP trophy for the World Series. Few players have ever been as instrumental in the outcome of the fall classic. Pitcher Steve Blass also had a remarkable Series: two complete games, two wins and a spectacular 1.00 ERA. "After the Series, I was numb for two days," he confessed.

The Pirate faithful pulled out all stops. The city of Pittsburgh turned into the city of parties and parades. Their Bucs had overcome overwhelming odds to bring home the first championship flag in 11 years.

Shortly after the last hurrah was shouted, Danny Murtaugh announced that he was stepping down as manager of the Pirates. Pirate fans, sad to see him leave, took satisfaction in realizing that the most popular Irishman ever to come from Chester, Pennsylvania, could leave while riding the crest of a wave.

Before the start of the 1972 season, baseball heard increased rumblings from the players. Spring training, normally a marketplace for optimistic predictions, became a feeding ground for discontent. When players dared to choose that time to walk off the diamonds in protest of the current pension plan, thus robbing baseball fans of this priceless moment of hope, the nation realized, more than ever before, that America's pastime would never be quite the same. Some of the more cynical truly felt they had arrived at an intersection of a bygone era marked by men who played solely for the love of the game, and the hard-core modern belief that baseball is just another business.

Marvin Miller, the players' representative, openly argued with club owners. The articulate Miller, who looked more like a Wall Street executive than a union representative, calmly voiced his positions to the press. He took up the cause of Curt Flood who, two years earlier, argued that baseball's reserve clause — which bound a player to a team even after he was eliminated from the playing roster — was unconstitutional and not in the best interest of either baseball or the player. Miller presented his arguments in a systematic manner that made owners appear to be greedy, pompous and arrogant. The players, he said, were no more than "slaves" (a claim initially used by Flood) in a system that was immoral.

Baseball owners, who formerly enjoyed support of the press and public, were challenged to respond with reason and empathy. They reminded anyone who would listen that they spent a lot of money in developing ballplayers through their minor-league systems; consequently, they were entitled to some protection of their investments.

The outsider didn't care who was to blame. Commissioner Bowie Kuhn expressed what was in the hearts of most baseball diehards: "Obviously the losers in the strike action taken tonight are the sports fans of America."

Negotiations ground to a halt. Egos were bruised. By the time the players union and the owners finally reached an agreement, baseball lost 13 days and a total of 86 games from its schedule.

The Supreme Court of the United States, meanwhile, refused to overturn the ruling against Curt Flood.

After fighting off the field ceased,

Bill Virdon, one of the heroes of the 1960 World Series, emerged as the new Pirate manager. His challenge was simple: Keep the momentum the team had established the previous year. What no one expected, however, was the tremendous surge of the Cincinnati Reds.

This is not to imply that Pittsburgh threw in the towel. The 1972 season produced a solid Pirate team and plenty of highlights for Bucs fans. To know that, you only have to look at the impressive batting averages compiled by Roberto Clemente (.312), Richie Hebner (.300), Gene Clines (.334), Manny Sanguillen (.298), Willie Stargell (.293), Al Oliver (.312), and Vic Davalillo (.318). Stargell led the power department with 33 homers and 112 RBI.

Steve Blass (19-8), Bob Moose (13-10), Nelson Briles (14-11), Dock Ellis (15-7) and Bruce Kison (9-7) led a talented mound staff.

The most unforgettable event of the 1972 campaign took

"The Great One"

"He played a kind of baseball that none of us had ever seen before — throwing and running and hitting at something close to the level of absolute perfection, playing to win but also playing the game almost as if it were a form of punishment for everyone else on the field." — ROGER ANGELL, NEW YORKER, 1971

place at Three Rivers Stadium on the evening of September 30. Fan-favorite Roberto Clemente insured his place in Cooperstown when he slammed a double to left-center field off left-hander Jon Matlack of the New York Mets. It was the 3,000th hit of his illustrious career. Baseball enthusiasts still remember the image of Clemente standing on second base, waving his hat in response to the five-minute standing ovation.

The Pirates won an impressive 96 games that year, good enough to win, again, the East Division championship. But Cincinnati's 99 wins indicated that they were a bit superior; their three victories in the League Championship Series amplified that claim.

Pittsburgh had tied the series after the first four games, thanks, in part, to home runs hammered by Sanguillen and Clemente. It looked as though the Bucs just might pull it out as they went into the bottom of the ninth inning of the fifth and final game leading 3-2. But perennial All-Star Johnny Bench led off the inning with a game-tying home run, and, with runners on first and third, pitcher Bob Moose let go a wild pitch that allowed the winning run to score.

Bill Mazeroski, hero of the '60 series and outstanding second baseman for the Bucs since 1956, played in only 34 games that year. "I knew the end was close," said Maz. His legs were giving out. When he announced his retirement in 1972, Pittsburgh had to say "Good bye" to one of the premier infielders the game has ever known.

The biggest crime of the 20th century, since the exploits of Bonnie and Clyde, is the failure of the

Baseball Writers Association of America to elect Bill Mazeroski to the Hall of Fame. Granted, Mazeroski was not a Babe Ruth-type home run threat (although he is probably best remembered for his World Series winning blast), and he did not hit over .300 in any of his 17 years as a player — all with Pittsburgh. But those who saw him play know that he was a textbook second baseman.

Veterans of the game insist that were Maz put at second base with any other team in history, the other guy would have to play in the outfield.

An eight-time Gold Glove winner, seven-time All-Star selection, he led the league in chances per game 10 times; in assists, nine times; in double plays, eight times. His career 1,706 double plays and single-season mark of 161 double plays remain major-league records.

Unfortunately, defensive skills are more difficult to evaluate than offensive ability. Record books may reflect a few numbers, such as an infielder's chances and errors, but they cannot tell just how many ground balls someone snagged that would have gone through for base hits were someone else at the position. That's a dimension of the game that can be measured only by someone who saw the player on a day-to-day basis.

Bill Mazeroski was the quintessential second baseman. Not only was he able to reach ground balls that nearly every other infielder would let dribble through for hits, he also turned a double play faster than anyone before or since. "It was as if his hands never touched the ball," claims Dick Groat, Mazeroski's

The 3,000th hit of Roberto Clemete — September 30, 1972.

partner in many of the twin-killings. "As soon as the ball reached his glove it was on its way to first base. Frankly, I never saw anything like it."

They called him "No Touch" because of his uncanny ability to catch and release the ball in one apparent motion. Veteran sports writer Bob Carroll called Maz "the daVinci of the double play."

Maz certainly was a gifted player. He must have exited the womb wearing an infielder's mitt. His training habits, however may have left something to be desired. Catcher Manny Sanguillen remembers: "Early in the morning, when we would all go out to eat breakfast, everybody ordered eggs, or milk or

oatmeal. Mazeroski would ask for two Budweisers and two large Kielbasa sausages at 8:00 in the morning."

Bill Mazeroski's number 9 was retired in 1987.

Pittsburgh went into mourning two times following the 1972 season. The first time was the result of the loss to Cincinnati in the post-season playoffs. The Bucs were so close. That gloom, however, could not begin to compare to the sadness Pittsburghers and baseball fans everywhere felt less than three months later.

On the morning of January 1, 1973, no Pirate fan was in a mood to celebrate the New Year. Headlines of the morning *Post-Gazette* told the shocking story: "Clemente Dies in Plane Crash." Fans poured over the news reports of how their beloved Roberto, the day before, had volunteered his time and effort to loading relief supplies for earthquake victims of Managua, Nicaragua, onto an airplane at the airport in San Juan, Puerto Rico. Clemente, witnesses said, heard that other supplies were stolen. He was sure nobody would steal from Roberto Clemente, so he climbed on board the plane to accompany the supplies to their destination.

The old DC-7, packed with five men and 16,000 pounds of supplies, was considered by the manager of Airport Aviation Services in San Juan unsafe and improperly loaded. Shortly after takeoff, the airplane bobbed and seemed to wheeze asthmatically for air. Suddenly, the engines burst into flames. The plane banked sharply to the left and plunged deep into the ocean. Roberto Clemente was dead. No one ever found his body.

He was only 38 years old.

During his 18 years with Pittsburgh, Clemente topped the .300 mark 13 times, won four National League batting crowns, batted .317, hit 240 home runs and knocked-in 1,305 runs. He also won 12 Gold Glove awards for his outstanding fielding. He hit safely in all seven games of both the '60 and '71 World Series, winning the Series MVP award in '71. He was selected 12 times to the All-Star Team and voted the National League's MVP in 1966.

Someone once said that if Roberto Clemente knew how to sing, Harry Belefonte would have to learn to play baseball for a living. He

redefined standards by which right fielders are measured.

His epitaph, on a memorial plaque in Puerto Rico, reads: "I want to be remembered as a ballplayer who gave all he had to give."

When Commissioner Bowie Kuhn heard about the Pirate star's death, he described baseball's premier right fielder in just eight words: "He had about him a touch of royalty."

That was Roberto Clemente.

Pittsburgh fans, players and management were still in mourning over the death of Roberto Clemente when the season began in 1973. Players wore number 21 on sleeves of their uniforms for the entire season. Pirate management voted to retire his jersey number. In the same year, baseball broke a sacred rule and admitted him to the Hall of Fame before completing the five-year wait for eligibility, making him the first Latin-American player to be voted into baseball's shrine to its immortals.

National recognition of Roberto's legacy following his death far surpassed that which he enjoyed while he was living. A middle school in Philadelphia was named in his honor, likewise a youth baseball league bore his name. Even the Federal Government added to his accolades when it issued a postage stamp featuring the likeness of this textbook right fielder.

The Pirates, in 1994, commissioned a more permanent shrine to the great Clemente. Sculptor Susan Wagner designed and molded a statue of Clemente showing the incandescent hitter in action. The statue stands outside Gate A of

Three Rivers Stadium as a final "Arriba! Arriba!" by the fans for this flamboyant, exciting and very proud baseball player.

Roberto Clemente possessed a healthy pride, especially when it involved his native land. For instance, he insisted on being called "Roberto," so that nobody would be allowed to forget his Puerto-Rican heritage. Pirate broadcaster Bob Prince was the only person who could call him "Bobby" and get away with it. Also, just months before his disappearance, Clemente envisioned a complex he dubbed "Sports City" where underprivileged youth in his homeland would have the opportunity not just to play baseball, but also to enjoy some quality time with parents, away from the pressures of the inner-city. Following the tragic accident, his wife Vera, spearheaded a campaign to build the complex. Today, Sports City covers over 300 acres of land. Along with her son, Roberto Jr., and sports agent Chuck Berry of Pittsburgh, Roberto Clemente's dream lives on through the Roberto Clemente Foundation that still gathers donations for his Sports City.

Life and baseball had to continue, however. Slugger Willie Stargell thrilled hometown fans during the 1973 season by hitting a major league-leading slugging average of .646 and 44 home runs. Four of the exact spots where his gigantic bombs landed were identified with painted numbers. In that way, fans who attended future contests could see for themselves just how far Stargell clubbed those drives.

Stargell demonstrated his power in other venues as well. For the

second time in his career, he poled one out of Dodger Stadium in Los Angeles — hitting the right field pavilion roof 470 feet away. No other player ever hit one out of that stadium until Dodger catcher Mike Piazza slammed one out in 1997. In 1993, Stargell also recorded 119 RBI — best in the National League. On July 11 he hit his 302nd career homer, making him Pittsburgh's all-time home run leader.

Right fielder Richie Zisk had a banner year in '73 when he hit .324, and center fielder Al Oliver clubbed 20 homers while hitting a healthy .292. A rookie outfielder from Calhoun, Mississippi, showing promise was Dave Parker. In 54 games he hit four home runs and batted a rather respectable .288.

Despite Stargell's prowess and solid performances from some of his mates, the Pirates were never able to climb beyond second spot in the standings. With 26 games remaining and only five games separating the top five teams in the Eastern Division, Manager Bill Virdon was discharged. Relieving him was

Pitcher Steve Blass (28) is in the arms of first baseman Bob Robertson as the Pirates celebrate winning the 1971 World Series. At left is Bill Mazeroski, hero of the 1960 World Series win for the Pirates over the Yankees. Clapping hands at right is Richie Hebner. Blass had a remarkable '71 World Series and a mysterious loss of control just two years later.

perennial "replacement manager" — Danny Murtaugh — who was brought back for his fourth stint as on-the-field leader.

Before he departed, Manager Virdon attempted to fill the gap remaining in right field by the untimely death of Roberto Clemente with catcher Manny Sanguillen. At times, the gifted athlete demonstrated his ability to adapt. At other times, he resembled . . . well . . . a catcher trying to play right field. Those who regularly watched the Bucs play claim that this experiment actually kept the Pirates from capturing first place. The team took on the appearance of a genuine contender for the National League flag only when Sanguillen moved back behind the plate where he belonged.

The biggest shock of the 1973

season was the pitching of Steve Blass. Without any logical explanation, something happened to the Pirates' ace of the moundstaff. The man who used to dominate the opposition with pinpoint control, suddenly could not throw strikes. He still possessed all the physical attributes of a solid pitcher. The fastball was there; his curve broke sharply, down and away. Even his patented "slop drop" brought "oohs" and "aahs" from the fans. But he could not, for some mysterious reason, find the strike zone. In only 88 innings pitched (compared to the 249 he tossed just a year before) he gave up 88 bases on balls (the same number he issued in all of '72). Consequently, the best he could do was post a 3-9 record and a whopping 9.85 ERA.

Blass pitched only five innings

the next year and gave up five earned runs. He retired from baseball and left the mystery of his sudden loss of control unsolved. Still, today, complete strangers approach him on the street and ask, "What happened to you in. . . ?" Before they have a chance to finish the question, Blass shrugs his shoulders and answers, "Frankly, I don't know. I wish I did."

In 1986, Steve Blass returned to baseball and the city he loves as a popular radio and television announcer for the Pirate Broadcasting Network — a position he currently holds.

The struggling Bucs dropped to third place before the conclusion of the '73 season, but the club showed enough talent to resurrect hopes in the hearts of players, fans and media for a pennant and World Series in the near future.

In 1974, Danny Murtaugh gave life to those hopes when he pulled yet another miracle from his Irish cap and led the Pirates to an 88-74 record — good enough to capture the East Division Crown.

Contributing to Murtaugh's "genius" was the fact that center fielder Al Oliver hit a blistering .321, while slugger Willie Stargell hit .301 and led the Pittsburgh club with 25 four-baggers.

Pitchers Jim Rooker (15-11), Jerry Reuss (16-11), Ken Brett (13-9), Dock Ellis (12-9), Bruce Kison (9-8), Dave Giusti (7-5), and rookie Larry Demery (6-6) provided a balanced attack from the mound.

It was a good year for Pirate fans, even though the team showed no one player who racked up "superstar" statistics.

The Bucs could have used a few

superstars in the National League Championship Series against Los Angeles; they were able to win only one game in the best-of-five contest. Their lone victory was a four-hit, 7-0 shutout tossed by Bruce Kison and reliever Ramon Hernandez. Richie Hebner and Willie Stargell homered for five of the Bucs' seven runs.

The 1975 campaign began as a year filled with promise. Dave "The Cobra" Parker applied all his skills to compile a .308 average and 25 home runs — good enough to win the National League slugging title with .541. Parker had a unique way of hitting; when he swung at a pitch, often his long muscular body seemed to uncurl as he powered long drives into right-center field. Hence the nickname: "Cobra." In addition, his sparkling play in right field reminded fans of another Pirate who used to wear number 21 and roamed the same outfield just three years earlier.

However, Pittsburgh fans chafed at some of his habits. This gregarious million-dollar player who earned in one year what most families would never earn in a lifetime, wore lavish jewelry, including a diamond-studded, gold necklace spelling out "C-O-B-R-A." To many Pittsburghers, this spelled "E-X-T-R-A-V-A-G-A-N-C-E." Most damaging to Parker's image was that he reportedly claimed to have a throwing arm as good as that of the immortal Clemente. This claim, in the eyes of many longtime Pirate supporters, bordered on blasphemy.

Willie Stargell showed his usual offensive punch with 22 homers and a .295 batting average. Manny Sanguillen also added fine numbers

DAVE PARKER

Slugger Willie Stargell shows that to be a success in hitting you must keep your eye glued to the ball.

with a solid .328. And, on September 16, Rennie Stennett became the first modern-day player to collect seven hits in a nine-inning game.

Starting pitchers Jerry Reuss (18-11), Jim Rooker (13-11), Bruce Kison (12-11), and relief specialist Dave Giusti (17 saves) were able to do what was necessary to keep the opposition in check.

The domination of Pirate pitching and hitting in the Eastern Division became most evident on September 16 that year when they shutout the Cubs 22-0 at Wrigley Field. After the Bucs scored nine runs in the top of the first, one writer observed: "Vendors were selling hot dogs to go."

None of that, sadly, was good enough to overcome Cincinnati's steamroller during the National League Championship Series. The Pirates never seemed to get untracked as they succumbed to the Reds in three straight games by the scores of 8-3, 6-1 and 5-3.

Following the 1975 season, Pirate management announced that Bob Prince, along with his sidekick, former Pirate pitcher Nellie King, would no longer serve as broadcasters for their games. That shocked not only Buc fans but the entire city. Willie Stargell still recalled that day in his autobiography: "He (Prince) was Pittsburgh's number one son. Pirate fans loved Bob and he loved being their announcer."

Bob Prince was a boy in a man's body. He was not above creating news as well as reporting it. In 1969, for example, he won a $20 bet by diving 90 feet into a swimming pool at the Chase Hotel in St. Louis.

"You could see his flashy sport coats coming from 10 blocks away," said longtime Boston Red Sox announcer Curt Gowdy. And Prince was never shy about creating his own fashion statement when he wore $500 Gucci shoes . . . and no socks. When questioned about this, Prince answered with a flip: "It's gauche to wear socks with Gucci."

Prince was a "homer" — i.e. he openly rooted for his Pirates.

"Calling a game with cold dispassion is a cinch," he said. "You sit on your can, reporting grounders and two-base hits lackadaisically. You've got no responsibilities. But rooting is tough. It requires creativeness. It also fulfills your function, which is to shill. You are the arm of the home club who is there to make the listener happy."

Like his predecessor, Rosey Rowswell, Prince brought to the game his unique descriptions of events. When one of the Pirates slammed a home run, Prince shouted: "You can kiss it good-bye." A soft fly ball to the outfield was "a can of corn." A Pirate hit into the gap was a "tweener." A "bug on the rug" was a ball hit to one of the outfield gaps on artificial turf. When a Pirate relief pitcher entered the game with men on base, he called for a "Hoover" or "vacuum" — his designation for a double play grounder. If Roberto Clemente made another one of his impossible catches or astonishing throws to nab an advancing runner, Prince merely intoned: "Bobby Clemente!" Everyone who knew Pirate baseball could picture it all. Finally, when the Bucs would

squeak out a victory with a last-minute run, Prince sighed with an aura of confidence: "We had 'em all the way."

As a result of continued pressure from the fans on the Pirate front office, Prince was finally brought back to the broadcast booth on May 3, 1985. Prince was jubilant. "You have given me back my life," he told the thousands who gathered at a special rally in his honor. That was a bittersweet day for the gregarious man they called "The Gunner." Bob Prince was suffering from terminal cancer. It was a fact he kept to himself.

Prince lasted only three games. He died on June 10. The headline of the next day's edition of the *Post-Gazette* read: Bob Prince dies, Bucs Broadcaster." That was only partially correct. Bob Prince was more than a broadcaster; he was the Pirates "voice."

Baseball recognized this when he was inducted into the broadcaster's wing of Baseball's Hall of Fame on August 3, 1986.

Before the start of the 1976 season, two pitchers — Montreal's Dave McNally and the Dodgers' Andy Messersmith — declared themselves "free agents," because they played the entire 1975 season without contracts. An arbitrator, Peter Seitz, who, by his own admission had limited knowledge about baseball, on December 23, 1975, made a landmark decision by siding with the pitchers. The owners, in protest, locked the players out of camp at the beginning of spring training.

"The Gunner"

Prince was never shy about creating his own fashion statement . . .

"You could see his flashy sport coats coming from ten blocks away,"

— CURT GOWDY
Boston Red Sox
announcer

The mission of Curt Flood had come to an end.

Commissioner Bowie Kuhn wielded his political muscle, stepped in, and got things back on track. After all, this was not a time for argument, but for celebration. It was the 100th season of major league baseball.

The 1976 *Pirate Official Scorebook* promised a season laced with power. On its cover were seven sluggers — Manny Sanguillen, Rennie Stennett, Richie Hebner, Al Oliver, Richie Zisk, Willie Stargell and Dave Parker — labeled as "The Lumber Company."

Right fielder Dave Parker certainly showed that he belonged as he hit .313 — his second year in a row batting over .300. His colleague in center, Al Oliver, hit a career-high .323.

The third outfielder, Richie Zisk, tied Bill Robinson for the Pirate lead with 21 home runs in '76, establishing him as a consistent home run threat. But Zisk was in the final year of his contract with the Pirates, and the Bucs knew that it would be only a matter of time before other teams would seek to pry away this gifted outfielder with an offer of more money.

Pitching prowess may not have been overbearing, but it was consistent. Victories were quite evenly divided among John Candelaria (16), Jim Rooker (15), Jerry Reuss (14) and Bruce Kison (14). Generating the most excitement, of course, was Candelaria's brilliant no-hitter on August 9. The "Candy Man" struck out seven and walked only one as he tossed the first no-hitter ever against the Los Angeles Dodgers.

More than one-million fans attended games at Three Rivers Stadium in '76. The Pirates certainly played heads-up ball, winning 92 games that year. But it was not enough to overtake superstar Mike Schmidt and his Philadelphia Phillies. The Bucs settled for second place in the East Division and were condemned to watch another year's World Series on television.

This year ended on a special note of sadness. The Pirate family lost one of its most beloved members.

For the last few months of the season, those closest to Danny Murtaugh knew something was wrong. He just did not look good. In lieu of the familiar, perky Irish impishness in his eyes, he was more sullen. He lost considerable weight. His walk no longer had its familiar bounce, and his pace grew increasingly slower. Whispers around Three Rivers Stadium predicted that he would not return the next year. On December 2, 1976, only two months following his last day in a Pirate uniform, Danny Murtaugh died of a heart attack at his home in Chester, Pennsylvania.

ElRoy Face thought Murtaugh was one of the smartest managers ever to guide a team: "If you did your job, he just left you alone. If you didn't he let you know. He knew his players, the ones he had to pat on the back and the ones he had to kick in the butt. He knew everything about them, on and off the field."

Pirate fans as well as the front office loved this beautiful Irishman. Danny Murtaugh's uniform number 40 was retired in 1977.

Replacing a cherished legend such as Danny Murtaugh was a

challenge that could be handled by few people. One of them, however, was Charles "Chuck" Tanner, who embodied a rare mixture of youthful exuberance and managerial savvy. There was only one problem. Tanner was under contract to manage the Oakland Athletics.

In one of the more bizarre trades in baseball, the Pirates had to send catcher Manny Sanguillen to the Oakland A's to get Chuck Tanner.

To bolster its pitching staff, the Pirates reluctantly traded the young, talented Richie Zisk to the Chicago White Sox for two veterans with modest-at-best statistics during the previous season. One was fire-balling, but erratic reliever Richard Michael "Goose" Gossage (9-17); the other was Terry Forster (2-12).

In his first season at the helm, Tanner's 1977 team won an impressive 96 games and finished second to the Phils.

Dave Parker came on stronger. He belted 21 homers and a National League leading .338 percentage. He was also busy on defense as he cut down 15 runners to lead all outfielders, and he led the league in put-outs with 389.

Shortstop Frank Taveras stole 70 bases, good enough to lead the league. Bob Robertson (.304 and a club-leading 26 homers), Rennie Stennett (.336) and Al Oliver (.308) also had solid years. Southpaw John Candelaria put all of his 6'7" body into the games when he won 20 and lost only 5. He led the league that year both in winning percentage (.800) and his career-best 2.34 ERA. On the plus side of the ledger were Jim Rooker (14-9), Goose Gossage (11-9 plus 26 saves), Grant Jackson (5-3) and Kent Tekulve (10-1). Terry Forster, in his only year with the Pirates, was 6-4, with a 4.45 ERA.

The next year, 1978, was "the year of the Cobra" as Dave Parker led the Pirates with 30 home runs and 117 RBI. He also led the National League with a .334 batting average and a .585 slugging average. It was good enough to win the National League Most Valuable Player Award. Unfortunately, he was the only Pittsburgh player to hit over .300. Old reliable Willie Stargell missed that plateau by only five points, although he did slug 28 homers.

In spite of his obvious talent at the plate and in the field, Dave Parker never seemed to hit it off with Pirate fans and media. He was big. He was cocky. He wore an earring. All three made him an ideal target for people with a steel-mill heritage.

A lot of this negative image was due to misinterpretations of his actions. For example, shortly after he arrived at the clubhouse, part of his routine was to psych himself up for the game by shouting: "I'm wall-to-wall and tree-top tall. Two things are for sure. The sun's gonna shine, and I'm goin' three-for-four." Some sports writers regarded this as boasting and let their feelings be known in print. Those who knew Dave Parker, including Roberto Clemente, Jr., testify that he was a gentleman who only wanted to do his best for the sake of the team. Parker

This powerful swing made 1978 the "Year of the Cobra."

often told Clemente Jr. that his biggest frustration was his failure to overcome the negative image that, somehow, dominated his coverage by the media.

Tearing up the basepaths that year was Omar Moreno who led the major leagues with 71 steals. Willie Stargell received a standing ovation on September 3 when he collected his 2,000th hit.

Prior to the 1978 season, pitcher Bert Blyleven was picked up from Texas in a trade for Al Oliver. It looked like a good move when the veteran right-hander posted a 14-10 record with a 3.02 ERA. Don Robinson (14-6) and John Candelaria (12-11) helped balance the starting rotation. Kent Tekulve was now named as the "stopper." He responded by appearing in a league-leading 91 games and registering 31 saves.

The Pirates finished in second place in the East, only one-and-a-half games behind Philadelphia. Although the players and the fans would have appreciated a championship in 1978, there was no doubt in anyone's mind that the Bucs had now formed a solid team that was a work in progress.

It was merely a matter of time. ■

Speedy Omar Moreno led the National League in stolen bases during the 1978 and 1979 campaigns.

"I want to be remembered as a ballplayer who gave all he had to give." –Roberto Clemente

CHAMPAGNE CORKS
AND BOTTLENECKS

" *We are fam-i-lee.*"

—PIRATE "THEME SONG"
FOR 1979

MORE LABOR-MANAGEMENT PROBLEMS started the 1979 season; this time they involved not players or owners, but umpires. On March 7, arbiters from both the National and American Leagues walked out of spring training because they had no contract. That left the duties of calling balls and strikes to semipro officials.

The strike continued into the official season. The "replacement umpires" missed too many calls, demonstrating just how important it is to have nothing but the best on the field calling balls and strikes. The strike lasted just a few weeks and the umpires returned after gaining nearly every concession.

Manny Sanguillen — the player swapped for Manager Chuck Tanner — was shipped back to the Bucs in 1978.

Pittsburgh fans again bought bottles of champagne and packed them in ice as they saw their team hang onto first place in the Eastern Division and finish the 1979 season two games ahead of a surging Montreal team.

If nothing else, the Pirates that year were the fashion plates of baseball. They donned an arsenal of uniforms that included yellow jerseys and white jerseys, yellow caps and black caps, yellow pants and black pants — enough for 64 possible combinations.

In 1990, Barry Bonds became the first player in history to hit .300 with 30 homers, 100 RBI and 50 stolen bases. It was this avalanche of offensive output that earned Bonds a well-deserved Most Valuable Player Award.

WILLIE "POPS" STARGELL

1979 PITTSBURGH PIRATES

Uniforms, however, don't win ball games; players do that. And the Pirates had more than their share of productive hitters. Big (6'5", 250 lbs.) Dave Parker and Willie "Pops" Stargell (6'2", 225 lbs.) provided awesome appearances every time they entered the batter's box. When Dave Parker announced his plans to become a vegetarian, pitcher John Candelaria asked, "What are you going to eat? Redwoods?"

Neither Stargell nor Parker showed mercy on opposing pitchers. "Pops" hit 32 drives out of the stadium and Parker chimed in with 25, to go along with his .310 average.

Other players emerged with career-high years. One was Phil "Scrap Iron" Garner, a second-sacker obtained from Oakland two years earlier, who hit .293, clubbed 11 home runs and knocked in 59 teammates. Another was shortstop Tim Foli picked up from the Mets shortly after the season began. Foli plugged a big hole at short. His fielding was brilliant. He hit .288. And, with limited physical abilities, this 6-foot, 190 pounder did everything he could to find a way to get on base. From August 18 to the last week in September, for instance, Foli never once fanned.

The balanced pitching staff of Blyleven (12-5), Candelaria (14-9), Kison (13-7), Bibby (12-4) Jackson (8-5) and Enrique Romo (10-5) kept the Pirates in nearly every ballgame.

(L–R) Front Row: Steve Nicosia, Batboy Steve Hallahan, Batboy Steve Graff, Phil Garner and Ed Ott.

Second Row: Ed Whitson, Trainer Tony Bartirome, Coach Al Monchak, Coach Harvey Haddix, Manager Chuck Tanner, Coach Bob Skinner, Coach Joe Lonnett, Jim Rooker and Enrique Romo.

Third Row: Grant Jackson, Rennie Stennett, Matt Alexander, Manny Sanguillen, Tim Foli, John Milner, Mike Easler, Dale Berra, Lee Lacy, Rick Rhoden and Traveling Secretary Charles Muse.

Back Row: Bill Robinson, Bert Blyleven, Omar Moreno, Dave Parker, John Candelaria, Jim Bibby, Kent Tekulve, Willie Stargell, Bruce Kison and Don Robinson.

Not all of the "Fam-i-lee" enjoyed talking to the press. Slugger Dave Parker refused to talk to the media and insisted that his bat would do the talking for him.

" When Willie walked into the clubhouse, everybody else stopped talking and waited for him to let us know what he had planned for that day."

—TIM FOLI

On many occasions, stringbean, submarine relief pitcher Kent Tekulve was the deciding factor. He was the ace of the bullpen with 31 saves in 94 appearances.

Both the inspiration and the solidifying element for the entire Pirate family on and off the field was Willie Stargell. "When Willie walked into the clubhouse," says Tim Foli, "everybody else stopped talking and waited for him to let us know what he had planned for that day."

Sometimes Stargell praised individual performances when, for example, he dispensed "Stargell Stars" to teammates who made exceptional plays or timely hits. The players, in turn, wore them proudly on their caps. When appropriate, he counseled them about how they could best approach the upcoming game.

One of the factors uniting both the team and the Pirate fans was a popular song recorded by Sister Sledge that contained the recurring theme: "We are fam-i-lee." Prior to games, spectators at Three Rivers Stadium who had never before met, held hands, swayed back and forth, and sang to the tops of their lungs the words of the song. Even some players who could not carry a tune in a bucket joined in. While this may have not sounded like the Mormon Tabernacle Choir, it was enough to ignite a contagious enthusiasm that had been missing for far too many years.

The city and the team became one. Both grew increasingly confident that nobody could overcome the "Fam-i-lee." It came as no real surprise to the Pittsburgh faithful,

therefore, when, in the 1979 National League Championship Series, their team won 3 games to 0 against Johnny Bench, Ray Knight, Joe Morgan, George Foster and the rest of the Cincinnati Reds, arguably baseball's best team of the 1970s. Willie Stargell slugged two key home runs and batted .455 as the Pirates outscored the Reds 15-5 in the series. "Scrap Iron" Garner hit .417.

"Ah," sneered the experts, "but wait until they meet Baltimore in the Series."

As was the case in 1971, on paper the experts had good cause to make that statement. The powerful Baltimore Orioles, led by scrappy Manager Earl Weaver and his stable of superstars were heavy favorites to capture the World Series crown. Sluggers Eddie Murray and Ken Singleton led a powerful offensive lineup. Pitcher Mike Flanagan led the American League with 23 wins.

Baltimore immediately came out swinging in their home park. In Game One, they blasted Pirate pitching for five runs and held off the Bucs the rest of the way for a 5-4 win.

The Bucs bounced back when pinch hitter Manny Sanguillen laced a timely single with two out in the ninth to win Game Two for Pittsburgh by a 3-2 score.

Baltimore's Kiko Garcia went four-for-four and knocked in four runs as the Birds bested Pittsburgh 8-4 in Game Three before a sold-out crowd at Three Rivers Stadium.

When Willie Stargell homered in Game Four, giving the Bucs a three-run lead, Pirate fans were certain the Series would be tied. Baltimore had other ideas. Pounding Pirate pitchers for a six-run eighth inning, the Birds topped the Bucs 9-6.

The Orioles enjoyed a three games to one lead. It looked as though it would be only a matter of time before the Pirates walked the plank, and the Orioles would taste sweet revenge for the humiliating defeat eight years earlier.

Suddenly, the World Series took on the excitement of watching a fighter, outclassed by a stronger opponent, get knocked down, only to rise off the canvas and come after his foe as if he were the one in change.

Willie Stargell was one of those who definitely took control. Almost single-handedly, he quietly instilled confidence in his teammates. He spoke to them as one having authority . . . as one who richly deserved the nickname, "Pops."

His counsel must have helped third baseman Bill "Mad Dog" Madlock (picked up from San Francisco the previous season) who got four hits, and Tim Foli, who knocked in three runs in the Pirates' 7-1 victory in Game Five.

Back in Baltimore, where the Orioles had only to win one game before its home crowd, the Bucs reached inside themselves for every ounce of motivation. John Candelaria and Kent Tekulve combined to blank the Orioles 4-0. The series was now tied.

Somehow, the wind blew no longer beneath the Orioles' wings. Willie Stargell's towering home run signaled to the world that the Pirates were a team of destiny. The Pirates used four pitchers that day, and when Kent Tekulve raised his arm in the air following the final out, the score was Pittsburgh 4, Baltimore 1.

Using the skills of a veteran psychologist plus the power of his awesome bat, this had to be Willie Stargell's finest hour. He hit .400 for the Series, smacked three home runs and knocked in seven runs. "Having Willie Stargell on your club is like having a diamond ring on your finger," said Manager Tanner in an interview for *Time* magazine.

Willie Stargell richly deserved his MVP award in both the National League Championship Series and the World Series — the first time that ever happened. His regular season .281 average, 32 homers and 82 RBI were enough to earn him a tie for the National League's Most Valuable Player Award. At age 39, he became the oldest player ever to win that honor.

Offensive punch during the Series came from other sources as well. Second baseman Phil Garner hit .500, and shortstop Tim Foli averaged .333. Together they combined for 22 hits and 10 runs in the seven games.

For the fifth time in their history, the Pittsburgh Pirates were Champions of the World.

The energy consumed by the come-from-behind Series victory seemed to sap strength from the 1980 Pirates. Manager Chuck Tanner's exhausted Bucs of that year captured the third spot in the six-team East Division race with an 83-79 record. The 40-year-old World Series hero and fan-favorite, Willie Stargell, suffered a knee injury that

Foli was a fan favorite.

Phil "Scrap Iron" Garner enjoys an impromptu shower during a post-game victory celebration during the '79 World Series.

year and was limited to 67 games and 11 home runs. That put much more pressure on Dave Parker, who hit 17 homers and batted .295.

Filling the gap left by Stargell was outfielder Mike Easler, who hit a career-high .338 and led the club with 21 round-trippers. Also having a banner year in 1980 was Leondaus "Lee" Lacy, another outfielder brought in from Los Angeles the year before, who hit .335. Omar Marino, the third outfielder with world-class speed, tied for the league-lead in triples (13) and a whopping 96 stolen bases, a Pirate record. In one game he swiped four bases — a club record that would stand for 17 years.

Right-hander Jim Bibby led the National League in winning percentage (.760) posting a 19-6 record. Other pitchers did not fair as well. Candelaria slipped to 11-14, Blyleven to 8-13, and Tekulve to 8-12.

At the conclusion of the 1980 campaign, San Diego's Dave Winfield entered the free agency market and was given a record $1.5 million contract for the next season. The struggling Pirates realized to an even greater extent that salaries for marquee players could threaten a team such as the Bucs that played in a smaller market.

The fans in Pittsburgh chose to honor their "Pops" on July 20, 1980. The celebration for Willie Stargell that evening was tempered, however, when a spectator threw a transistor battery at outfielder Dave Parker.

"I could hear it whiz over my head," said an angry and confused Parker. "That could have killed me." According to eyewitnesses, the battery hit the ground and bounced another 200 feet toward the infield. Afterward, Parker exploded to the press: "This is baseball, not war. I'm not going out there, especially at home." Then Parker, who had a $6 million contract, said he would welcome a trade "whenever it can be arranged."

That irritated the Pirate faithful. For years both the fans and the media accused Parker of not playing up to his potential, thus certainly not earning his high salary. People could understand his fear after coming so close to being hit by a thrown battery, but when he claimed to be afraid to leave the dugout and appear on the field in front of the hometown Pirate fans, from that day on, Dave Parker and Pittsburgh were never on speaking terms.

The greatest threat to baseball since the 1919 "Black Sox" scandal came at the start of the 1981 season. America's favorite summer sport was interrupted when Marvin Miller and his Major League Baseball Players Association voted to strike. Initiating the eight-week strike, which began on July 12 and lasted until the owners' strike insurance ran out, allegedly was some fine print in free agent contracts.

When baseball finally resumed after 713 canceled games, a so-called "split season" was declared in which the "first half" winners would meet in a best-of-five playoff with the "second half" winners. This make-shift remedy did little more than infuriate fans throughout the nation

Doug Drabek shows his Cy Young-Award-winning form.

Catcher Steve Nicosia and Pitcher Kent Tekulve celebrate the last out in Game 7 of Pittsburgh's World Series victory over the heavily favored Orioles in 1979.

who had, until this year, regarded baseball as one of the unchangeables in an era of constant change.

The Pirates finished third in the East Division in the first half and sixth in the second half, with a season-long total record of 46 wins, 56 losses.

Bill Madlock led all hitters in the National League with his .341 average, and catcher Tony Peña, in his first full season, hit an even .300.

Toward the end of 1981, the Bucs brought up rookie Johnny Ray, a solid second base prospect from Chouteau, Oklahoma. Ray seemed to know his way around the keystone sack and showed promise as a dependable player with a bright future.

Heading the mound staff was Rick Rhoden (who later became one of the nation's top celebrity golfers), an acquisition from the Dodgers in '79. He led the team with only nine wins. That is not too surprising if you consider that, due to the short-ened season caused by the strike, no pitcher during 1981, in either league, won 20 games.

Baseball fans are a forgiving bunch. Willing to put their animosity behind, they filled ballparks in record numbers in 1982. The Pittsburgh faithful also supported their Pirates to the tune of over one million paid admissions.

In spite of the fact that fan support was there, Pittsburgh could end the season no better than fourth in the East Division, eight games behind the eventual World Champion St. Louis Cardinals.

Lanky (6'4", 175 lbs.) relief pitcher Kent Tekulve pitched in more games (85) that year than any other National League pitcher. Tekulve, much like Cincinnati's Ewell "The Whip" Blackwell who pitched in the '40s and early '50s, threw with a mean, side-arm motion that was disarming to batters. Hitters described the experience as watching a man pitch a baseball at you while he was falling out of a tree.

Topping the club in the home run department with 31 blows for the circuit, was Jason Thompson, a 6'4" first baseman from Hollywood, California. Thompson, who came over to the Bucs from Detroit in 1980, had a graceful swing and was a consistent long-ball threat.

The Pirates needed as many new sources of power as they could find. After playing in only 74 games that year, Willie Stargell, now 42 years old and hobbled by a bad knee, announced his retirement from baseball.

Willie Stargell spent 21 seasons in a Pirate uniform, a club record. While his 1,936 strikeouts rank him second only to Reggie Jackson (2,597) among major league hitters, Willie Stargell is best remembered for two things. The first was his offensive punch. In 2,360 games he batted .282 with 475 home runs, 1,540 RBI and seven post-season home runs. The seven-time All-Star is the Bucs' all-time leader in home runs, RBI and extra base hits; he also ranks in the Pirates' top 10 in games, at bats, runs, hits, singles, doubles and total bases. In 1979, when he shared the Most Valuable Player Award with Keith Hernandez, he went on to earn MVP honors in both the League Championship Series with Cincinnati and the World Series victory over the Baltimore Orioles.

The second legacy of Willie Stargell was his mature leadership both on and off the field. His gift of leadership was due, in part, to his ability to keep things in perspective. Teammate Tim Foli recalls that if Pops fanned with two outs and a runner in scoring position, he never went into a rage. Instead, he calmly removed his batting helmet, placed it on the ground beside his bat and ran out to his position at first base. "Baseball is supposed to be fun," said Stargell. "The man says 'Play ball,' not 'Work ball.'"

In short, Wilver Dornel Stargell gave to the Pittsburgh Pirates a dimension that most clubs will never possess — majesty.

The Pirates retired his number 8 jersey in 1982. Six years later, during his first year of eligibility, Willie Stargell became the 17th Pirate to be elected to Baseball's Hall of Fame in Cooperstown.

Financial problems still dominated the Pirate franchise in 1982. Management did what it could to bring in additional revenue. In September of that year, the Stadium Authority of Pittsburgh offered million-dollar "medallions" that would feature the logos of supporting companies. These gold medallions would be displayed at the stadium for 10 years. Using a combination of diplomacy and sales excellence, the Authority was able to gain positive response from 14 corporations.

Those positive vibes carried over to manager Chuck Tanner who shot a bit of life into the Pirates in 1983. He guided them to second-place in the East Division on the shoulders of Madlock's fourth and final National

League batting title. The compact third baseman, with an even more compact swing, hit .323 and pounded 12 homers. Adding to the offensive punch was Lee Lacy, who hit an impressive .312.

In 1983, Jason Thompson again led his team with 18 home runs and second baseman Johnny Ray led the National League with 38 doubles. Slugger Dave Parker, on more than one occasion, heard a chorus of "boos" from the hometown crowd, as he complied a rather disappointing (for him) season with 12 home runs and an average of .279.

In the pitching department, Larry McWilliams, picked up from Atlanta the year before, and John Candelaria led the club with identical 15-8 records.

The Pirates never came close to giving their fans hope for a pennant in 1984. They were out of the running from the very beginning, eventually ending the season in sixth (last) place in the East Division standings, 21½ games behind Chicago.

Perennial All-Star Dave Parker was traded to Cincinnati before the season. Management was concerned not only about his huge salary demands, but also about his sour relationship with the fans and, by his confession, his use of cocaine during the 1983 season.

Manager Chuck Tanner, however, was pleased with the performance of

Team Captain Willie Stargell said "It's 'play ball' not 'work ball.'"

Coach Gene Lamont congratulates Jay Bell following a home-run.

and John Tudor (in his only year with the Bucs) all had identical 12-11 records.

Two black eyes were given baseball in 1985. The first came on August 6 when the Players Union voted to walk off the fields. Donald Fehr, now executive director of the Union, and Lee McPhail, representative of the team owners, locked horns over financial issues. Fan resentment was loud and clear. Talks were resumed instantly, but that, alone, seemed to satisfy no one.

Former Pirate Pitcher Rip Sewell was resting in his home in Plant City, Florida. Disease had taken both of his legs, but he was still able to shoot a competitive game of golf. When learning about the newest strike, Sewell, in characteristic fashion, commented on the demands of the players: "First the players want a hamburger, and the owners give them a hamburger. Then they want a filet mignon, and they gave them a filet mignon. Then they wanted the whole damn cow, and now that they got the cow they want a pasture to put her in. You just can't satisfy them, and I have no sympathy for any of them."

The strike was settled in two days. Baseball continued with virtually no changes in the contract agreement between owners and the players union.

The second scandal to rock the baseball world had a Steel City connection. Curtis Strong, a former caterer in the Philadelphia Phillies' locker room, was charged with selling cocaine to various players. A trial was held in Pittsburgh at which several Pirate players, including slugger Dave Parker, testified that

second-sacker Johnny Ray who hit .312 and, again, led the National League with 38 doubles. Ray also set a major-league record by recording game-winning RBI in six consecutive games. Lee Lacy earned his pay checks as he led the club with a .321 average. At the same time, Pirate management had to be more than a little concerned about the elbow injury that sidelined last year's batting champion, Bill Madlock, and reduced his average to a mere .253.

Rick Rhoden's 14 victories were enough to lead the club in pitching. Larry McWilliams, John Candelaria

they, too, purchased controlled substances from the caterer. Strong was found guilty and sent to prison. Although none of the players were indicted, the entire incident became a public relations disaster for baseball.

The Bucs of 1985 offered few positive results to heal the wounds of disgruntled Pirate loyalists; the team's performance on the field did little to generate fan enthusiasm. Once again, Pittsburgh languished in the basement of the East Division and ended the year 43½ games behind front-running St. Louis. Only 737,900 paying customers came to Three Rivers Stadium in '85. It was the lowest attendance reported by any team in the National League that year. Bucs first baseman Lee Mazzilli commented: "Some people have those games where you guess the number of people in the park. Here you have to identify them, too."

Outfielder Joe Orsulak (.300), in his first full season with the Pirates, led his club in hitting. Bill Madlock, hitting only .251, was shuffled off late in the season to the Dodgers. Jason Thompson stroked only 12 home runs but that was better than any other Pirate in '85.

Rick Rhoden slipped to a 10-15 record and a disappointing 4.47 ERA. Rick Reuschel, picked up from the Cubs at the beginning of the year, led the Pittsburgh club with 14 wins. Unfortunately, right-hander Jose DeLeon's 2-19 record gave him the dubious distinction of ending the season with the lowest winning percentage (.095) in National League history.

The time was ripe for a change; nobody knew that better than

manager Chuck Tanner. Shortly after the last out was recorded for the dismal season, Tanner resigned as manager of the Pirates and signed-on to become manager of the Atlanta Braves. He took with him as one of his coaches, fan-favorite Willie Stargell.

A concern growing rapidly in the Pirate front office was not just the play on the field; it was also the financial status of the club. Owner Dan Galbreath grew weary of the struggle to balance the budget. In 1985, there- fore, he put the team up for sale after nearly 40 years as its owner. A consortium of private investors and the City of Pittsburgh paid him $21.8 million for the Pirate franchise and, with the help of Mayor Richard Caliguiri, was able to borrow another $20 million through the city's Urban Redevelopment Authority. Malcom "Mac" Prine was named President and CEO. His first year — 1986 — proved to be not very profitable; the club ended the season $7.1 million in the red.

On the playing field, 41-year-old Jim Leyland became the Pirates' new manager in 1986. Leyland, whose only previous big-league experience was as a third base coach, was able to generate seven more wins than the year before. But his Bucs still led the league with their 98 losses. As might well be expected, this wasn't the sort of record good

JAY BELL

enough to pry the Bucs out of last place in the East Division.

Leyland and his Pirates were able to lure a shade over one-million paid fans into the ballpark in the '86 season, a testimony to the continued loyal support of Pittsburghers for their Buccos. That attendance figure, however, was still the lowest number for any team in the majors that year.

Only one regular player — Johnny Ray — hit over .300 and that was by a mere one percentage point. Infielder Jim Morrison, in his fourth year with the Bucs, led the club with 23 homers and 88 RBI. First baseman Sid Bream, obtained from the Dodgers late in the season the year before, hit only .268, but demonstrated a zest for play that delighted Pittsburgh fans and media.

Reliever Rick Rhoden recaptured his spot at the top of the heap of pitchers with his 15-12 record, but the other "RR man,"

Barry Bonds was a

terror at bat . . .

Rick Reuschel, dropped to a 9-16 record.

A nagging weakness of the '86 Bucs was defense. A league-leading 143 errors contributed to their sour record. As one disgruntled fan put it, "They had better defense at Pearl Harbor."

A new face to the Pirate lineup that year was Barry Bonds, whose father, Bobby, had been an outstanding player for the Giants 20 years earlier. Although he hit only .223 during his rookie year, young Barry displayed a quick swing and significant power (16 homers) that made Manager Leyland realize here was a future candidate for stardom. Another youngster showing promise was a late-season pickup from the White Sox named Roberto "Bobby" Bonilla, a 24-year-old switch-hitting, long-ball threat who was comfortable playing either third base or the outfield.

In 1987, Barry Bonds, in fact, led his team in homers (25) and increased his batting average by 38 points.

Joining Bonds in the outfield for the 1987 season was an established regular who came from the Cardinals — Andy Van Slyke — whose .293 average and 21 home runs added more punch for the Bucs. In his first full season with Pittsburgh, young Bobby Bonilla also demonstrated that he, too, belonged in the big leagues by hitting an even .300 and slamming 15 homers.

Others showing some spark that year were Mike LaValliere, a spray-hitting catcher, who also posted a .300 average and Alfredo Pedrique, a Venezuelan shortstop acquired from the Giants, who hit .301 in 88 games.

Although their hitting may have been noteworthy, the Pirates lacked the sort of mound strength that would allow them to be taken seriously in 1987. The ace of the staff was rookie Mike Dunne with a 13-6 record and 3.03 ERA. The only other positive record that year belonged to Rick Reuschel who, once again, got over the .500 average with an 8-6 mark and a pretty fair 2.75 ERA. Reuschel, however, spent only part of the year with Pittsburgh; he was traded in August to San Francisco.

Sid Bream, who continued to please the crowds with his energetic play, hit .275 and 13 round-trippers. He also led the league in errors for first basemen (17).

Throughout the entire 1987 campaign, the Pirates seemed never able to settle on a consistent lineup. An outspoken Andy Van Slyke quipped: "We had so many people coming in and out they didn't bother to sew their names on the backs of uniforms. They just put them there with Velcro."

Adding to the plagues of '87 was some internal bickering. Syd Thrift was General Manager, but Pirate President Mac Prine insisted that he be the one to approve all organizational and personnel moves.

Financial woes still dominated the concerns of the Pirate front office. Carl Barger was named interim president in 1987, but the club continued to lose money. Pirate ownership seriously considered moving the team to a more lucrative venue.

Instrumental in keeping the Pirate club in Pittsburgh was the hands-on involvement by Mayor Caliguiri.

Both he and Carl Barger devoted countless hours to this mission.

The faith in the franchise by Caliguiri, Barger and the rest of the consortium would be tested over the next few years.

In short, 1987 was not a season which will go down in the annals of

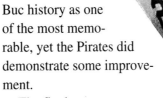

Buc history as one of the most memorable, yet the Pirates did demonstrate some improvement.

The final season stats for '87 show that the team fell just two games short of .500 and ended the season in a tie with Philadelphia for fourth place in the East Division, 15 games behind division-leading St. Louis.

During the 1988 season, the Pirates displayed signs of maturity. Not only were they winning more games, they posed a genuine threat to the New York Mets who had moved to the first place spot. The Mets, led by manager Davey Johnson, had a powerful lineup of players such as Darryl Strawberry (with his league-leading 39 home runs), Kevin McReynolds and Gregg Jefferies. The team won a whopping 100 games that year.

The Pirates, with an 85-75 record, ended 15 games out of first for the

. . . and on the bases.

Lloyd McClendon enjoyed his greatest moments of glory.

second year in a row, but displayed the same combative spirit that propelled previous Buc teams to World Series crowns.

At the top of the club in home runs were the big three — Van Slyke (25), Bonds (24) and Bonilla (24).

Doug Drabek, now in his second year with Pittsburgh, led the team with a 15-7 record. His colleague, John Smiley, had 13 wins. Bob Walk finished with 12, and Jeff Robinson had 11.

The fans identified with the 1988 Pirates who seemed to enjoy playing the game and seldom took themselves too seriously. Ex-Cardinal Andy Van Slyke compared the '88 Bucs with his former team: "With the Cardinals, everybody would be reading the business section to see what their stocks were doing. You get to this locker room in the morning, and everybody is looking at the sports page to see if Hulk Hogan won."

The enthusiastic play of the team and their second-place finish in 1988 were impressive enough to give the fans and management renewed hope. They dreamed that another World Championship might be waiting just around the corner.

The only trouble with beautiful dreams is that, sooner or later, you must awaken to reality. The reality in this case was that the Pirates simply did not have the muscle in '89 to maintain the momentum of the previous season. A frustrated

General Manager Larry Doughty joked: "Baseball is supposed to be a non-contact sport, but our hitters seem to be taking that literally."

Outside of backup catcher Mike LaValliere (.316), no Pirate was able to hit .300 or better that year. Bobby Bonilla hit a team-leading 24 homers, but also led all National League third-sackers with 35 errors.

Jay Bell, received in a trade with Cleveland, showed promise as a solid defensive shortstop. Andy Van Slyke also displayed some spectacular play in center field, and led the National League in throwing runners out (5) after catching a fly ball.

Pitching had not

Andy Van Slyke peppered his remarks with memorable one-liners, yet he made certain that he was prepared for each game.

improved enough to be overpowering. Drabek was 14-12, Walk was 13-10 and Smiley was 12-8. Jeff Robinson, who was a focus of the Pirates' hope for the future, fell to a 7-13 record with a 4.58 ERA.

Even the normally composed Jim Leyland yielded to the frustration of the season when, following one game in July, he screamed at his players: "You are a bunch of losers. All you care about is your own stats. You're worse than a watered-down expansion team. You're giving up. You've got no pride, no dignity, no guts."

The mediocre season still brought over 1.3 million fans into Three Rivers Stadium. Fan and media support were there, although wins were mighty scarce. The Pirates finished 74-88 for a fifth-place spot in the East Division, 19 games behind the first-place Cubs.

Baseball in 1990 was still shooting itself in the foot. Whenever it seemed as though players and owners were winning back the loyal fans who had supported our national pastime, one of the two camps elected to flame the fires of controversy. After failing to sign a new collective bargaining agreement, the owners locked players out of spring training camps. Both sides remained at impasse until the disputes were resolved in mid-March. Baseball had only two-and-a-half weeks to get ready for a delayed opening day.

Fans grew increasingly angry and frustrated. They labeled both players and owners "greedy." Lucrative television contracts, on the surface, seemed to guarantee profits for owners. Several players were earning more than $3 million a year; Jose Canseco, for example, signed a

pact with the Oakland A's for $23.5 million over five years. "Ballplayers and deer hunters are alike. They both want the big bucks," said General Manager Larry Doughty.

Resembling a sick patient who suddenly takes a turn for the better, the 1990 Pittsburgh Pirates sprang to life with the vim and vigor of a reborn religious convert. Jim Leyland's boys played with serious determination to get the job done each time they stepped between the foul lines. They did so with the help of both the year's best everyday player and pitcher.

Right-hand fire-balling Doug Drabek led the National League that season with a winning percentage of .786 (22-6). That accomplishment, combined with his 2.76 ERA, was good enough to earn him the coveted Cy Young Award. Veteran relief specialist Neal Heaton, now in his second year with Pittsburgh, racked up 24 saves and a 12-9 record.

Of all the stars in the Pirates' heaven that year, none shown brighter than Barry Bonds. This speedy outfielder was praised by much of the media as the best all-around player since Roberto Clemente. His record supports this accolade. He not only showed consistency at the plate (.301 average, 33 homers and a league-leading .566 slugging average), but also sparkled in the outfield with diving catches and a powerful throwing arm that enabled him to gun-down a league-tying 14 runners brazen enough to try for one base too many. That helped earn for him the Gold Glove Award.

In 1990, Barry Bonds became the first player in history to hit .300 with

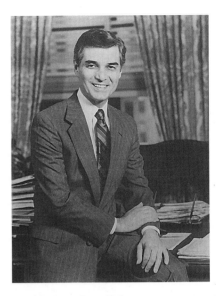

A great deal of credit for keeping the Pirates in Pittsburgh goes to former Mayor Richard Caliguiri.

Resembling a sick patient who suddenly takes a turn for the better, the 1990 Pittsburgh Pirates sprang to life with the vim and vigor of a reborn religious convert.

Manager Jim Leyland was not afraid to express his opinions following a disputed call.

30 homers, 100 RBI and 50 stolen bases. It was this avalanche of offensive output that earned Bonds a well-deserved Most Valuable Player Award.

Bobby Bonilla also added punch with 32 homers, as did Andy Van Slyke (another Gold Glove Award winner) with 17, and Sid Bream with 15.

The Pirates certainly hit their share of home runs in 1990 (a team total of 138), but they were also able to subdue their league rivals with a whopping total of 288 doubles — far more than those hit by any other team during 1990.

Catcher Don Slaught, whom the Pirates got from the Yankees in a trade for Jeff Robinson prior to the season, was a rock-steady backstop who hit .300 in 84 games.

With Jay Bell at short and fourth-year Pirate Jose Lind at second, the Bucs had a middle-of-the-diamond defense that would be the envy of any manager. Perhaps that was one reason Jim Leyland received the Manager of the Year award in 1990.

The West Division Cincinnati Reds, however, defeated the Buccos four games to two in the National League Championship Series. Contributing to the Pirates' demise in this series was weak hitting — a team batting average of only .194. Especially disappointing was the output of their two stars — Bonds (.167) and Bonilla (.190). Neither of them hit a home run during the six games.

In spite of sterling individual performances throughout the regular season, the 1990 Pirates were sentenced to join the ranks of those who chant the saddest words in baseball: "Wait 'til next year."

But, the operative question was: would there be a next year? In 1990, with home attendance surpassing two million and the Bucs winning the National League East championship, the club still showed a $7 million loss due, in part, to skyrocketing player salaries. "The past few years has shown the wisdom of former mayor Richard Caliguiri's dream to save the Pirates," said Albert Neri, press secretary for Mayor Sophie Masloff. Frederick "Fritz" Huysman, Assistant Managing Editor/Sports for the *Pittsburgh Post-Gazette*, agrees. He witnessed close-up the struggles the team and city had with financial problems. Huysman thinks had it not been for Mayor Caliguiri, the Pirate franchise would not have been saved for Pittsburgh.

President Carl Barger was still faced with a dilemma in 1991. He admitted that what was done to restore the franchise over the past five years was "a miracle." He questioned, however, how the Bucs, with limited financial resources, could afford to retain free agents such as Barry Bonds or Bobby Bonilla. "Pittsburgh demands winners," he observed. "I get letters praising us for our stand on high salaries, then there is a P.S. — 'Please sign Bonds and Bonilla.'"

The Pirates did remain in Pittsburgh in 1991, but at a substantial cost. An arbitrator awarded Doug Drabek $3.35 million dollars for the '91 season. Barry Bonds received $2.3 million and Bobby Bonilla got $2.4 million — substantially less than each was seeking.

Some of that investment paid dividends as more than two million fans flocked to Three Rivers Stadium during 1991. The Pirates appeared to be on a roll. They left the opposition far behind, winning the National League East by 14 games.

Barry Bonds (.292, 25 homers) and Bobby Bonilla (.302, 18 four-baggers) once again led the Pirate attack.

Bonds emerged as one of the most exciting players in baseball during the 1991 season. The Bucs' charismatic left fielder topped the National League with a .410 on-base percentage and was second in both walks (107) and RBI (116). He also swiped 43 bases.

Barry Bonds sometimes irritated opposing pitchers when, after he clubbed a home run, he would circle the bases very slowly. Even some of the Pittsburgh media thought this was a display bordering on arrogance. In responding to criticism of his actions, Bonds was able to laugh it off. He once compared himself to Olympic champion Carl Lewis: "He makes his living running fast and I make mine running slow."

Jay Bell added to the power department with 16 home runs and paced all shortstops with 164 hits. His normally steady fielding became suspect, however, when he led all National League shortstops with 24 errors.

The most pleasant surprise of all was the addition to the lineup of a native Pittsburgher with a familiar sounding name: John Paul Wehner (pronounced "Waner"). Although he possessed only average native skills, he won the hearts of Pirate fans with his hard-nosed determination to

succeed. "That scrappy kid will grab a ground ball with his teeth if that was the only way to make a play," claimed Manager Leyland. Wehner's .340 average gave Pirate fans even more reason to cheer his play.

Southpaw pitcher John Smiley took advantage of his raw talent and some breaks that went his way to post a 20-8 record, good enough to tie Jose Rijo of Cincinnati in winning percentage (.714). He also tied Atlanta's Tom Glavin for the number of wins. Another left-handed pitcher, Zane Smith (16-10), was exceptionally sharp with his control as he led the league with a stingy 1.14 walks per nine-inning contest.

In post-season play it was, as Yogi Berra would say, "*deja-vu* all over again." The Atlanta Braves, the previous season's last-place team, led in 1991 by sluggers David Justice, Ron Gant, Terry Pendleton and Brian Hunter and a solid pitching staff, defeated Pittsburgh four games to three — the

. . . more than

two million fans

flocked to Three

Rivers Stadium

during 1991.

Cy Young Award-Winning Doug Drabek

last, a masterful six-hit shutout tossed by John Smoltz.

Shortstop Jay Bell led all players with 12 hits and a .414 batting average during the seven games. Pitchers Doug Drabek and Zane Smith allowed less than one run per game in the two contests they each started for Pittsburgh, but reliables Bobby Bonds (.148) and Andy Van Slyke (.160) succumbed to the "curse of the playoffs" and failed to perform up to their standards. Bobby Bonilla hit .304 over the seven games, but was unable to hit one ball out of the park.

Pittsburgh Pirate fans again threw their hands toward heaven and asked the gods of baseball: "What do we have to do to win a World Series?"

Alas, the answer to that question was not revealed in 1992. Catcher Don Slaught (.345) and center fielder

BOBBY BONILLA

Andy Van Slyke (.324) led the Bucs to another East Division Championship. Barry Bonds chipped in with a .311 average and a team-leading 34 homers and 103 RBI. He led the league with a slugging average of .624. He also joined his father, Bobby, as well as Willie Mays, Howard Johnson and Ron Gant, as a player to have two 30-home run, 30-stolen base seasons.

Doug Drabek (15-11) displayed remarkable control with a very respectable 2.77 ERA. Randy Tomlin (14-9) and Bob Walk (10-6) also kept the opposition in check.

The National League Championship Series provided one Pirate player his greatest moments of glory. Lloyd McClendon, in his second year in a Buc uniform, hit a whopping .727 in 11 at-bats during the series, including a home run. It was a great way to mark McClendon's last season in the major leagues. For the rest of the Pirate squad, however, the NLCS was nearly a copy of the one a year earlier. Again, some key Pirate players failed to perform up to expectations during the series. Jay Bell, for instance, batted only .172 and Doug Drabek could do no better than post an 0-3 record.

Nonetheless, as late as the ninth inning of the final NLCS game at Atlanta's Fulton County Stadium, Pittsburgh fans thought their prayer requests for a World Series berth were finally granted. Leading the same Atlanta Braves by a score of 2-0, the Pirates needed just three outs to capture the National League crown. Unfortunately, they managed to get only two. Doug Drabek (15-14 that season) pitched masterfully until the ninth, when he loaded the bases with nobody out. Stan Belinda (6-4) was brought in from the bullpen. Belinda got two quick outs (one, a sacrifice fly), before little-known Francisco Cabrera of Atlanta hit a pinch-hit single. One runner easily scored the tying run, and former Pirate Sid Bream, running on a bad leg, hobbled toward home plate. With an awkward slide, Bream crossed the plate. Umpire Randy Marsh hollered: "Safe." It was a close call but, in spite of the outcome, even the most die-hard Pirate fan had to admit it was the right call.

Braves fans cheered lustfully. Pittsburgh fans sank in silent resignation. Higher powers then us mortals must have known all along who was going to win. The Pirate faithful only wondered why those gods of baseball were so cruel as to let them wait until the very last minute.

Three years of frustration — coming so close to the World Series only to lose in the playoffs — can sap the enthusiasm out of even the best players. That record must certainly have affected two of the Pirates' established stars — Barry Bonds and Bobby Bonilla — who left for greener pastures immediately following the '92 season. Bonds signed a lucrative contract with San Francisco; Bonilla also landed a seven-figure deal with the Mets.

Pirate President Carl Barger could have sent the Pirates packing in 1991. "But we have no intention of doing so," he promised Buc fans.

CEO Douglas Danforth sought ways to reduce the financial anxieties, even attempting to obtain reduced rent at Three Rivers Stadium.

A rather youthful (44-year-old) Mark Sauer was brought in from the Cardinal organization as new President and CEO in late October. Immediately he sized-up the situation. "We don't have the resources of some other teams. The development of young players is our key to success," he said. He was right. Although the Pirates had 2.4 million in attendance during the '91 season, the club lost $2.9 million.

Talk around the hot stove leagues that winter concentrated not on runs and base hits as much as on finances. Not helping the Pirate cause in 1992 was a six-month newspaper strike. Attendance dropped to 2.1 million and the club lost an astonishing $13 million. Tension with local politicians increased when the City sued the Pirate organization for $1.26 million in unpaid rent. The Bucs countered with the claim that the city reneged on promises to maintain the stadium as a "first class" facility.

This infighting generated a negative feeling about baseball around Pittsburgh. It may well have affected the play of the Bucs who dropped to fifth place in the National League East with a mediocre 75-87 record. It may also have affected the attitude of the fans. On June 4, when Bobby Bonilla returned to Pittsburgh as a member of the Mets, he was soundly booed. One fan even hit him on the head with a golf ball. Bonilla was forced to wear a batting helmet while in the field.

The only Pirate to put up significant numbers was shortstop Jay Bell who had 187 hits (good enough for fourth best in the league). He batted .310, hit nine homers and had just as many triples to earn him a tie for third in the league. Third baseman Jeff King showed he was a "comer" with a .295 average and five home runs.

Knuckleballer Tim Wakefield, in his second year with the Bucs, threw

Pirate President Carl Barger could have sent the Pirates packing in 1991, "But we have no intention of doing so," he promised Buc fans.

Barry Bonds seems to be frustrated during the '92 NLCS at his failure to contribute to the Pirates' offense.

171 pitches in a 10-inning win over the Braves in April of that year. But the ball didn't always dance his way as he concluded the season with a 6-11 mark.

Pittsburgh hosted the All-Star Game in 1994, but the Pirates did not win the World Series in 1994. Nor did any other team. This was the year of the most infamous of all baseball strikes — one that nearly spelled the death of major league baseball.

On August 12, major league players voted to stop play for the eighth time since 1972. Fans and media shared two emotions: a mutual disgust at what was happening and a growing frustration because nobody could do anything about it.

Prior to the strike, both the National and American leagues voted to divide into three divisions — the East, Central and West. Pittsburgh was in the Central, along with Cincinnati, Houston, St. Louis and Chicago.

Sharing a division with fewer teams did little to improve the Pirates' standing over the previous year. The Bucs were 53-61 in 1994, good enough for only fourth place, 13 games behind division-leading Cincinnati. The Bucs tied the Cubs for the lowest team batting average that year (.259). Once again, Jay Bell was the only player to post significant numbers in any category when he tied for second in the league with 35 doubles.

It was a sad year for the Pirates.

It was a sad year for baseball. ■

MANAGER JIM LEYLAND

CHAPTER 15

VISIONS OF McCLATCHY

"*We're here to stay!*"

—KEVIN McCLATCHY, 1997
responding to a reporter's
question about the future of
the Pirates in Pittsburgh

*T*HE STRIKE OF **1994** left baseball in a funk. By spring training the next year, players and owners were still far apart in negotiations. Good-faith bargaining gave way to insults levied by both sides through the media. Dirty laundry was hung out for every fan to see. Each side grew increasing stubborn, dug in their heels and refused to acknowledge the demands by the other. Even the most optimistic of fans knew the impasse would not be resolved before opening day. The best slogan of the year was published by *Sports Illustrated* — "Major League Baseball: No Balls and a Strike."

Major league clubs then opened their spring-training camps to anyone who wanted to audition. The Grapefruit League began preseason play with so-called "replacement players." With few exceptions, the caliber of talent shown by these minor leaguers and sandlot players in no way came close to that of established major leaguers.

The strike finally was settled not at the bargaining table, but in a courtroom. A U.S. District court, on March 31, forbid owners from implementing new financial working conditions. Both owners and players were ordered to revert to the rules of the previous season.

Kevin McClatchy purchased the Pittsburgh Ball Club in February 1996. Although the Bucs had a string of losing seasons and a huge loss of fan support, McClatchy was a man on a mission.

Jay Bell was one of the Pirate stars sacrificed during the "fire sale" prior to the 1997 season.

Eighteen games were trimmed from the 1995 schedule and teams were given time to prepare for the season. This time, baseball fans were not ready to forgive. Over the seven months of the strike, they grew increasingly tired, as many said, of listening to "arguments between billionaires and millionaires." They accused team owners of being gluttonous financial vampires, seeking to drain the last possible dollar out of the sport. They also labeled the players as egotistical, overpaid, selfish rogues, earning millions of dollars for playing a kid's game and refusing to sign a young fan's baseball without being paid for the autograph.

Many heretofore loyal Pirate fans echoed the feelings of the rest of the nation. "I don't care if I ever see a game, again," they said. At the same time, loyal fans, such as Rich Corson of McMurray, attended as many games as possible. "The Pirates have been and always will be my team," he said.

On Opening Day at Three Rivers, fans were given souvenir flags for promotional purposes. To show their frustration at the current state of affairs, many of the fans tossed the plastic sticks onto the playing field, holding up the action for more than 15 minutes.

A few of the "replacement players" were impressive enough to receive big-league contracts. Their entrance into the majors, however, was not enjoyable. They were shunned by their teammates who openly called them "scabs."

Throughout the 1995 season, marked by fan apathy and growing distrust of both owners and players,

some of the Pirates played respectable ball. Outfielder Orlando Merced hit .300 and rapped 15 home runs. Jeff King played at least one full game at every infield position, and hit a club-leading 18 homers.

Southpaw Denny Neagle showed his All-Star credentials with a 13-6 record, tying Atlanta's Greg Maddux with 209.2 innings pitched. Had he pitched every game, the Bucs could have bettered their 58-86 record of that year. By ending the season in last place in the Central Division, 27 games behind Cincinnati, the Pirates, as a team, did little to overcome the mounting frustration and ire of diehard baseball fans in the Steel City.

Adding to the dark clouds of fan discontentment in Pittsburgh was the announcement that, with a debt approaching $60 million, the Pirate front office seriously was searching for someone with deep pockets to buy the franchise. The City of Pittsburgh, with the urging of Mayor Tom Murphy, offered $3.5 million through lease concessions at Three Rivers Stadium to help cover the club's financial losses. President Mark Sauer was reluctant to accept an additional $6.4 million offered by the mayor's office because attached to it was a string that would block the club from moving to another city before 1997.

Finally, a buyer was found and accepted by all parties. In February 1996, 32-year-old Kevin McClatchy, an ambitious visionary from a newspaper family in Sacramento, California, purchased the Pittsburgh Ball Club for a reported $90 million. Close friends counseled him that he was tossing his money down the

drain, because the Bucs had a string of losing seasons and a huge loss of fan support due to the 1994 strike. McClatchy, however, viewed this as a challenge. Even before the first pitch was tossed on opening day, McClatchy did everything he could to stir the waters of excitement for Pirate fans.

His real challenge, as it turned out, was to win ball games. In 1996, most Pirate players flew as high as cement kites — with two exceptions. Jay Bell started his eighth consecutive season at shortstop, the longest such streak since Dick Groat (1955-

1962). He led all major-league shortstops with a .986 fielding percentage and 478 assists. He also had his best year in the RBI department with 71.

Bell's close friend, Jeff King, set career-high marks for homers (30), RBI (111) walks (70) and stolen bases (15). He became the ninth player in Pirates' history to hit at least 30 home runs in a season; it was the most since Barry Bonds slugged 34 in 1992 and the most by a right-hander since Dick Stuart slammed 35 in '61.

None of Bell's achievements

Orlando Merced receives congratulations following one of his 15 home runs in 1995, but it was not enough to make fans forget about the '94 strike.

Southpaw Denny Neagle was the Pirates' top pitcher and was named on the 1995 All-Star roster. He, too, walked the Pirate plank in the giant sell-off prior to '97.

were good enough to lift the Pirates beyond a 73-89 record and out of the Central Division basement.

The next year — 1997 — would be crucial to the future of the Pirates and their involvement with the City of Pittsburgh. The Pirate faithful continued to love the game of baseball. Most of them treasured fond memories of their beloved Bucs. They talked about the dazzling play of Pie Traynor at third, about the mighty home runs hit by Ralph Kiner and Willie Stargell, and, of course, the dramatic World Series blast by Maz. At the same time, they still smarted from the pain caused by the players' strike in '94. The bitter aftertaste of that strike affected, to a special degree, those who called Pittsburgh their home. The people of Allegheny County embody an industrial city mentality. They vividly remembered how their fathers and grandfathers worked hard in the steel mills and coal mines just to earn enough money to put bread on the table and make the mortgage payments. If anything remained after the bills were paid, fathers and mothers would treat their children to a game at Forbes Field where, for less than $20, they all enjoyed a memorable night at the ballpark. To people of this heritage, absolutely no logic could explain why baseball player,

earning over a million dollars by playing a game, would want to go on strike.

The Pirates' second consecutive last-place finish in the Central Division in 1996 didn't help matters.

Kevin McClatchy, nevertheless, kept his eyes glued on the potential of his club. In 1996 he announced his vision of a new stadium, designed specifically for baseball, to be built adjacent to the Sixth Street Bridge. The new ball park, with fewer than 40,000 seats, would create a more intimate atmosphere. The fans could be seated close to the action as they are at Fenway Park and Wrigley Field. An unobstructed picture of the field from each seat would be enhanced by the panoramic view beyond the outfield walls of the Allegheny River and the city's skyline.

McClatchy later announced his commitment of $35 million toward the construction of this classic Forbes Field-type design with all the modern amenities. A new park would help in keeping major league players in Pittsburgh and ensure that the organization could field a championship caliber team year-in and year-out. "The Pirates' ownership group is committed to this region long-term," said the aggressive Pirate owner.

At the moment, however, Kevin McClatchy had to concentrate on rebuilding a ballclub. Before the end of the '96 season, he met with Manager Jim Leyland and General Manager Cam Bonifay about the free agents they wanted to select to set the team on a winning track. Everyone agreed that to turn the team around, some serious changes were

The Pirates' broadcast team: (L-R) Lanny Frattare, Bob Walk, Steve Blass and Greg Brown.

needed. The discussion, however, generated absolutely no consensus as to precisely what changes had to be made. Leyland sought more talent, an approach that surely would cost the club more money; McClatchy, in turn, announced that the Pirate Baseball Club had to limit its total salary package for the next season to $10 million. Instead of adding proven players, the Pirates were compelled to let go their most talented (and most expensive) athletes. The team slashed its payroll by trading away such veterans as pitcher Denny Neagle, outfielder Orlando Merced. According to Kevin McClatchy, this was only the beginning.

That was all Manager Leyland could take. He was frustrated after years of working with young talent, grooming them to major league

status, only to have them traded, sold or released because of high salary demands. Certainly he realized that Pittsburgh, a small market by comparison, was unable to compete in salary-bidding wars with larger franchises, yet he felt he owed it to himself to pilot a team with enough financial backing to guarantee not only consistency, but also a chance to win a pennant. He announced before the end of the season that this would be his last year with Pittsburgh. He would start the 1997 season at the helm of the power-laden, affluent Florida Marlins.

On December 13, shortstop Jay Bell and first baseman Jeff King were traded to the Royals for infielder Joe Randa and minor-league pitchers Jeff Granger, Jeff Martin and Jeff Wallace. Only Randa made the parent club.

Agile third baseman Jeff King was also traded prior to the '97 season.

JOSE GUILLEN

on McClatchy and the rest of the Pirate owners. Should they search for more supportive venues?

With the hope that it would add a shot of life to dwindling attendance, major-league baseball that year broke a long-standing tradition by allowing inter-league play before the World Series. Baseball purists opposed this move, arguing that it would take away from the appeal of the World Series. Yet, marked increases in attendance at games featuring inter-league rivalry demonstrated that fans around the country, including the Pirate faithful, welcomed an opportunity to see, in person, stars from the other league. In Pittsburgh, for example, a three-game Labor Day series with the nearby American League Cleveland Indians attracted a total of 126,191 fans — an average of 42,000 per game.

Kevin McClatchy and his crew realized that an easy solution to the Pirates' monetary uncertainties would be to move the team to a more lucrative area of the country. McClatchy, however, gave his word to the people of Pittsburgh: "We are here to stay." So, in 1997, the Pirates introduced a new manager, new uniforms (a black home uniform jersey that incorporated red into the official colors for the first time in a half century, and a pin-striped road uniform), a new logo (a swashbuckling, snarling buccaneer wearing a red bandanna), and a renewed effort to win back fan support. Most importantly, they approached the game with a new attitude.

Much of that new attitude was generated from the new Pirate skipper. Gene Lamont became the

According to some critics, this was not a trade; it was a fire sale. In all, the team traded eight veterans who were earning $17 million for 14 younger, far less expensive players.

All of this did little to create instant fan interest. Many of the Pirate faithful reacted in the worst way possible — with apathy. Pittsburghers adopted an "I don't care" attitude.

During the first month of the 1997 season, Pittsburgh recorded the lowest average attendance — 12,600 per game — of any team in the National League. Through the same number of home games Colorado filled its stadium with nearly four times that number. Pressure mounted

Infielder Tony Womak shows his enthusiasm for the game each time he's on base.

24th manager in Buc history when he replaced the popular Jim Leyland. He had served as Pittsburgh's third base coach from 1986-1991 and again in 1996. He managed the Chicago White Sox from '91 until mid-season '95, compiling an impressive 258-210 record and Manager-of-the-Year honors in 1993.

Lamont didn't seek the post as manager of the Bucs. "I never heard of anybody getting a job he applied for," he said. Yet when he was offered the position, he boldly promised to deliver a team that was "exciting and aggressive."

Lamont was on the same page as Pirate ownership. "Kevin McClatchy is dedicated to getting this done the right way," he said. "People are going to realize that Kevin was the one. He needs to receive credit for that. This ownership group has talked a lot about getting a new ballpark; I think they'll get it done."

One of Lamont's first decisions was to hire as pitching coach, the 1982 American League Cy Young Award winner Pete Vukovich. This 43-year-old native of Johnstown, Pennsylvania, won the respect of the fans, the media and the mound staff as he developed the talents of Jon Lieber, Esteban Loaiza, Jason Schmidt and Francisco Cordova.

Slowly, the club generated fan interest. People around the city talked about their Bucs in a spirit reminiscent of the glory days of the 1960s and 1970s.

Enthusiasm for the "New-Look Bucs" was enhanced by the upbeat descriptions of Lanny Frattare, the "Voice of the Pirates" since 1976. As with previous announcers such as

Rosey Rowswell and Bob Prince, Pirate fans grew familiar with his unique expressions such as: "Go, ball. Get outta' here."

Joining Lanny Frattare in the booth were Steve Blass, 10-year veteran of the Pirate pitching staff and '71 World Series hero; Bob Walk, another former pitcher who spent 10 of his 14 big-league years with the Bucs; and Greg Brown, a native of Mechanicsburg, who had previously worked as a color commentator for the Buffalo Bills.

Increased efforts to win back fan support ranked at the top of the Pirates' list of priorities. Loyal support through game attendance is the backbone of most ballclubs. That's especially true with Pittsburgh and its limited television coverage.

Kevin McClatchy did all he could to rekindle fan enthusiasm for the Bucs. He spearheaded a grass roots campaign as he spoke at local Rotary, Kiwanis and Lions clubs throughout the Tri-state area, telling the story of the Pirates with the zeal of a missionary. He appeared on radio and television talk shows to share his dreams for the future. He sponsored special "days" at the ballpark. In addition to the typical "Cap Day" and "Ball Day" held at other parks, McClatchy's menu included "Fishing Rod Day," "New Logo Sweatshirt Day," and "Dog Tag Night." Many of these events were staged in cooperation with the Pirates' loyal booster — Giant Eagle stores — along with other Pittsburgh businesses.

The Pirate front office also introduced a year-round community involvement program called "Pirates

Manager Gene Lamont proved to be popular with fans and players. His success in 1997 earned him a contract extension through the year 2000.

Partners" in which players, coaches and alumni made personal appearances throughout the greater Pittsburgh area in support of civic and charitable organizations.

One particular display of fan appreciation came on May 9 when players greeted fans at all four gates in an impromptu "Meet the Fans" event. They shook hands with the people and posed for photos. One 16-year-old who had just had his picture taken with rookie Jose Guillen crystallized the feeling of the fans: "This is great. This is the best Pirates team ever."

On February 11, 1997, the Pirates invited back home the legendary Willie Stargell as a Special Assistant to the General Manager. "We are extremely proud to have Willie Stargell back as a member of our organization," said McClatchy. "He always represented the Pirates and the city of Pittsburgh with an unmatched level of class both on and off the field."

Finally, the new attitude of 1997 was one that contradicted everything else happening in baseball that year. In an era when owners and baseball, in general, made decisions as to what might be in the best interest of the sport or of a team without thinking past the next five minutes, Kevin McClatchy was willing to establish and implement a more effective, long-range plan.

Ever since baseball's old reserve clause was deemed illegal by Peter Seitz back in 1975, established players could shop around for teams that would pay the highest dollar. Many owners were willing to part with those dollars. They believed they could buy instant pennant contenders. These baseball owners, therefore, dug deep into their financial coffers for more money, and incurred more debt in order to buy name ballplayers for salaries that would equal the assets of a small country.

Prior to the '97 season, for example, the Chicago White Sox wooed away from the Cleveland Indians their most notable slugger, Albert Belle, for a cool $55 million, five-year contract. The average salary for a major-league player in 1997 was over $1.2 million.

Neither Kevin McClatchy nor any of his partners were able to match that kind of expense. It was a matter of geography, nothing else. The Steel City, with less than a half million people living inside its limits, was not a gold mine in terms of revenue. Other cities such as New York, Chicago, Philadelphia and Los Angeles far outranked Pittsburgh in terms of both fan and dollar potential.

Someone might argue that Cincinnati was similar in size to Pittsburgh, but the Reds could draw from other cities such as Indianapolis, Louisville and Columbus. Pittsburgh's nearest large city is Cleveland, and Cleveland already had a pretty solid ballclub.

Pirate management decided on a daring approach. If you cannot play the game by the rules of the other owners, you make your *own* rules. The plan was simple. Instead of paying multi-million-dollar contracts to established semi-super-stars,

Jim Leyland did not have to ponder his future very long. Shortly following his resignation as Pirate manager, he was signed to lead the Florida Marlins to the 1997 World Championship.

ESTEBAN LOAIZA

General Manager Cam Bonifay and his staff promoted relatively untested minor-league players who were lean, mean and hungry. They included three pitchers from Mexico — Esteban Loaiza, Francisco Cordova, and Ricardo Rincon (affectionately called "The Three Amigos") — outfielder Jermaine Allensworth (who played in 61 games for the Bucs in '96), and second-year catcher Jason Kendall. The only free agent on the '97 squad was shortstop Kevin Elster, and the only million-dollar players that year were Elster and outfielder Al Martin. Of the 25-man roster, 19 were either rookies or second-year players.

Not everyone applauded this move. Even before the first pitch of opening day in 1997, certain so-called baseball experts laughed at the very mention of the Pirates. One reporter predicted the Pirates would lose 110 games in '97. But when the Bucs won their first game of the season against San Francisco, most of the critics suddenly quit vocalizing their predictions.

On April 11 — opening day at Three Rivers Stadium — 43,128 paid admissions showed support for

In an effort to build fan support, Pirate players look forward to signing autographs for baseball's fans of the future.

Slugging first baseman, Kevin Young, plays with an all-out enthusiasm for the game.

their Bucs. A 7-1 loss to the Dodgers sent them home disappointed, yet they appreciated the "wall-to-wall" enthusiasm of the new-look Pirates. They knew they were witnessing the beginning of a new era.

The tenacity of the young Bucs brought back memories of old-timers who played the game simply because they loved the sport. That refreshing spirit converted even the sharpest critics. During spring training, sports reporters labeled the Pittsburgh ballclub "nobodies." By May 1, as the Pirates were playing .500 ball, many of the same reporters hedged their bets referring to these players as "upstarts." On May 10, the Associated Press release featured seven words in its lead paragraph that few thought would ever be written in 1997: "The Pittsburgh Pirates are in first place."

Reporters who had written them off before the first day of spring training, now had to admit that these former "no-name" youngsters had developed into viable "contenders." The most common question asked by delighted fans was: "Can you believe this?"

Like a thunderbolt, just when the Pirates were getting used to being in first place, within a one-week period in May, the team lost three instrumental players. Center fielder Jermaine Allensworth broke his left hand. Shortstop Kevin Elster — the glue to the infield who had seven team-leading home runs — broke his left wrist, and outfielder Al Martin injured his right wrist. Later, in August, first baseman Kevin Young — the club's leader in home runs at the time — tore a ligament in his right thumb, requiring surgery. All were placed on the disabled list. "Now we have to dig even deeper into ourselves to see what we're made of," said Manager Gene Lamont.

In spite of these setbacks, the Bucs continued to keep pace with the rest of the National League Central Division. "We have no secret, no magic formula," said Al Martin. "We scratch and claw to score runs. We know if we don't hustle, we don't score."

Not just the city, but others throughout the nation, now rooted for the underdog Pirates. True baseball fans appreciated seeing players, sans pompous attitudes, willing to play ball for less than grotesque salaries. On top of this, the Bucs continued to win. By All-Star break, they led the National League Central Division. The team had become "The Little Engine that Could."

That's baseball.

This became most evident on the evening of Saturday, July 12. For the first time in 20 years, Three Rivers Stadium was completely sold out for a non-opening day game. Fans flocked to see their Bucs revive the spirit of playing for the love of the game. And they were amply rewarded with a 10-inning, no-hit, no-run ball game tossed by Francisco Cordova and Ricardo Rinon. It was the first combined, extra-inning no-hitter in major league history. The excitement was further enhanced when newcomer Mark Smith won the game with a dramatic, pinch-hit, three-run homer.

Paul Meyer of the *Pittsburgh Post-Gazette* wrote that the Pirates were making the word "unbelievable" a cliché.

"The team is like a bunch of crazed dogs," said first baseman Eddie Williams.

"This is definitely a storybook," exclaimed infielder Joe Randa.

The September 17, 1997, edition of *USA TODAY* named the Pirates its "Organization of the Year." The paper praised the leadership of General Manager Cam Bonifay and Paul Tinnell, director of the farm system, for their efforts in generating an array of blue-chip prospects.

On October 21, *The Sporting News* selected Senior Vice President and General Manager Cam Bonifay as its Major League Executive-of-the-Year. Bonifay was the second Pirate executive to win the coveted award; Joe L. Brown received the honor in 1958.

Whatever superlative or elation anyone chose to make, the bottom line was this: The Bucs were able to field a competitive team of scrappy,

"in-your-face" athletes who were there because they wanted to play in the big leagues. As a result, the team the experts predicted would finish dead last spent 40 days of the '97 season leading the Central Division and finished the campaign in second place, only five games behind the Central Division Champion Houston Astros.

The Pirates generated a new level of excitement for both fans and players. In an era when loyalty to a team normally means "Wait until there's a better offer," high-profile players such as Al Martin elected to turn down higher salaries to remain in Pittsburgh — a city he loves.

The '97 Bucs offered plenty of thrills to Pirate fans. Generating excitement each time he was on the basepaths was the Bucs' All-Star second baseman Tony Womack, who swiped a league-leading 60 bases — more than any Pirate since Omar Moreno in 1979.

Leading the club in batting was Turner Ward with a .353 average. Joining him in the .300-or-better department were Joe Randa (.332), Kevin Young (.300) and newly-acquired veteran shortstop Shawon Dunston (.300). The home run leader was Kevin Young with 18.

Pitching was balanced. Tying for wins (11) were Francisco Cordova, Esteban Loaiza and Jon Lieber.

Even the most calloused observer had to agree that the battling Bucs certainly were not playing ball in '97 just to fill their wallets. Pittsburgh's payroll was the lowest of any major league club that year. In fact, Albert Belle's 1997 salary with the White Sox surpassed the entire payroll of the Pirates team for the year.

The September 17, 1997, edition of USA TODAY named the Pirates its "Organization of the Year."

The PirateFest has become an annual event that draws crowds in excess of 20,000 in early winter. One of the attractions is the opportunity to receive an autograph by one of the current or former Pirate players.

How did Pittsburgh fans react to all this? The total home attendance for 1997 was 1,657,022 — the sixth highest total in team history. The gain of nearly 325,000 fans over the previous season was the third largest increase among all the National League teams.

Based on the amazing performance of Pittsburgh's team in '97, the Pirates head into the future with renewed vigor and determination. They know that other teams are more experienced and have a lot more money at their disposal. But the Bucs are dedicated to make a definite impact in the league and on baseball.

Other teams may be Goliaths by comparison. But every time one of those clubs meets up with Pittsburgh, the Pirates have one pointed warning: "Watch out, Goliath. Little David just got into town!" ■

The excitement generated by the Bucs in 1997 brought fans back to Three Rivers Stadium.

NO-HITTERS (9 OR MORE INNINGS) IN PIRATE HISTORY

DATE	BY	OPPONENT	SITE	SCORE
9-20-07	Nicholas Maddox	Brooklyn	Pittsburgh	2-1
5-6-51	Cliff Chambers	Boston	Boston	3-0
5-26-59	Harvey Haddix	Milwaukee	Milwaukee	0-1*
9-20-69	Bob Moose	New York	New York	4-0
6-12-70	Dock Ellis	San Diego	San Diego	2-0
8-9-76	John Candelaria	Los Angeles	Pittsburgh	2-0
7-12-97	Francisco Cordova and Ricardo Rincon	Houston	Pittsburgh	2-0

Haddix pitched 12 perfect innings and lost his no-hit bid and the game in the 13th inning.

GOLD GLOVE AWARDS

Bill Mazeroski	1958, '59, '60, '61, '63, '64, '65, '66, '67
Harvey Haddix	1959, '60
Bobby Shantz	1961
Roberto Clemente	1961, '62, '63, '64, '65, '66, '67, '68, '69, '70, '71, '72
Bill Virdon	1962
Gene Alley	1966, '67
Dave Parker	1977, '78, '79
Tony Peña	1983, '84, '85
Mike LaValliere	1987
Andy Van Slyke	1988, '89, '90, '91, '92
Barry Bonds	1990, '91, '92
Jose Lind	1992
Jay Bell	1993

RETIRED NUMBERS

1	William Meyer
4	Ralph Kiner
8	Willie Stargell
9	Billy Mazeroski
20	Harold "Pie" Traynor
21	Roberto Clemente
33	Honus Wagner

MOST VALUABLE PLAYER

Paul Waner	1927
Dick Groat	1960
Roberto Clemente	1966
Dave Parker	1978
Willie Stargell (tie)	1979
Barry Bonds	1990, 1992

PIRATES IN THE HALL OF FAME

Listed in order of induction and showing years with the Bucs

1936	Honus Wagner (1900–1917)
1937	Connie Mack (1891–1896)
1945	Fred Clarke (1900–1915)
1946	Jack Chesbro (1899–1902)
1946	Rube Waddell (1900–1901)
1947	Frankie Frisch (1940–1946)
1948	Pie Traynor (1920–1937)
1952	Paul Waner (1926–1940)
1954	Rabbit Maranville (1921–1924)
1955	Dazzy Vance (1915)
1956	Joe Cronin (1926–1927)
1956	Hank Greenberg (1947)
1961	Max Carey (1910–1926)
1962	Bill McKechnie (1922–1926)
1964	Burleigh Grimes (1916–1917, 1928–1929, 1934)
1964	Heine Manush (1938–1939)
1965	James "Pud" Galvin (1887–1889, 1891–1892)
1966	Casey Stengel (1918–1919)
1967	Branch Rickey (1951–1955)
1967	Lloyd Waner (1927–1941)
1968	Kiki Cuyler (1921–1927)
1969	Waite Hoyt (1933–1937)
1971	Jake Beckley (1888–1889, 1891–1896)
1971	Joe Kelley (1891–1892)
1973	Roberto Clemente (1955–1972)
1973	George Kelly (1917)
1975	Billy Herman (1947)
1975	Ralph Kiner (1946–1953)
1976	Fred Lindstrom (1933–1934)
1977	Al Lopez (1940–1946)
1980	Chuck Klein (1939)
1985	Arky Vaughan (1932–1941)
1988	Willie Stargell (1962–1982)
1995	Vic Willis (1906–1909)
1996	Jim Bunning (1968–1969)
1996	Ned Hanlon (1889, 1891)

MANAGER OF THE YEAR

Billy Meyer	1948
Jim Leyland	1990, 1992

CY YOUNG AWARD

Vernon Law	1960
Doug Drabek	1990

THE BUCS' FANS BILL OF RIGHTS

1. We pledge to follow a proven model to rebuild this franchise into a championship team.

2. We pledge to keep baseball affordable for everyone in Pittsburgh, especially families.

3. We pledge to work to secure a private-public financing package to build a new baseball-only ballpark in Pittsburgh.

4. We pledge to make baseball fun in Pittsburgh.

5. We pledge to work with area youth organizations to encourage baseball enthusiasm.

6. We pledge to work with local officials to explore new transportation plans so that everyone can come see the Pirates.

7. We pledge to work with the Pittsburgh business community to make Pirates baseball a greater economic plus for the region.

8. We pledge to talk Pirates baseball as often as we can to anyone who will listen.

9. We pledge that we will do anything we can to cultivate your trust and support for the Pirates.

10. We pledge that we will not move the Pirates from Pittsburgh.

— KEVIN McCLATCHY
CEO AND MANAGING GENERAL PARTNER
PITTSBURGH PIRATES

INDEX